Bārasa Aṇuvekkhā of Kundakunda

By the Same Author

Pañcāstikāyasāra of Kundakunda: Building of the Cosmos (2024)

Advaita Vedānta and Jaina Advaita (2024)

Ratnakaraṇḍa Śrāvakācāra: Spiritual Life of the Householder(2022)

Perspectives in Jainism (2017)

The Essence of Jaina Scriptures: Pravacanasāra of Kundakunda (2014)

The Art and Science of Self-Realization: Puruṣārtha-Siddhyupāya of Amritachandra Suri (2006)

Fundamentals of Jainism (2005)

Salvation through Self-Discipline: *Niyamasāra of Kundakunda* (2005)

The Enlightened Vision of the Self: *Svarūpa Sambodhana of Akalaṅka Deva* (ed.) (2005)

Spiritual Enlightenment: *Paramātma Prakāśa of Yogindu Deva* (ed.) (2000)

Spiritual Insights: Iṣṭopadeśa and Samādhi Śataka of Pūjyapāda (ed.) (2000)

Bārasa Aṇuvekkhā of Kundakunda

— Twelve Facets of Reality —

Edited, Translated and Commentary by
Jagdish Prasad Jain

DK PRINTWORLD
Publishers of Indian Traditions

Cataloging in Publication Data — DK
[Courtesy: D.K. Agencies (P) Ltd. <docinfo@dkagencies.com>]

Kundakunda, author.
Bārasa aṇuvekkhā of Kundakunda = Twelve facets of reality / edited, translated and commentary by Jagdish Prasad Jain.
pages cm
English and Prakrit (Prakrit in Devanagari and roman).
Includes bibliographical references and indexes.
ISBN 9788124613047 (HB)

1. Digambara (Jaina sect) – Doctrines. 2. Meditation – Jainism. 3. Kundakunda. Bārasāṇuvekkhā. I. Jain, Jagdish P., 1930-2019, editor, translator, writer of added commentary. II. Kundakunda. Bārasāṇuvekkhā. III. Kundakunda. Bārasāṇuvekkhā. English. IV. Title. V. Title: Twelve facets of reality.

LCC BL1380.D53K86 2025 | DDC 294.493 23

ISBN: 978-81-246-1304-7
First published in 2025

Printed and published by:
D.K. Printworld (P) Ltd.
Regd. Office : "Vedaśrī", F-395, Sudarshan Park
ESI Hospital Metro Station, New Delhi - 110015
Phones : (011) 4172 2626, 98713 94815
e-mail : indology@dkprintworld.com
Web : www.dkprintworld.com

Contents

Part Two: Bārasa Aṇuvekkhā
(Text, Transliteration, Translation and Commentary)

List of Abbreviations

AC	Amrtachandra
BA	*Bārasa Aṇuvekkhā* of Kundakunda
Bha	*Bhagavatī Ārādhanā*
Jña	*Jñānārṇava* of Shubhachandra
JS	Jayasena
KA	*Kārttikeyānuprekṣā* of Svami Kumar
Mar	*Maraṇa-Samādhi*
MK	*Maraṇakaṇḍikā* of Acharya Amitgati
MP	*Mokṣa-Mārga Prakāśaka* of Paṇḍit Ṭoḍarmal
NS	*Niyamasāra* of Kundakunda
PKS	*Pañcāstikāyasāra* of Kundakunda
PSU	*Puruṣārthasiddhyupāya* of Amritachandra
RKS	*Ratnakaraṇḍa Śrāvakācāra* of Samantabhadra
SAS	*Sarvārthasiddhi* Commentary on *Tattvārthasūtra* of Pūjyapāda
SS	*Samayasāra* of Kundakunda
TRV	*Tattvārtha-Rājavārttika* Commentary on *Tattvārthasūtra* of Akalaṅka
TS	*Tattvārthasūtra* of Umāsvāmi or Umāsvāti
TSV	*Tattvārthaśloka-Vārttika* of Vidyānandi

Introduction

THE term *aṇuvekkhā* has several spellings in Prākr̥t, viz. *aṇuppehā*, *aṇupehā*, *aṇuvehā*, *aṇuppekkhā*, *aṇupekkhā* and *aṇuvekkā*. Its Sanskrit counterpart is *anuprekṣā* (and not *anutprekṣā*) from the root *ikṣ* with the propositions *anu* and *pra*, meaning to ponder, to reflect, to think repeatedly, etc.

The term *anuprekṣā* is used in nearly a dozen works dealing with reflections/contemplations. Kundakunda's *Bārasa Aṇuvekkhā* (Jain, M. 1949) uses *anuprekṣā* in ninety verses while Vaṭṭakera's *Mūlācāra* (Manikchandra 1923) uses it in seventy-five verses (693–768). In *Bhagavatī Ārādhanā* (Sivarya 1990) (also known as *Mūlārādhanā*), Sivarya uses the term in 160 verses (1715–1875) and *Maraṇa-samādhi* in sixty-nine verses (569–638). Svami Kumar's *Kārttikeyānuprekṣā* (1945), which is wholly devoted to *anuprekṣās*, uses it in 491 verses. *Jñānārṇava* (Shubhachandra 1975) uses the word *bhāvanā* in 202 verses. Other works which use the word *anuprekṣā* are *Tattvārthasūtra* (IX.7) of Umāsvāmi or Umāsvāti (Jaini 1956); *Sarvārthasiddhi* commentary of Pūjyapāda (1944) on *Tattvarthasūtra; Tattvārtha-Rājavārttika* commentary on the *Tattvārthasūtra* by Akalaṅka (1993) and *Tattvārthaśloka-Vārttika* on *Tattvārthasūtra* by Vidyānandi (1918).

Thus, many Jaina texts deal either exclusively or to a substantial extent with *anuprekṣā*; some of them being older than even *Tattvārthasūtra*.

Bārasa Aṇuvekkhā of Kundakunda is an important Prākr̥t text, which is solely devoted to the twelvefold reflections/contemplations. The printed text shows a total of ninety-one *gāthās* (verses).

However, a palm-leaf manuscript with a Kannada gloss from the Lakṣmīsena Matha, Kolhapur, lists only eighty-seven verses and omits four *gāthās* (35, 41, 45 and 67). This is similar to *Kāttigeyāṇuppekkhā* 104, 90 and 91 (which specifies Kundakunda-*munināthа* as the author), and has a different *gāthā* instead of number 19 which happens to be identical with verse 3 of *Daṁsana-pāhuḍa*. There seem to be three facets of the antiquity about this work.[1] First, some of the *gāthās* are common with *Mūlācāra* VIII; they are possibly ancient traditional verses. Second, five of its verses (25-29) are quoted in the same order in *Sarvārthasiddhi* II.10 of Pūjyapāda. Third, the method of exposition is quite traditional and dogmatic. For instance, Pūjyapāda seems to have been indebted to Kundakunda for some of the ideas and similes (like *jala-budbuda*).

Kundakunda's exposition uses the terms *niścaya naya*, *vyavahāra naya* and *śuddha naya*. Apart from his discussion about transitoriness, etc. of external adjuncts, he insists on meditation for the *ātman*, which he states is eternal, the ultimate shelter, unique on account of the distinguishing characteristics, distinct from all others. *Ātmā*, he argues, should not be lost sight of in the transmigratory existence of births and deaths. It is worthy of being realized in this universe. Unlike the body, *ātmā* is pure and distinct from the influx (*āsrava*), stoppage (*saṁvara*), bondage (*bandha*) and shedding of *karmas* (*nirjarā*). Realization of *ātmā* in purity by a monk or a householder is essential for attaining spiritual happiness. Self-realization is the ultimate and the only object of twelvefold reflections. Unlike other commentators who obscure the central theme of self-realization by being engrossed in didactic exhortations, Ācārya Kundakunda does not lose sight of this. The *anuprekṣās* emphasize the wide purpose of religious practices, including meditation, renunciation, atonement for sins as well as maintaining an equanimous attitude.

Mūlācāra of Vaṭṭakera (1923), containing eight chapters and seventy-four verses, is devoted to a discourse on the twelve

---

[1] Upadhye, 1935, *Pravacanasāra*, Introduction, p. 40. For the age of Kundakunda, see ibid.: 10ff.

anuprekṣās or *bhāvanās*. In their exposition of *anuprekṣā*, both *Bārasa Aṇuvekkhā* and *Mūlācāra* have some common verses either in part or in full.

Differences in the Approach of Kundakunda and Vaṭṭakera

There are several marked differences in both the approach and some details regarding *anuprekṣās* in the expositions of Kundakunda and Vaṭṭakera. For instance, Kundakunda emphasizes the positive aspects of *anuprekṣās*. The *ātman* as such must be realized. He also introduces several *nayas*. His description of *dharma* encompasses duties of both monks and householders.

Vaṭṭakera, on the other hand, does not go beyond the literal and dogmatic meaning of each *anuprekṣā*. His primary focus is on the ascetic life. His exposition of *bodhi-durlabha* (rarity of enlightenment, wisdom or true insight of the reality of things and of the right path of liberation) is more of a traditional nature and reminds one of canonical descriptions. Vaṭṭakera prefers the term *aśubha* (inauspicious). For Kundakunda, *aśubha* signifies *aśuci* (impurity). In fact, Kundakunda confines himself to bodily impurity without any reference to *artha* (satisfaction of economic needs), *kāma* (sex), etc. which prominently figure in *Bhagavatī Ārādhanā* and *Maraṇa-Samādhi*.

According to Kundakunda, *saṁsāra* is of five kinds (verse 24). For Vaṭṭakera, however, *saṁsāra* is of four kinds or of six kinds (with reference to *aniyoga-dvārā*) or of many kinds with reference to *gatis* (nos 14-15). Ācārya Vasunandī, who is aware of the fivefold *saṁsāra*, includes *bhava* (implied by *ca*) under *bhava*.

Bhagavatī Ārādhanā of Sivarya devotes nearly 160 verses (1715–1875) to the exposition of the twelve *anuprekṣās*. These contemplations are introduced as *ālambana* of *dharma-dhyāna* (in the manner of *thanaṁga*) under its *saṁsthāna-vicaya* variety. In his exposition, Sivarya impresses us more as a poet than either a dogmatist or a teacher. His style is fluent, simple and lucid, and with the racy flourishing embellishes his composition with strings of striking *upamās* (similes, comparisons) (at times studiously collected) and *rūpakas* (metaphors) many of which are used by subsequent authors. Sivarya mentions a large number of objects of comparison drawn from different walks of life to highlight the transient character of things. In view of the helplessness of persons in the face of kārmic consequences, he urges everyone to seek shelter in *darśana, jñāna, caritra* and *tapas* (austerities). Kundakunda goes one step further and emphasizes the significance and rarity of discriminative insight (enlightenment) or *bheda-vijñāna* (*Bha* 1746 and *BA* 13).

If *Maraṇa-Samādhi* emphasizes helplessness in the face of death, Sivarya emphasizes the same in the face of kārmic consequences. One is really alone and lonely; relatives are not dependable, much less the body; and it is the *dharma* consisting of faith, knowledge and conduct that accompanies the soul (cf. *Bha* 1752 and *BA* 20).

Contact with people here in different parts is similar to a meeting of birds on a tree at night. Individuals have different temperaments, and their mutual attachment is necessarily utilitarian. *Saṁsāra*, which is fivefold, is a dangerous wilderness or an unfathomable ocean in which one drifts by one's own *karmas* through various forms of life. A person wanders in *saṁsāra* in different places, with changing body forms and varying aptitudes. He is constantly pursued by death and suffers manifold miseries. *Karmas* constantly entrap the soul, which, in its pursuit of pleasure, suffers infinite pain in this endless *saṁsāra*.

Under *lokānuprekṣā* (contemplation of the nature of the universe), Sivarya provides a more detailed explanation about changing human relations (e.g. by the story of Vasantatilaka), various births and worldly conditions, instead of cosmological details.

Dharma alone is *śubha* (auspicious), while *artha* (satisfaction of economic needs) and *kāma* (sex) are *aśubha* (inauspicious): the body is all impure. An unguarded soul is like a leaky boat in which the kārmic fluid easily flows or similar to an oily surface to which the kārmic dust clings. The human life should be used to eradicate the causes of the influx (*āsrava*) of *karmas* which are all-pervasive. It is essential to stop (*saṁvara*) of the influx of *karmas* by curbing the senses, passions, etc. *Karmas* either get destroyed in their own way after giving the fruit or through the practice of penances.

While discussing *dharma*, Sivarya does not distinguish between *sāgāra-dharma* (a householder's religion) and *anāgāra-dharma* (religion of an ascetic), but speaks of it in general. *Dharma* is supreme and thereby human beings attain the highest bliss. *Dharma* preached by the Jina is compared with a wheel in this manner.

Enlightenment and religion are something rare and accidental for a soul overwhelmed by *karmas* and constantly moving in *saṁsāra*. It is like the yoke and yoke-pin. It comes together on a vast sea: fortunate are those who have acquired it.

One is not quite certain about the relative chronology of Kundakunda, Sivarya and Vaṭṭakera. A comparative study of their exposition of *anuprekṣās* is nevertheless interesting. Though the works of this trio are related, they have their own individuality. They enumerate the twelve *anuprekṣās* in the same sequence and share many common ideas. While Kundakunda addresses both monks and householders, Sivarya and Vaṭṭakera focus on ascetics, which is akin to canonical texts.

Kundakunda and Sivarya speak of the fivefold *saṁsāra*. In this context, the latter seems to quote a few verses from the former (*BA* 26-27 or *Bha* 1776 and 1778). Verse 1824 of Sivarya also occurs in *Pañcāstikāyasāra* (Chakravartinayanar 1975) where Amritachandra calls it *Siddhāntasūtra*, possibly an ancient verse inherited in traditional memory.

Some *gāthās* of Kundakunda have a close resemblance to those of Sivarya (cf. *BA* 13, 48-49 and 67 respectively with *Bha* 1746, 1825-1826 and 1847). Between Vaṭṭakera and Sivarya, two verses are almost common (*Mūlācāra* 65[2] and 67 respectively with *Bhagavatī Ārādhanā* 1867 and 1870); both of them use the term *loga-dhamma* (*Mūlācāra* 28 and *Bhagavatī Ārādhanā* 1811); and there are some *gāthās* which show many common ideas and expressions (cf. *Mūlācāra* 17, 26-27, 31-32, 37, 43-44, 50, 56-57, 61 and 66 respectively with *Bhagavatī Ārādhanā* 1789, 1799, 1802-1803, 1814-1815, 1821, 1828, 1837, 1851, 1853, 1857 and 1869).

Some of the verses of Sivarya's *Bhagavatī Ārādhanā* are similar to a few verses in *Maraṇa-Samādhi* (cf. *Bha* 1776, 1822, 1837 and 1870 with *Mar* 598, 618, 621 and 634). These three texts, along with the section on *bhāvanās* in *Maraṇa-Samādhi*, are the basic fountainhead which have fostered the subsequent thoughts about *anuprekṣās*.

Jñānārṇava (or *Yogapradīpādhikāra*) of Shubhachandra (1927) is a solid and significant treatise on *yoga* (meditation), written in fluent Sanskrit and full of didactic fervour. As an authoritative work on *dhyāna*, it is only natural that it incorporates a discussion of the twelve *anuprekṣās*. Interestingly, Shubhachandra prefaces *Jñānārṇava* with an elaborate discussion of *anuprekṣās* (which he calls *bhāvanās*) and asserts that they lead to the cleansing of the heart and steadiness of the mind. They are, in fact, the "beautiful steps leading to the terrace of liberation" (*Jñā* II.5-7). In all, around 88 verses (*Jñā* II.5 onwards), which are mostly *anuṣṭubh* but occasionally have longer metres, are devoted to these topics of reflection, which primarily address the ascetic. Shubhachandra refers to the fivefold *saṁsāra* in the *aśucitva bhāvanā*. He devotes more attention to bodily integrity, along with a long, general essay on the tenfold *dharma*. Details of his discussion on the *loka* (world or universe) are more cosmological.

Use of the Term Bhāvanā

The term *bhāvanā* is used in various contexts in Jaina terminology. It came to be gradually used in the sense of *anuprekṣā*. Subsequently, *bhāvanā* practically replaced *anuprekṣā*, especially in Hindi and Gujarati literature (Upadhye 1983: 9-12).

Literally speaking, whatever is to be reflected upon would be called *bhāvanā*. In this way, *anuprekṣā* came to be equated with *bhāvanā* in course of time. The term *anuprekṣā* occurs in *Thanaṁga* and *Ovavaiya Suttam* (Suru 1931) as well as Sivarya's *Bhagavatī Ārādhanā*. Kundakunda's verse[2]:

> *bhavahi anupekkhāu avare pannīs bhāvanā bhavi,*
> *bhava rahiana kim puna bahirliṅgena kayavvam* ।
> — *Bhāvapāhuḍa*, v. 96

clearly illustrates how the term *bhāvanā* could have come into vogue instead of *anuprekṣā*. In Sanskrit, it means "meditate" (*bhavai*) on the twelve reflections (*anuprekṣās*) and the twenty-five *bhāvanās* (of the five vows); what can external form do for a person devoid of mental purity?

Though not as a direct synonym for *anuprekṣā*, Kundakunda incidentally uses the word *bhāvanā* (*BA* 46) in concluding his exposition of *aśucitva*. Vaṭṭakera however has clearly used the term *bhāvanā*. *Kāttikeyāṇuppekkhā* uses both the terms (*KA* 87 and 94) though it seems to prefer *anuprekṣā*. In *Maraṇa-Samādhi* and *Jñānārṇava*, the term *bhāvanā* has practically taken the place of *anuprekṣā*. Subsequently, it became more and more popular.

In Hindi, hundreds of *bhāvanās* have been composed by Bhudhar Das, Yugalji, Mangat Rai, Daulatram, Roopchand, Dyanatrai, Budhajan, Deepchand, etc. Of these, the *bhāvanā* of Bhudhar Das and Yugalji are more popular.

Bhāvanā, Pandit Sadasukhdas Kasliwal observes, is the foundation of the whole *dharma* (i.e. righteousness and piety). It is from *bhāvanā* that brightness or brilliance of the states-of-evolution (*pariṇāma*) takes place. *Bhāvanā* alone leads to the absence of a deluded view. It leads to the *pariṇāma* of moral self-restraints like non-violence. It leads to vows (*vrata*) becoming more resolute

---

2 See Kundakunda, *Ashta Pahuda*, p. 24, Sonegar: Shri Digambar Jain Svadhyay Mandir Trust.

(*dṛḍha*). *Bhāvanā* also enhances and fosters *vītarāgatā* (freedom from attachment).

Moreover, from *bhāvanā*, due to the absence or lack of inauspicious meditation, auspicious meditation (*dharma dhyāna*) is enhanced. For instance, from *bhāvanā*, one experiences the Self. Thus, *bhāvanā* alone gives rise to thousands of good qualities. Being aware of this reality, one should not give up contemplations (*bhāvanās*) even for a moment.

When *bhāvanā* is present in the mind, one's thoughts and actions as well as their fruits are similar. The fruits of actions done with good *bhāvanās* are also good. However, action motivated by evil thoughts blight this world as well as the next one.

There is a complete psychological, systematic order of the particular practice of the twelve contemplations (*bhāvanās*) in Jaina tradition. The practice of these *bhāvanās* has great significance in enfeebling mental and subconscious compulsions. The primary intention behind a *bhāvanā* is the restraint of the processes (*vṛttis*) of the mind (*citta*), which is the seed, the organ, the aggregate of the cognitive, volitional and emotional activities, functions and processes of the individual. The mental processes are perception, inference, testimony, perverseness/error, thought construction (*vikalpa*) and memory.

Absorption in a particular *bhāvanā* leads one to become transformed in a similar form.

Bhāvanās are the mental processes for their flowing in a particular direction. A *bhāvanā* is the construction of a strong situation by the repetition of any thought. It is a power which can be used in different forms. In fact, the use of a *bhāvanā* facilitates the transformation of one's nature (*svabhāva*) and spiritual development. By the inspiration of *bhāvanās*, all activities can be managed. There is only one formula — the construction of the mind and to make or fashion its mobility in a particular direction (Muni Kishanlal 1994: 110-111).

A *bhāvanā* is very significant in spiritual practice (*sādhanā*). It is a powerful medium for the eradication of evil habits and the formation of new habits. The transformation of an individual's personality can be done through *bhāvanās* (Mahaprajna 1995: 62-63).

The twelve *bhāvanās* have a calming effect on mental agitations arising from the separation of desired things and the conjunction of undesired ones, and tolerance of fortitude (*dhairya*) in calamities. They give rise to attachment from sensual pleasures and passions like anger and lead to fondness for righteousness and piety (*dharma*). As a result of pondering over these *bhāvanās*, the infatuation for life in fear of death is enfeebled.

In *Bārasa Aṇuvekkhā* 90, Acharya Kundakunda states:

> Of what use is the lengthy chatter? The excellent souls who have liberated themselves in the past, thereby attaining the liberated state of *siddha*, and those who will liberate themselves in the future — all that is due to the majesty of *anuprekṣās*.

The twelve *bhāvanās* are the subject matter of one's meditation, and how to occupy one's mind with useful, religious, beneficial, peaceful, spiritually-advancing, *karma*-preventing thoughts. They assist in spiritual progress, produce detachment and enable aspirants to move from the realm of desire to the path of renunciation. They are reflections upon the fundamental facets of life. They seek to develop purity of thought and sincerity in the practice of religion.

Anuprekṣās, according to Acharya Mahaprajna, is thinking/ contemplation on a particular subject which frees the mind of its infatuation. Repeated thinking on a subject/idea influences the mind. Such thinking or practice is called *bhāvanā*. However, to change one's habits, one takes recourse to *anuprekṣā*, which may be termed as "suggestology". It is being employed for curing ills. It is the technique of auto-suggestion in which a person makes a suggestion to oneself. Hypnotism is carried out on the basis of suggestion.

The technique of *anuprekṣā* is an infallible method of bringing about a change in one's character and for dissolving one's false assumptions and preconceptions as well as negative thoughts.

Bhāvanā means contemplative meditation. It implies total identification with and concentration on the subject or the goal chosen. It is the exercise of willpower behind the process of change. It changes both consciousness as well as the environment. Even the most complex habit can be changed through the exercise of *bhāvanās*.

Bhāvanās are the principal medium of brainwashing. Go on repeating one thing time and again. Keep reiterating it. A moment eventually comes when old ideas are shed and new ideas get established in the mind. It is the path of the soul's transformation.

Bhāvanās imply the transcendence of the conscious mind and the awakening of the subconscious mind to establish it firmly in the subconscious mind (Mahaprajna 2010: 1-19).

Just as negative thoughts over a period of time become so deeply entrenched in the mind that a specific groove is created in the brain that makes one behave in a certain way, often against his/her wish; similarly, contemplations repeated over time create brain patterns of positive thoughts.

Pondering over *bhāvanās* enables one to have greater understanding of the reality (*vāstavikatā*).

Bhāvanā is a preliminary step of meditation (*dhyāna*). Due to repeated contemplations, the fire of passions like anger is extinguished, attachment to other substances is dissolved, the darkness of ignorance is stamped out and attachment arises against deluded assumptions due to the exhibition of the reality of the situation. As a result, the path of happiness, peace and supreme well-being is facilitated.

In *Kārttikeyānuprekṣā*, *anuprekṣās* are said to be the mother of happiness or bliss. Acharya Padmanandi in *Pañcaviṁśati* states that the contemplation of *bhāvanās* is the cause of the destruction of *karmas*. The *anuprekṣās* have great significance in the destruction of *karmas*, in the acquisition of *samyak darśana* and non-attachment (*vītarāgatā*).

Saṁvara (stoppage) of the influx (*āsrava*) of *karmas* is accomplished by the contemplation of these *bhāvanās*.

Dhammapada 282 says:

> From earnest contemplation is wisdom born, from lack of earnest contemplation wisdom wanes. It is said that from *bhāvanā* arises liking for what is to be aspired for (*upādeya*) and what is to be discarded (*heya*).

The equanimity, contemplations (*bhāvanās*) enable one to attain mental peace and tranquillity even in adverse circumstances. Due to this equanimity, the mind transcends the constricting thoughts and all partial viewpoints of the soul being bound or not bound (*SS* 141) and of preferences, bias or partiality of likes and dislikes, friendship or enmity, happiness and unhappiness, honour and dishonour, etc. In other words, one is free from such attachment. Such a transcendental and equanimous Self is the true reality or the essence (*sāra*) of *samaya* (soul substance or the Self) — *samayasāra* — and he alone is qualified to be characterized by enlightened worldview (*samyak darśana*) and enlightened knowledge (*SS* 151). An enlightened Self is endowed with the potency of knowledge and detachment (*vairāgya*) (Amrtachandra 1964: 136).

In *Pravacanasāra* 7, *dharma* (righteousness and piety) is described or defined as equanimity and equanimity is said to be a state-of-evolution of the soul, in which it is free from infatuation (*moha*) and mental agitation or disturbance (*kṣoba*). The equanimous Self, which is free from *moha*, is also free from a sense of mineness (*mamakāra*) [that this body, etc. is "mine or me"] as well as arrogance or pride (*ahaṁkāra*) — the two sons of *moha* (*Tattvānuśāsana* 13-14). Of these two, the former gives rise to attachment (*rāga*) and the latter to aversion (*dveṣa*) (*Tattvānuśāsana* 16), which are the causal conditions (*hetu*) of bondage (*bandha*) of *karmas* and transmigration into four conditions of existence (hell, heaven, human and sub-human) (*Tattvānuśāsana* 18). The destruction of these *bandha-hetu*, leads to liberation (*Tattvānuśāsana* 23).

Apart from practice (*abhyāsa*), detachment (*vairāgya*), knowledge (*jñāna*) and concentration (*dhyāna*), the other means of the subjugation and conquest of the mind, include thinking, contemplation/reflection (*anuprekṣā* or *bhāvanā*) of transitoriness (*anitya*), etc. as well as non-attachment to sense objects (*Tattvānuśāsana* 79).

A person who conquers the mind is considered to be the conqueror of senses (*jitendriya*) (*Tattvānuśāsana* 76). Desire for sense objects creates mental agitations and frenzy. With total restraint of mind, the soul (*puruṣa* or seer) is established in his own true nature (*Yogasūtra* 1.3).

A person who gives up all desires is devoid of possessiveness (*saṅga-tyāga*) and expectations is in reality consciousness of the knowing nature *jñāyaka* (*SS* 210-213). Such a person who is free from the sense of mineness (*nirmama*) (*SS* 36-37 and 73 and *Gītā* II.71) and devoid of arrogance (*ahaṁkāra*) attains peace, tranquillity or "quietitude" (*Gītā* II.71). Desire, possessiveness and ego do not belong to the *jñāyaka*, who introspects the body, the sense organs, and the mind. Such an *asaṅga* or *niḥsaṅga* or *nirgrantha* person invariably conquers the mind and the senses (*Tattvānuśāsana* 75).

The term *muni* is very often used in Jaina scriptures (e.g. *SS* 151). One becomes a *muni* because of *mānasa-śīlatva*, i.e. the practice of reflection or rumination. This *manana* (reflection) must remain steady, constant, stable and firm. A person, who has a steady, not a restless mind, remains steady and poised. He never swerves from its axis (*sthira mana*). The *manana* or *munitva* will be quite pronounced in such a person with a stable mind. Those *munis*, who are absorbed in the supreme reality or divine state of the Self, attain liberation (*nirvāṇa*) (*SS* 151).

It is, thus, obvious that *anuprekṣā*, first as an attendant cause of meditation and then as a part of religious study, has grown in popularity in Jaina literature from the earliest to the latest times. What were once stray topics of Śramaṇic (ascetic) poetry, quite suited to Jaina ideology, were soon codified and enumerated in twelve *anuprekṣās*. This trend has conveniently included ideas conducive to renunciation (say as in the *saṁsāra*) and to the elaboration of Jaina dogmatic details (as in the *āsrava*, etc. and in the *loka*). Apart from independent treatises and substantial expositions, manuals of conduct for monks and laymen, narrative tales and the *Purāṇas* and even stylistic *kāvyas* have given place in them to be exposition of *anuprekṣā*. In the growth, propagation/elaboration of Jaina ideology, the exposition of *anuprekṣā* has become an important branch of literature in Prākr̥t (including Apabhraṁśa), Sanskrit, Kannada and other modern Indian languages.

Kinds of Bhāvanā

It is obvious from the above discussion that the twelve *anuprekṣās* (*bhāvanās*) of *adhruva/anitya*, etc. are not the only *bhāvanās*. Verse 96 of Kundakunda's *Bhāva Pāhuḍa* makes it quite clear that apart from the twelve *anuprekṣās*, there are twenty-five meditation (*bhāvanās*) (five each in case of each of the five vows prescribed for householders and ascetics/monks) in order to make the five vows stable, lasting, enduring (*sthira*) pertaining to *ahiṁsā*, etc. These are enumerated in *Caritra Pāhuḍa* 32-36 and *Tattvārthasūtra* VII.4-VII.8.

Thus, the five meditations (*bhāvanās*) for the non-violence (*ahiṁsā*) vow against injury are: (1) self-restraint of speech (*vacana guptī*); (2) self-restraint of mind (*manoguptī*); (3) carefulness in walking (*iryā-samiti*); (4) carefulness in lifting and laying down things (*ādāna-nikṣepaṇa samiti*); and (5) thoroughly seeing to one's food and drink (*alokita panā bhājana*) (*TS* VII.4).

The five meditations for the vow against falsehood are: (1) giving up anger (*krodha*); (2) giving up of greed (*lobha*); (3) giving up of fear or cowardice; (4) giving up of frivolity (*hāsya*); and (5) speaking in accordance with scriptural injunctions (*anuvīcī bhāṣaṇa*) (*TS* VII.5). (According to verse 33 of *Caritra Pāhuḍa*, it is infatuation (*moha*).)

The five meditations for the vow against theft are:

1. residence in a solitary place, like a mountain, cave, etc. (*śūnyāgāra*);
2. residence in a deserted place (*vimocita vāsa*);
3. residence in a place where one is not likely to be prohibited by others, nor where one should be likely to prohibit others (*paroparodhakaraṇa*);
4. purity of alms (*bhaikṣya śuddhi*) (*TS* VII.6); and
5. purity in taking food, *eṣaṇā śuddhi* in *Caritra Pāhuḍa* 34.

The five meditations for the vow against unchastity (*abrahmacarya*) are:

1. renouncing of reading or hearing stories (*kathā*) exciting attachment for women;
2. renouncing of seeing/looking, observing (*nirīkṣaṇa* in *TS* VII.7) and *ālokana* in *Caritra Pāhuḍa* 35) the beautiful bodies of women;
3. renouncing of thinking over or remembrance of past enjoyment of women (*pūrvaratānusmaraṇa*);
4. renouncing of exciting and aphrodisiac drinks (*vṛṣyastarasa*); and
5. renouncing of beautifying one's own body (self-adornment) (*sva śarīra saṁskāra*) (*TS* VII.7) (residing in the dwelling place connected or attached to women in *Caritra Pāhuḍa* 35).

The five meditations for the vow against attachment or mental clinging to worldly belongings/objects or possessiveness which entraps the soul from all sides are:

1. giving up or self-denial of attachment (*rāga*);
2. aversion (hatred) (*dveṣa*);
3. in the pleasing (*manojña*); and
4. displeasing (*amanojña*) (worldly) objects of the five senses (*TS* VII.8) (of sound, touch, taste, form/appearance and smell in *Caritra Pāhuḍa* 36).

In addition to the above twenty-five *bhāvanās*, the destructive or dangerous (*apāya*) and censurable (*avādya*) character of the five faults, like injury or violence, five sins, or to be meditated upon for the strengthening of the five vows (*TS* VII.9). One must also meditate that the five faults, injury, etc. are a personification of pain/misery (*duḥkhameva*) (*TS* VII.10) since they themselves are the veritable wombs of misery. For the apprehension of the miseries of the world (*saṁvega*) and non-attachment to sense pleasures (*vairāgya*), one should meditate upon the nature of the world (which is transitory and full of misery) and of our physical body (which is impure) (*TS* VII.12).

According to Pandit Sadasukhdas, whenever there is bonding (*bandhana*), dependence, anger, pride, deceit and greed (passions) and misery or suffering in the world, it is due to acquisitiveness (*parigraha*). Moreover, sensual pleasures only lead to misery or suffering since they are accompanied by obstacles/distractions, interrupted or terminable and the causes of bondage (*PS* 76).

Various kinds of useful and significant reflections (*bhāvanās*) may be mentioned as follows:

1. The twelve reflections (*bhāvanās*) of *adhruva/anitya*, etc.
2. The twenty-five reflections (*bhāvanās*) of the five vows (*TS* VII.1) and the accompanying meditations (*TS* VII.9, *TS* VII.10 and *TS* VII.12) described above (see *supra*).
3. The four reflections/meditations (*bhāvanās*) (*TS* VII.11) as follows:
   a. amity, fellow feeling, friendship or benevolence (*maitrī*) for all living beings (*sattva*), i.e. being a friend of all, an enemy of none. Reflection of *maitrī bhāvanā* leaves no room for harm, deceit or quarrelsome with anybody. *Maitrī* will lead us to be tolerant, forgiving and caring for one another;
   b. *pramoda* (*mudita*), i.e. delight, appreciation or admiration of the merits of the good qualities of others, who are better qualified

or more advanced than ourselves (*guṇādhika*). It corrodes one's own pride, conceit and jealousy;

c. *karuṇā* (feeling of compassion and mercy or kindness or pity) for those in distress or afflicted; and

d. *madhyastha* (tolerance, indifference, equanimity) towards uncivil, ill-behaved or perversely inclined (*Bhāvanā Dvātriṁśatikā* (1975) of Ācārya Amitgati).

These four *bhāvanās* are the golden principles for social intercourse and a happy and peaceful life.

4. The sixteen reflections (*bhāvanās*) (*TS* VII.24 and *SAS*, pp. 260-261) which bring about the influx of *tīrthaṅkara-nāma-karman* are as follows: purity of worldview (*darśana-viśuddhi*). Without the nearness of the Omniscient Lord (Kevalī) or all-knowing masters of scriptures (*śruta-kevalī*) one does not have purity of the states-of-evolution capable of bondage of *tīrthaṅkara* species of *karma*.

Darśana-viśuddhi is equated with enlightened worldview or right belief (*samyak darśana*), which has five prerequisites and eight characteristics. The five prerequisites are:

a. control or subsidence of anger, etc. passions (*praśama*);
b. enthusiasm for righteousness and positive motivation (*saṁvega*);
c. detached, objective or balanced view of things and disinterest in sensual pleasures in worldly possessions (*nirveda*);
d. compassion (*anukampā*); and
e. conviction or acceptance of reality as it is (*astikāya*).

The eight characteristics called component parts (*aṅgas*) of *samyak darśana* are:

1. freedom from all doubt (*niḥśaṅkita*);
2. freedom from worldly desires (*niḥkāṅkṣita*);
3. freedom from repulsion (*nirvicikitsā*);
4. freedom from superstitious beliefs and folly;

5. tendency to cover up or hide the faults and shortcomings of others (*upagūhana*); it is also said to be *upabṛhana*, i.e. cultivation of virtuous dispositions of honesty such as *ahiṁsā*, forgiveness, modesty and straightforwardness;
6. stabilization of those faltering in their righteous pursuits and re-establishing them on the path of righteousness and truth (*sthithikaraṇa*);
7. disinterest affection for others (*vātsalya*); and
8. propagation of the values of life and path of liberation (*prabhāvanā*).

Without *samyak darśana*, there is neither the householder's *dharma* nor the *dharma* of saints. Without *samyak darśana*, the knowledge is bad/defective and the conduct is bad/defective.

The belief that Jaina Tīrthaṅkaras are the true gods, the glorious Divine Lords worthy of worship, Jaina Śāstras are the true scriptures and that Jaina saints are the true preceptors, is called right faith, i.e. *samyak darśana*. The true believer must be free from three kinds of stupidity, follies or foolishness (*mūḍhatā*) and eight kinds of pride (*Ratnakaraṇḍa Śrāvakācāra* 4).

The three kinds of foolishness are:

1. *Loka-mūḍhatā*: Bathing in [the so-called sacred] rivers (such as the Ganges) and oceans, setting up heaps of sand and stones [as objects of worship], immolating oneself by falling from a precipice or by being burnt up in fire (as in *satī*) are some of the common follies (*loka-mūḍhatās*) (*RKS* 23).
2. *Deva-mūḍhatā*: Worshipping with desire to obtain favour of deities whose minds are full of likes and dislikes is called folly of devotion to false divinity (*RKS* 23).
3. *Guru-mūḍhatā*: This consists of the worship of false ascetics revolving in the wheel of *saṁsāra* (births and deaths), who have neither renounced worldly attractions or goods, and occupations nor *hiṁsā* (causing injury to others) (*RKS* 24).

The saints who have eradicated all traces of pride from their souls describe *mada* (pride) as the intoxication of the Self in respect of eight particulars:

1. learning;
2. worship;
3. family;
4. tribe;
5. power;
6. affluence or accomplishments;
7. religious austerities; and
8. person (*RKS* 25).

Sixteen Bhāvanās

1. By giving up or abandoning six kinds of *anāyatana* (perversity, i.e. perverse resting place or abode) also purity of the *darśana* (*darśana-viśuddhi*) takes place. The six *anāyatanas* are: (1) perverse divinity (*kudeva*); (2) bad or perverse preceptor (*kuguru*); (3) perverse or defective scriptures (*kuśāstra*); and those who are devoted to or followers of the above three, thus making up six.

Those who are endowed with attachment, aversion, lust, anger, greed and weapons do not obtain true *dharma*. They are therefore *kudeva anāyatana*.

Those, who are desirous or covetous of the five sense objects, have acquisitiveness, and those committing and commissioning sinful activities (*ārambha*), wearing clothes and devoid of *dharma* are *kuguru*, i.e. not true preceptor (*guru*).

Kuśāstras are those who give inspiration of sinful activity of violence, increasing the force of attachment, aversion and lust, expound or describe completely one-sided thoughts.

Those who are devotees of Goddess Padmāvatī or Khetrapāla are devoid of *dharma*. Those who serve with devotion to *kugurus*; those who read *kuśāstra* and have devotion for them are one-sided persons, are the other three *anāyatanas* (Jain, J.P. 2022: 69).

2. Another *bhāvanā* is reverence for the (enlightened knowledge, etc.) path of liberation (*vinaya sampannatā*). According to Pandit Sadasukhdas Kasliwal, *vinaya-sampannatā* is of five kinds:

a. *darśana vinaya* (keeping one's faith free from the faults of doubt, etc.);
b. *jñāna-vinaya* (to make efforts towards adoration of enlightened knowledge (*samyak jñāna*) and hearing and reading of Jaina scriptures, etc.);

c. *caritra-vinaya*, i.e. acquisition of right conduct according to one's capacity and to reduce one's craving for sense objects (*viṣaya*) and passions like anger;

d. *tapa-vinaya*, i.e. having contentment in *viṣaya* and make efforts in meditation and study (*dhyāna-svādhyāya*); and

e. *upacāra-vinaya*, i.e. modesty of humility (*vinaya*), prayer, adoration or homage (*vandanā*) and praise (*stavana*) of the five most revered souls (*pañca parameṣṭhi*) after establishing the names. *Upacāra-vinaya* is of many other kinds like

   i. *loka-vinaya* (becoming courteous after extreme absence of eight prides and thinking that wealth, youth and life) is ephemeral and dependent on *karmas*. This *vinaya* is like fire for burning the tree of the cycle of births and deaths and is principal in the three universes;

   ii. *deva-vinaya*, i.e. contemplating the Omniscient Lord Arihanta and his eulogy or praise and paying homage;

   iii. *guru-vinaya*, i.e. adoration of the preceptor;

   iv. *śāstra-vinaya*, i.e. courtesy and respect for scriptures;

   v. *niścaya-vinaya* is the humility in respect of the Self (*ātmā*), thinking that it does not get misery of transmigration due to delusion, passions, etc.;

   vi. *vyavahāra-vinaya*, in which passion of pride is reduced and one speaks sweet words to all; and

   vii. *vacana-vinaya*, i.e. not to show disrespect even to the deluded person and speak sweet words.

3. *Śīlavrateṣuanaticāra*: faultless observance of the five vows and subdual of passions like anger.

4. *Abhīkṣana jñānopayoga*: ceaseless pursuit of right knowledge pertaining to the Self's own psychic principles of states (*svatattva*) of the nature of *jīva*, etc. objects (*padārthas*) (*SAS*, p. 261).

5. *Saṁvega*: perpetual apprehension of worldly/mundane miseries (*saṁvega*).

6. *Śaktitastyāga*: renunciation (*tyāga*) is giving charity (*dāna*), which

is of three kinds (giving of food, giving of fearlessness and giving up of knowledge) (*SAS*, p. 261) according to one's capacity.

7. *Śaktitastapa*: the practice of austerities or penance (*tapa*) or causing suffering to the body being well disposed to the path of liberation (*SAS*, p. 261) according to one's capacity.

8. *Sādhu samādhi*: protecting and reassuring the saints or removing their troubles while they are engaged in observing penance (*SAS*, p. 261).

9. *Vaiyāvrātya*: serving the meritorious and removing any trouble faced by them (*SAS*, p. 261).

10. *Arahanta bhakti*: devotion with the impurity of psychic dispositions of Arahanta or the Omniscient Lord.

11. *Ācārya bhakti*: heads of the order of saints (*ācārya*).

12. *Bahuśruta bhakti*: those engaged in teaching of saints (*upādhyāya*).

13. *Pravacana bhakti*: those engaged in teaching of scriptures.

14. *Āvaśyaka parihāni*: not neglecting one's six essential daily duties according to time. The six essential or obligatory duties are:

   a. worship of the worthy Lord (*deva-pūjā*),
   b. respecting and serving the preceptor (*gurūpāsti*),
   c. study of scriptures (*svādhyāya*),
   d. self-restraint (*saṁyama*),
   e. austerities of penances (*tapa*), and
   f. giving of donation or charity (*dāna*).

Of these six, austerities are of two kinds: external and internal. The external austerities are of six kinds (*TS* IX.19):

   i. fasting or absence from food (*anaśana*);
   ii. reduced diet or taking part of a full meal (*avamaudārya*);
   iii. voluntary limiting the range of choice or the variety of seeking food (*vṛtti parisaṁkhyāna*);
   iv. giving up delicacies or a stimulating diet (*rasaparityāga*);

v. sleeping or residing in a lovely place, free from insect afflictions and all disturbances (*vivikta śayyāsana*); and

vi. bodily discomforts (*kāya-kleśa*).

The internal austerities are also of six kinds (*TS* IX.20):

i. expiation or atonement (*prāyaścitta*);

ii. reverence, veneration or respect (*vinaya*);

iii. serving the meritorious (*vaiyyāvṛtya*);

iv. study (*svādhyāya*), which is of five kinds (*TS* IX.25):

   a. reading (*vācana*);
   b. questioning or enquiry (*praccehana*);
   c. reflection (*anuprekṣā*);
   d. memorizing (*amānya*);
   e. lecturing on righteousness (*dharmopadeśa*);

v. renunciation is attachment (vyutsarga); and

vi. meditation (dhyāna).

Meditation (*dhyāna*) is of four kinds (*TS* IX.28): (i) mournful (*ārta-dhyāna*); (ii) cruel or wrathful meditation (*raudra dhyāna*); (iii) virtuous or righteous meditation (*dharma-dhyāna*); and (iv) pure or whole meditation (*śukla-dhyāna*);

15. propagation of righteousness (*dharma*) and path of liberation through knowledge, austerities, giving charity or worship of the worthy Lord (*jinapiya*).

16. affection (*vātsalya*) for coreligionists (*sādharmī*).

Even one of these sixteen *bhāvanās*, if properly contemplated/ reflected and with enlightened worldview (or right belief), brings about the inflow of the *tīrthaṅkara* body-making (*nāma*) *karma*.

Bhagavatī Ārādhanā

Bhagavatī Ārādhanā, also called *Mūlārādhanā* by Acharya Sivarya, also called *Śivakoṭi*, written in Prākṛt, describes the twelve *anuprekṣās* in the same order as *Bārasa Aṇuvekkhā* of Kundakunda (mentioning *adhruva*, not *anitya* as first *anuprekṣā*) with one difference, viz. in place of *aśuci* of Kundakunda, *Bārasa Aṇuvekkhā* mentions *aśubha*. In addition to describing twelve *anuprekṣās*, *Bārasa Aṇuvekkhā* also describes five contemplations (*bhāvanās*), which are to be given up or to be discarded, and the sixth *asaṅkliṣṭa bhāvanā* (contemplation), i.e. one devoid of affliction, suffering, wretched or difficult to grasp (*uleṣa*) *bhāvanā*, which again is of five kinds which are to be grasped (*grāhya*), contemplated or reflected.

Maraṇakaṇḍikā

Maraṇakaṇḍikā (*MK*) of Acharya Amitgati (2004: 75-84) is the Sanskrit rendering or version of *Bārasa Aṇuvekkhā*. It does not describe the twelve *anuprekṣās* but describes only the five *bhāvanās* that are to be given up and the sixth *asaṅkliṣṭa bhāvanā*, which again is of five kinds.

Bhāvanās to Be Given Up

The five *bhāvanās*, which are to be given up, are:

1. *kandarpa bhāvanā*: a person of unsteady and fickle mind and one who indulges in tales of laughter and arousing of curiosity or interest (*kautuka*) puts others in astonishment (*Bha* 182);
2. uncivilized speech, mixed with excessive laughter due to attachment is *kandarpa*. And bad action or movement (*kuceṣṭā*) of the body with sexual inclination is *kaut-kucya*. One who engages in these two always indulges in culpable or sinning (*kilviṣi*) *bhāvanā*, in which one blames the knowledge of the scriptures (*śruta-jñāna*), a deceiver regarding the Omniscient Lord, *dharma*, i.e. conduct of non-attachment and cheats his *ācāryas* and all the saints;
3. *abhiyoga bhāvanā*: in which one makes use of *mantras* for gain of money or sensual pleasures, indulges in magical powers

(*bhūti karma*) such as unrestrained (*niraṅkuśa*), imbued with scolding, abuse and resentment (*ākrośī*) (in *MK*) (*nirdaya*);

4. *āsurī bhāvanā*: in which one is engaged in attached or stipulated (*anubodha*) anger and quarrel/strife (*kalaha*). He also earns his living by making use of astrology and palmistry, etc. and one who is devoid of compassion or piety (*nirdaya*), unrestrained (*niraṅkuśa*), imbued with scolding, abuse and resentment (*ākrośī*) and does not repent even after causing trouble or hardship to others; and
5. *sammohī bhāvanā*: in which one lectures on an evil path (*unmārga*) of deluded view and lack of moral self-restraints, spoils/corrupts the path of liberation (*mokṣa mārga*) of triple jewels of enlightened worldview, knowledge and conduct, thereby being destroyer of *mokṣa mārga* and one who deludes people with perverted knowledge.

A person who, after giving up the above-mentioned five distressful and wretched (*saṅkleśa*) *bhāvanā*, one who acquires the *asaṅkleśa bhāva* in which one engages in five carefulness (*samiti*) and three self-restraints (*guptī*) of mind, speech and body [is free from all possessiveness (*parigraha*) and has apprehension of worldly miseries (in *Maraṇakaṇḍikā*)] should engage himself in the five *bhāvanās* which are worth acquiring.

Bhāvanās Worth Acquiring

The five *bhāvanās*, worth acquiring, are:

1. *Bhāvanā pertaining to tapa* (*austerities*): Due to this *bhāvanā*, one is indifferent or not interested (*vimukha*) in sense pleasures, desirous of voluntarily adopting peaceful death (*samādhi* or *sallekhanā*) and intolerant of hardships (*pariṣaha*) practitioner of austerities (*tapasvī*), and he engages in the triple jewels (*ratnatraya*) of enlightened worldview, knowledge and conduct in *Maraṇakaṇḍikā*.

2. *Śruta bhāvanā or jñāna bhāvanā*: The functional role (*kārya*) of

śruta is knowledge of scriptural contemplation (*śruta bhāvanā*), i.e. the constant practice of the meanings of the scriptures, the saint devolves into enlightened knowledge, enlightened worldview, or right belief, austerities and moral self-restraints (*saṁyama*). [Also he accomplishes on his own promises/vows (*pratijñā*) without thought-constructions (*vikalpa*) and mental agitation and distress (*ākulatā*). *Śruta bhāvanā* is engaging oneself repeatedly in the meaning of the scriptures. In other words, repeatedly pondering over the meanings of scriptural sentences on hearing them is knowledge reflection. After acquiring *jñāna bhāvanā*, austerities (*tapa*) and self-restraints (*saṁyama*) deserve to be worshipped (*bhajanīya*). Where there is *tapa* and *saṁyama*, necessarily there are *jñāna* and *darśana* (intuition) *bhāvanā*, because *tapa* and *saṁyama* are the functions (*kāryas*) thereof (in *Maraṇakaṇḍikā*).

3. *Sattva bhāvanā*: This contemplation states that even when one is afflicted or oppressed by the celestial beings or tormented by terrible living beings, one, being fearless and tolerating sufferings, the entire burden of the responsibility of the self-restraints (*saṁyama*) (*Bha* 198). One is not infatuated or deluded in face of the onset of the awesome disturbance (*upasarga*) and does not deviate from *sattva bhāvanā* (*Bha* 199).

In *Maraṇakaṇḍikā*, the following is added: Using or applying without fear during the time of protecting fostering (*pratipālana*) of the basic and primary restraints/virtues (*mūla guṇas*) and subsidiary or secondary qualities (*uttara guṇas*) is *sattva bhāvanā*. Due to the powers (full force, i.e. *bala*) of the *sattva bhāvanā*, the saints are not deviated from the self-restraint (*saṁyama*) even on the onset of somewhat terrible disturbances (*upasarga*) caused by human, subhuman or celestial beings and inanimate accidents.

4. *Ekatva bhāvanā:* In *ekatva* contemplation, one does not have attachment in *kāmabhoga*, i.e. those which are enjoyed due to one's own desires such conceived, imagined or intended (*saṅkalpita*) in

mind, food and drink, women, etc. group of *kāmabhoga*, which are the means of one's happiness (*sukha*), (the particular or distinctive affection (*prīti viśeṣa*) relating to external objects is said to be *sukha*) in a collection or a multitude of people (*saṅgha*) and the physical body. He also adopts the most excellent conduct by delighting his mind in the attachment (*Bha* 202).

In this *bhāvanā*, one contemplates that one is only alone (*akelā*) or solitary in all conditions or situations (*avasthās*). No one is mine. And I do not belong to anyone.

Contemplation of the (transcendental) pure nature of the Self without the help of other is called *ekatva bhāvanā*, which removes the infatuation of ignorance of perverted knowledge (*ajñāna*).

To the above, *Maraṇakaṇḍikā* adds: "One contemplates on *ekatva bhāvanā* in order that there is no attachment or attraction (*āsakti*) in the enjoyment of objects such as food, drink and women (*kāmabhoga*), in pleasures of the sense objects. The body is also inconsequential (*akiñcitkara*)." The definite intention or resolve (*saṅkalpa*) that other people or inanimate objects are beneficial or do disservice or harm to me is the cause of attachment and aversion; hence, one should get rid of such *saṅkalpa*. By the constant practice of this *ekatva bhāvanā*, one is not attached to any object and, as a result, one's freedom from worldly desires (*vairāgya*) is increased.

5. *Bhāvanā pertaining to steadfastness or being resoluteness* (*dhṛti*): This means not being fearful on the onset of sufferings. That which creates fear in people with small/little power/strength at seeing the massive array of hardships/sufferings (*pariṣaha*) (see *TS* IX.9), which is combined with great warriors of awesome disturbance (*upasarga*, see *supra*). However, the resolute saints by fighting against them (*upasarga* and *pariṣaha*) and attaining victory over them accomplish their cherished purpose or aim (*manoratha*) of voluntary and peaceful death by gradual fasting (*sallekhanā*).

Let people wander or roam about forever in an enlightened

worldview, knowledge and conduct as a result of the above-mentioned five *bhāvanās*.

The twenty-two hardships or sufferings (*pariṣaha*) are (*TS* IX.9):

1. hunger;
2. thirst;
3. cold;
4. heat;
5. insect bites;
6. nakedness;
7. ennui, dissatisfaction (*arati*);
8. women;
9. *caryā*, i.e. walking too much and feeling fatigue;
10. *niṣadya* (sitting). Not to disturb the posture of meditation, even if there is danger from a lion, a snake, etc.;
11. *śayyā* (sleeping) resting on the hard earth;
12. *ākrośa* (abuse);
13. *vadha* (beating);
14. *yācanā* (begging);
15. *alābha* (failure to get alms);
16. *roga* (disease);
17. *trāṇasparśa* (contact with thorny shrubs, etc.);
18. *mala* (dirt), discomfort from dust, etc.;
19. *satkārapuraskāra* (respect and disrespect);
20. *prajñā* (concert of knowledge);
21. *ajñāna* (perverted knowledge); and
22. *adarśana* (perverted or deluded belief).

A person interested in liberation should endure/tolerate the sufferings. A person who tolerates those sufferings, and whose great mind is free from distress (*saṅkleśa*), is a person imbued with great inhibition (*saṁvara*) due to stopping or preventing (*nirodha*) of the influx of attachment, etc. psychic states-of-evolution (Pūjyapāda 1944: 330, 335).

Fourfold Bhāvanās of Jinasena

In the context of the progress of *dhyāna*, Jinasena introduces fourfold *bhāvanās* connected with (a) *jñāna*, (b) *darśana*, (c) *caritra*, and (d) *vairāgya*.

The first (*Jñāna*) consists of *vācana*, *pracchanna*, *anuprekṣāṇa*, *upadeśa* (see *supra*) and *dharma-āmnāya*, which are the varieties of *svādhyāya* or study according to *Tattvārthasūtra* IX.25.

The second consists of *Saṁvega*, *praśama*, *stithairya*, *asammūḍhatva*, *asmaya*, *āstikya* and *anukampā*. Four of these, viz. *saṁvega*, *praśama*, *āstikya* and *anukampā*) (see *supra*), along with *nirveda* characterize *samyaktva* (enlightened) worldview or right faith (*savaya pa0nnatti* (55ff) and *viṁśati-viṁśikā* (VI.10-14 of Haribhadra; and also *SAS* on *TS* I.2, see *supra*) and the remaining three cover some of the *aṅgas* of *samyaktva* (*sthairya* = *asaṁśaya ruciḥ*, *asammūḍhatva* = *amūḍha-dṛṣṭi* and *asmaya* (*RKS* 4, 11, 14, 25, etc.) (Jain 2022).

The third (*Caritra*) consists of the five *samitis*, three *guptīs* and putting up with *pariṣahas*, which along with *dharma*, *anuprekṣā* and *caritra* are, according to *Tattvārthasūtra* IX.2, the causes of *saṁvara*.

The last *bhāvana*, i.e. *vairagya*, consists of the non-attachment for the pleasures of senses, constant thought in the nature of the body and pondering over the character of the universe. (*Tattvārthasūtra* mentions some of these, see *TS* VII.2 and *SAS* on the same.) These *bhāvanās* contribute to mental peace.

6. Contemplations are reflections (*bhāvanās*), which are helpful and useful in moral and spiritual development and advancement, such as *Samayasāra* 38 and *Niyamasāra* 102. In *Samayasāra* 38, it is stated:

> I (*aham*, the Self) is *ekko* (alone, solitary, unique), indeed pure, having intuition and knowledge, always non-corporeal or formless, and not even an iota or the minutest part of any other (*anya*) belongs to me or is mine.

Niyamasāra 102 describes the Self ("I", *aham*) as:

> "ever one" and "eternal", characterized by knowledge and intuition. All other remaining *bhāvas* (psychic states or dispositions) are external [i.e. other] (*para*), including other substances (*para-dravya*) and *para-bhāva* (psychic states which are other than my nature, the transcendental pure nature; all of them are having the characteristic of being a coincidence or matter of chance (*saṅjoga*).

Samayasāra describes the *ekatva-vibhakta* Self: unity or oneness (*ekatva*) with its transcendental, pure nature and distinct (*vibhakta*) from other substances (*para-dravya*) and *para-bhāva*, including attachment, aversion, etc. *Samayasāra* verses which can serve as appropriate contemplations in the field of spiritual development are 3-4, 16, 36-44, 49-56, 73-74, 144, 181-186, 188-189, 277 and 297-299.

Niyamasāra verses (39-49, 80-82, 100-102, 104 and 106), *Pravacanasāra* verses (7, 160 and 192), *Pañcāstikāyasāra* verses (27, 106, 154, 158 and 167) and *Samayasāra Kalaśa* verses (10, 131 and 239) of Amrtachandra (1964) can also serve as reflections (*bhāvanās*) regarding spiritual development. Of course, *Bārasa Aṇuvekkhā* as a whole, especially verses 4, 6-7, 13, 20-21 and 60, is also relevant for that purpose.

Meanings of Anuprekṣā/Bhāvanā

Anuprekṣā, as already stated, means to ponder, to reflect, to think repeatedly. Many commentators have endorsed this meaning, which have now and then amplified it according to the context.

Pūjyapāda's commentary on the *Tattvārthasūtra* (*Sarvārthasiddhi* on IX.2) interprets *anuprekṣā* as "pondering on the nature of the body and other substances".

According to Svami Kumar (*Kārttikeyānuprekṣā* 97), *anuprekṣā* is defined as "pondering on the right principles".

According to Siddhasena (1930: 181), this repeated pondering develops suitable mental states.

Nemicandra (on *Uttarādhyayana* 29.22) explains it as *cintanika*, reflecting that *anuprekṣā* covers comprehension-cum-visualization with a concentrated mind is clearly hinted by Asadhara (2018: 414).

Subhachandra (in his commentary on the *Kārttikeyānuprekṣā*) further expands its scope by saying that one has to reflect on the various principles and this continued reflection involves constant awareness of the nature of things.

Vaṭṭakera in *Mūlācāra* states that the person, who thinks, ponders, reflects or meditates upon the Self (*ātmā*) by these *anuprekṣās*, obtains liberation by becoming pure, devoid of all *karmas* (*Mūlācāra* 37).

According to Vijayamati's *Ātmānubhava*, reflection or thinking over (*manana*) of the nature of objects by understanding them is experience. For a person desirous of happiness, it is compulsory to reflect on the basic principles of life and things (*tattva-cintana*). The experienced person exerts to dive deep repeatedly in the real/true nature of objects when knowing them. In spiritual language, it is called *anuprekṣā* or *bhāvanā*. A *bhāvanā* is thinking over repeatedly of *tattvas*.

By *tattva-cintana*, Vijayamati adds, one's conviction or reverential belief (*śraddhā*) becomes firm, permanent. *Saṁvega* (energy, enthusiasm and motivation for the accomplishment of the objective or apprehension of miseries of the world (*TS* VII.12) and ever-present fear of the cycle of transmigration) and *vairāgya* (detachment from the world) are fostered. Knowledge becomes pure. There is progress and conduct. Life becomes firm and stable (*sthira*). One obtains happiness through a mature manner of acting.

There is also another aspect for its meaning when it is used in connection with *svādhyāya* (study of scriptures), *anuprekṣā* (pondering) on what one is learnt being one of its important factors. The *Bhāṣya* and *Sarvārthasiddhi* commentaries on *Tattvārthasūtra* IX.25 have stressed this meaning while discussing *svādhyāya*. Sometimes both the aspects, especially with the later commentators, have got mixed up.

Significance of Bhāvanās in the Modern Context

The contemplations, called affirmations (*bhāvanās*) by Dennis T. Jaffe and Cynthia D. Scott, play a significant role in inculcating a realistic perspective and a positive attitude in our life and help in obtaining *samyak darśana*. Thoughts, actions and happiness are inextricably linked with one another. If one thinks negatively, one cannot hope to act in a positive manner and thereby achieve peace, prosperity and happiness in life.

Samyak darśana (right perception, enlightened worldview) enables us to view life and its problems in a *realistic* perspective. It facilitates the adoption of a positive or right attitude in life. Thoughts, actions and happiness are inseparably linked with one another. If one thinks negatively, one cannot hope to act in a positive manner, and thereby achieve peace, prosperity and happiness in life.

Negative thoughts begin to sound monotonously alike after a while. That is because they *are* very much alike after a while. The chief characteristic of negative thoughts is that they are generally wrong. They are a distortion or exaggeration of the truth. That is at least partly because they tend to be automatic. That is, they simply leap into your mind unbidden; they are not conclusions you have reached through reason and logic. In fact, in a sense, they are not "thinking" at all.

How do "thought therapists" go about reshaping these negative, self-defeating, soul-saddening thought patterns?

The point is to put your life and your problems in a *realistic* perspective. Like a reporter, scientist or detective, you are looking to find the true facts of the case, to apply the principles of hard science to your own thought processes.

The plan of attack is in three phases. Gary Emery[3] says that they are awareness, answering and action.

AWARENESS

Vague, unfocused negative thoughts that lurk just below the surface of consciousness cause more harm than those that are dragged out into the open. So the first step out of the rut of depression is to become aware of what you are actually thinking and feeling.

Sometimes that is more difficult than it sounds, since these thoughts tend to be disguised. Emery suggests using a sort of "instant replay" technique, thinking back to what crossed your mind just before a mood change or a physical sensation life fatigue, heaviness or butterflies in the stomach.

Another way to become more aware of your negative thoughts is simply to count them.

"It is important to 'concretize' these negative thoughts", agrees Dr Freeman. One of the simplest ways is to write them down. We try to help patients separate thoughts into three distinct aspects: what the situation is, what are feeling about it and what are saying to yourself (your thoughts)."

Most of us do not consider situations objectively; instead, we load them up with all kinds of projections and judgements, Freeman says. You may think, for instance, "I am waiting for my girlfriend to call me but she probably won't because she knows I am a loser". The first step to strip away everything except the plain, simple facts: "I'm waiting for my girlfriend to call". Next, you sift your experience in search of your true feelings. "The first thing you come up with maybe, 'I feel like a loser', close but I submit that sort of feeling,

---

3 Gary Emery, cited in "New 3-Point Planto Chase Away the Blues!", *Weekly World News*, 18 June 1996, p. 16.

that's a thought," Freeman says. "Then it's, I feel as if she'll never call" — again, not a feeling, a thought. Finally, you let go, I feel sad. "OK — that's the feeling."

Then you got to tune into your self-talk concerning the situation. I have concluded your girlfriend is not going to call? If she is late, has it ever happened before? What reasonable expressions are there to account for the fact that she is late calling? In short, Freeman says, you got to *examine the evidence*. You have got to drag your negative thoughts into court, put them on the witness stand and confront them with the facts. Usually, they wilt under the pressure.

Emery, when counselling a woman who was depressed because she believed no man would ever want to marry and divorce with two children, told her to go to the library to look at the statistics. She found that women with children were actually *more* likely to find new mates than childless single women of the same age.

ANSWERING YOUR NEGATIVE THOUGHTS

Once you have identified and clarified the thought patterns that are making you feel bad, you got to answer them back. One of the best ways to pry open the close circle of negative thoughts is to learn to ask yourself good questions. Become a hard-nosed prosecutor and drill your negative thoughts but good. What is the evidence that I am such a worthless person? Am I confusing a mere thought with a fact? Am I overlooking my strengths? Exactly what is a distortion in my thinking? Am I exaggerating or over-generalizing? And so on.

A good way to clarify this process for yourself, Dr Beck suggests, is to divide a piece of paper into two columns and write out a more balanced, fact-based, realistic answer beside each of the current negative thought. A gloomy, lonesome housewife may think, "I'm neglected because nobody wants to be around me". But in the opposite column, if she gave little thought, she would answer, "Mary hasn't called because she's in the hospital. Judy is out of town, and Helen really *did*, but I forgot about that."

Occasionally, Emery says, you may be so upset that no reasonable answer comes immediately to mind. So postpone answering – wait an hour or two or set aside a certain time each day to write out your answers. One of his patients, expanding on this idea, created a "witness box" in which she deposited all the thoughts and ideas that bothered doing the week. On Wednesdays, she opened the box, tore up the thoughts that were no longer a problem and tried to constructively answer those that still were.

TAKING ACTION

It is not enough to simply answer your negative thoughts – you have to act on your thoughts and beliefs. In a way, Emery points out, acting out your written answers to negative, self-defeating thoughts is a way of "reality testing" them to see if they are really true. How do you know for sure that you "cannot" speak in public unless you try? Or that you will be rejected if you introduce yourself to someone you are attracted to? (It is possible you really cannot speak in public and you really will be rejected – but you will never know until you try).

For people mired in a deep mud of depression, Dr Beck suggests working up an activity schedule or a weekly calendar with each day divided into two-hour-long boxes. The idea is to schedule something throughout the day and keep a record of how well you did with each task – perhaps by rating the amount of pleasure of sense of accomplishment it gave you on a scale of one through five.

This simple calendar can help in many ways. It gives you the true facts about what you actually do during the day – demonstrating to many depressed people that their lives are not as bleak or empty as they had imagined. It helps you retake control of your life by breaking the rut of inactivity. And it helps you see clearly what gives you pleasure and satisfaction.

By becoming *aware* of your negative thoughts, *answering* them with a more realistic, constructive and adaptive view, and taking *action* to break out of the self-imposed trap, you can get control over depression and anxiety.

Eight Rules of Effective Affirmation

The rules of effective affirmations are described below:

1. Place yourself in a receptive state of mind. It is a deep state of relaxation. (The best of the relaxation techniques) or simply take a few moments to get your body and psyche ready to receive new information. Before you begin, you need to tell yourself you are ready.

2. Make your affirmations short, clear, unambiguous and specific. Down complex desires and changes into smaller, simpler directives.

3. Phrase formations in the present tense. You are creating them as a psychic reality that will exist from the moment you state them to yourself.

4. Phrase positively, as what you want to do. Avoid negative words like "stop", "not" or "do not". State what you actually want to think, feel and do instead.

5. When you repeat your intentions, try to suspend your doubts and inhibit a tendency to make a negative or doubting commentary. Do not undercut or undermine your affirmations. If you begin to think negatively, say "no" or "stop" to yourself, and continue the affirmation.

6. You should feel positive, expansive and supportive as you say them.

7. Write down your sets of affirmations and place the list where you will see it repeatedly during the day. You need to keep reminding yourself of them to make them concrete and real for you.

8. Make affirmations are continuing, ongoing part of your life (cited in Jain, J.P. 2001: 21).

Talking Back to the Internal Critic

Once you have learned to recognize distorted thinking, you also have to learn how to push it out of your mind (Jain, J.P. 2001: 22).

Here is an example of a three-column chart approach. See you suddenly realize you are late for an important meeting. Your heart sinks and you are equipped with panic. This is what your chart might look like:

Automatic self-critical thought

1. I never do anything right.
2. I am always late.
3. Everyone will look down on me.
4. I will make a fool of myself.

Self-cognitive distortion

1. Overgeneralizing.
2. Overgeneralizing.
3. Overgeneralizing, either/or thinking fortune-telling.
4. Fortune-telling.

A rational response

1. Nonsense! I do a lot of things right.
2. I am not always late. That is ridiculous. Think of all the times I have been on time. If I am late more than often than I would like, and work on this problem and develop a method for being more punctual.
3. Someone may be disappointed that I am late, but it is not the end of the world. Maybe the meeting would even start on time.
4. Come on, now, I am not a fool. I may appear foolish if I come in late, but this does not make me a fool. Everyone is late sometimes.

In regard to negative thoughts, Antaraatma Swamiji observes: "Understand that no negative thought has any effect if you do not own it and act upon it" (2005: 25). You are not responsible for the arising of any thought. Your responsibility commences from the time you act upon it. The difference is crucial (ibid.). One should always keep in mind that like positive affirmations or thoughts, negative thoughts, over a period of time, become so deeply entrenched in the mind that a specific "groove" is created in the brain that makes you behave in a certain way. If one does not contemplate on positive thoughts, he will be subjected to negative thoughts. Of the 70,000 to 80,000 thoughts per day, with 80 per cent of those being negative and 95 per cent being repeated, special effort with determination is required to eradicate the negative thoughts and to create brain patterns of positive thoughts (Taneja 2015). Joseph Goldstein (2002: 140-141) states that when the thoughts go unnoticed, they have compelling power, they become the dictators of the mind. Yet when they are noticed, we realize the only power thoughts have is the power we give them.

In a recent study published in the *Journal of Cognitive Neuroscience*, researchers found that several areas of our brain show greater activity in response to stimuli that are

> more negative than positive. Whenever there is anything negative in our life we focus on it with all our attention and energy and in the process of developing an obsession towards it. Bad feelings and negative thoughts then engulf our mind leading to sadness and depression.
>
> — Cited in Sharma 2017

We have immense potential to rewire the brain's biology and transform ourselves.

It is true that feelings, thoughts, volitions and experiences are all conscious phenomena. However, many of our preferences, thoughts, feelings and intentions form without our conscious participation, with the result that people are driven by what they feel, not by what makes sense. As Gautama Buddha said, "Your worst enemy cannot argue as much of your own unguarded thoughts". Many of our thoughts are not the product of "you" but rather of "your brain", neuroscientist David Eagleman says. Although

> we may feel that we are independently making judgements, forming opinions and choosing certain actions and not others out of our own free will, in fact, all of us are deeply driven by biological impulses,and genetic predispositions and programmes are heavily skewed to act on certain directions.
>
> — Cited in Nadkarni 2011

Daniel Kahneman (2011: 86) has shown that humans often make "irrational" choices. He has given a full catalogue of the biases, shortcuts and cognitive illusions to which our species regularly succumbs.

The problem as to who (the brain or the conscious being) plays the major role in mental thinking and judgements, etc. is resolved by the Jaina concept of the mind. This concept speaks of the physical mind and the psychic mind and maintains that the mind is a vehicle or instrument of both conscious entity and unconscious or sub-conscious brain processes.

Neuroscientist Benjamin Libet has conclusively proved that while a mental "wish to act" is initiated unconsciously and influenced and induced by new-physiological processes or brain states,

> the conscious veto is a control function, different from simply becoming aware of the wish to act. The conscious decision to veto could be made without direct specifications for that decision by the preceding unconscious processes.

Such a view, Libet states, "allows genuine conscious free will to be a controlling agent in the performance of a voluntary act" (2003: 24-25).

Recent pioneering experiments in neuro-plasticity have shown that the hardware of the brain is not fixed and immutable, that the brain and the mind interact, and that "mental training can also change the brain" (Begley 2007: viii). The brain's biology can be moulded and by what we feel, think or do.

Moreover, since we are the architect of our own destiny, we are neither helpless in the hands of external environment nor a slave to our internal, subconscious compulsions, instinctive urges and impulsive drives, the neurobiological processes or brain states.

Dennis T. Jaffe and Cynthia D. Scott (2001: 16-17) state:

> We live in a world where it is commonplace to blame others for our shortcomings, where negative messages about our own powers and worth are common. . . . The unintended messages we often get from our parents, teachers, and our employers are that we are not competent or not good. We take these messages into ourselves and repeat them until they become reality for us. We become powerless, incompetent, incapable of responding to things, thereby giving up all sense of power.

Jaffe and Scott have defined affirmations (*bhāvanās*) as

> positive personal statements that modify negative personal beliefs and expectations, and motivate and influence us in new directions. — Cited in Jain, J.P. 2001: 16

When practised properly and often (i.e. repeated to the Self several times a day), they have a significant bearing in countering negative thoughts and feelings, changing our perspective in life and to reprogramme our minds for more positive results which too can become "our internal reality".

For instance, think of short positive statements, such as "I am strong and competent", "I am happy with my work" or that "I am healthy and full of energy", rather than "I feel like a loser" or that "I feel sad", as the modern psychologists Jaffe, Scott, Emery and others say (Jain, J.P. 2001: 16-21).

As Jaffe and Scott explain:

> Spend a few more on several times a day slowly, repeating your affirmations to yourself. As you repeat them, try to imagine how that information is — or can be — in your life; you might imagine the formation as it comes to be part of your life. Actually see yourself changing.

Clinging to the past or fantasizing about the future prevents a genuine experience of reality or an objective assessment of situation. It is therefore necessary for the mind to be disengaged from all sorts of expectations, preconceived notions, projections and judgements to have clarity of vision. Since we come across numerous situations in life, there are as many facets of reality as there are contexts or situations.

The Position of Anuprekṣās in Jaina Thought

The *anuprekṣās* are, in general, topics of meditation or for reflection, twelve in number and embrace a wide range of subjects practically covering all the principles and cardinal teachings of Jainism.

It is interesting to study the position of *anuprekṣā* in Jaina thought or in the schemes of Jaina principles.

The shedding of *karmas* (*nirjarā*) is rendered possible through penance (*tapas*), of which internal penance includes study (*svādhyāya*) and *dhyāna* (meditation) (see *supra*). The study of the sacred lore is of five kinds (see *supra*). The latter is of six varieties of which *sajjhaya* (study of the sacred lore) is the fourth and *jñāna*, concentration or meditation, is the fifth:

1. *vanaya*, reading or reciting;
2. *paḍipucchana*, questioning or injuring on a doubtful point;
3. *aṇuppehā*, reflection and meditation on what is studied;
4. *pariyattana*, memorizing or proper recitation; and
5. *dhamma-kaha*, lecturing or delivering sermons (see *TS* IX.25).

Of the four *dhyānas* (*TS* IX.28), *dharma* and *śukla* deserve a detailed scrutiny in this context. The *dharma-dhyāna*, which is of four kinds (*TS* IX.36), has four characteristics (*lakkhaṇa*), fourfold support (*ālambana*), viz. *vācana, pracchana, āmnāya, dharmopadeśa* (see *supra*) (*TS* IX.25) and four attendant reflections (*anuprekṣā*):

1. *anitya*,
2. *asaraṇa*,
3. *ekatva*, and
4. *saṁsāra*.

Similarly, *śukla-dhyāna* is of four kinds (*TS* IX.39). It has four characteristics, fourfold support and four attendant reflections, viz.:

1. *anyatva*,
2. *aśubha*,
3. *anantavattiya*, and
4. *vipariṇāma*.

According to *Bhagavatī Ārādhanā*, reflections or contemplations of various *anuprekṣās* are closely associated or connected with *saṁsthāna-vicaya* (nature and constitution of the universe) and *dharma-dhyāna* (righteous concentration or meditation) (*Bha* 1709).

Thus, *anuprekṣā*, reflection on or pondering over certain topics, has been closely associated with both *śukla-dhyāna* and *dharma-dhyāna*, especially with the latter so far as the standard list of *anuprekṣās*, in parts or as a whole, is concerned.

Sivarya, in his *Bhagavatī Ārādhanā*, while describing *dharma-dhyāna*, thinks almost in similar terms. According to him, *anuprekṣā* is the last *ālambana* (the first three being *vācana*, *pracchana* and *āmnāya*) (see *supra*) of it under its fourth variety or stage, viz. *saṁsthāna-vicaya*, which consists in meditating on the constitution of the universe is conceived in Jainism (Sivarya 2004: *Gāthā* 1710, 1875-1876, etc.).

Sivarya gives an elaborate exposition of the twelve *anuprekṣās*, the contemplation on which being a supplementary discipline. In his description of *śukla-dhyāna*, there is no difference to *anuprekṣās*.

According to *Tattvārthasūtra* IX.2, *anuprekṣās* are mentioned among the agencies that bring about the stoppage of the influx of *karmas* (*saṁvara*), the remaining being *guptī* (self-restraint of mind, speech and body), *samiti* (carefulness in walking, etc.), *dharma* (righteousness), *pariṣaha-jaya* (conquering of sufferings) and *caritra* (conduct). All the commentators elaborate the discussion about *anuprekṣās* only in this context. The *sūtras* mention *anuprekṣās* under *svādhyāya* (*TS* IX.26) where the meaning is slightly different, but do not refer to them under the discussion of *dhyāna* (meditation) (*TS* IX.28ff.).

Thus, *anuprekṣā* occupies a significant position in Jaina ideology. It is conducive to the stoppage of the influx and shedding of *karmas*; it supplements the discipline of meditation; and it is one of the forms of the study of the sacred lore. Its twofold connotation, noted above, depends on its association with meditation or study.

The Purpose and Scope of Anuprekṣās

The object of *anuprekṣās* and their effect on the soul aspiring after liberation is explained at length in *Uttarādhyayanasūtra* XXIX.22:

> My pondering [on what he has learned] in use in the form of old with the seven kinds of *karma*, except the *āyuṣka* (have upon the soul); he shortens the duration when it was to be a longer one; he mitigates their power when it was intense; (he reduces their sphere of action when it was a wide one); he may acquire *āyuṣka-karma* or not, but he no more accumulates *karma* which produces unpleasant feelings, and he quickly crosses the very large of the fourfold *saṁsāra* which is without beginning and end.

The ultimate objective of *anuprekṣās* (contemplations) is the stoppage (*saṁvara*) of the influx of and the shedding of *karmas* (*nirjarā*). As intermediary steps, many a virtue is developed by the soul by contemplating on one or the other *anuprekṣā*.

Anuprekṣās serve as potent factors leading to spiritual progress. When one is impressed by the transient nature of worldly objects and relations, one directs one's attention from the outward to the inward: the attachment for the world is reduced giving place to liking for a religious life which alone can save the soul from *saṁsāra* and lead it on to liberation. By this contemplation, the relation of the Self with the universe is fully understood: the mind becomes pure and equanimous; attachment and aversion are subjugated; renunciation rules supreme; and in pure meditation the *ātmā* is realized.

The scope of the religious topics covered by the twelve *anuprekṣās* is rather vast. When one realizes that worldly objects are transitory and relations temporary, one develops a philosophical yearning to solve the problem of life and death. The individual, often under the pressure of his predispositions, thinks, talks and acts. As a result, this incurs numerous *karmas*; one cannot escape the consequences thereof. Being the architect of his own fortune, one can never escape one's *karmas* without experiencing their fruits.

Being in the company of *karmas* from beginningless time, the soul's transmigratory struggle has been going on for a long time. It is high time for the Self to realize itself as being completely different from its associates, both subtle and gross. To realize the potential of the effulgence of the Self, one has to understand the deregatory nature of its accessories like body, etc. The causes of the kārmic influx have to be eradicated and the stock of binding *karmas* has to be eliminated. A detailed contemplation on the universe in its manifold aspects helps one to understand the Self. This understanding is something rare and only attained after considerable effort along the religious path that has been preached by teachers who have lived what they preached and became ideals, after attending the bliss of liberation, for all the aspirants.

The *anuprekṣās* are of significant value in one's career in all the stages of religious life and spiritual progress. According to Krishna K. Handiqui (1949: 293):

> They are in the nature of reflections on the fundamental facts of life, and remind the devotee of the teachings of the Master on the subject of rebirth, *karma* and destruction, equanimity and self-control, the glory of the law and the final goal. They are no doubt designed to develop the contemplative faculty of the *yogī*

> and they recall the starting point of *dhyāna*. But they have also great moral significance inasmuch as they are meant to develop purity of thought and sincerity in the practice of religion.

The aspirant is advised that the twelve contemplations are to be meditated wilfully. Action wilfully performed is enthusiastic and deliberate, declares Acharya Kundakunda. Every aspirant who seeks liberation must constantly contemplate on these fundamental realities. These twelve sublime mental reflections set the seeker on the path leading to salvation (Dharma Raja 1990: 2-3).

Significance, Value and Purpose of the Twelve Bhāvanās

According to *Jñānārṇava*, the purpose of the twelve *bhāvanās* like *anitya* is to create or produce detachment or freedom from worldly desires (*vairāgya*), body and sensuous pleasures or sense enjoyments (*bhoga*) in order to enable living beings to focus on concentration or meditation (*dhyāna*). Thus, the twelve *bhāvanās* are said to be the only cause that foster *vairāgya*.

The possessiveness (*parigraha*) regarding union of wealth, grains, wife and relatives in the world causes sadness, dejection and despair (*viṣāda*). The body is afflicted with diseases. Death is ever ready to devour you. And misfortunes or disasters lead to rancour in you. The hellish sufferings are terrible. And the *bhoga* deceive you like a dream (*Jñā* 1).

Jñānārṇava 2 states:

> Oh Brother! Why don't you engage yourself in your well-being by seeing the frustration or distress of sense objects, and why don't you think of the nature of things (*vastu svarūpa*) or principles (*tattva*), and also why don't you know the strange or unusual nature of the world (*saṁsāra*); so this is your mission, mistake or error (*bhūla*).

The contemplation of twelve *bhāvanās* is also meant for the purification of one's mind or psychic states (*Jñā* 5).

In *Tattvārthasūtra* IX.2, *anuprekṣās* are mentioned among the agencies that bring about the stoppage (*saṁvara*) of the influx of *karmas*, the remaining being self-restraints of the mind, speech and body (*guptī*), the five carefulness in walking (*samiti*), forgiveness, ten kinds of righteousness and piety (*dharma*), conquering twenty-two kinds of sufferings (*pariṣaha-jaya*) and conduct (*caritra*).

Thinking and reflecting on previously read or studied subjects is *anuprekṣā*. By constantly thinking and pondering over *anuprekṣās*, a living being (*jīva*) enfeebles/deadens the excessive, serious or very thick bondage of knowledge-covering, etc. and seven species of *karmas*, excluding lifespan *karmas*. Their long-term duration is reduced to a brief, less or short-term duration. The intensity is also enfeebled or reduced.

The mind, speech and *karma* (activity) are the three sources of the tendency/inclination of the mind (*pravṛtti*), which flows towards auspicious as well as the inauspicious. *Bhāvanās* now account for turning of the source of *pravṛtti* towards the auspicious or inauspicious. The *pravṛtti* of activity (*kartā*) is through *bhāvanās*. If the flow of *bhāvanās* is inspired by auspicious mental activity (*citta-vṛtti*) and continues with high and pure psychic dispositions, then it blossoms the path of happiness and peace (Jain, Duli Chand 1993: 7 and 151).

The mind is to be sufficiently harmonized and integrity in order to help the mind receive, reflect, simulate and express. When something is exposed to us with clarity, first of all we are to receive it well. After receiving it, we must reflect or contemplate upon, ruminate over, analyse and finally make it our own. That is called assimilation. Comprehension and assimilation are great gifts of spirituality. After it is a simulated, one will find it begins to express itself.

The age-old habit of constant involvement with the objects of the world is the cause of desires. An impure mind is full of desires and the mind rid of desires is verily pure. Making the mind free of desires is tantamount to making it reflect and contemplate on the subject within constantly.

The contemplation of twelve *bhāvanās* is the most popular subject for religious persons. By repeatedly pondering over them, the fire of passions like anger and pride calms down/subsides, attachment is destroyed, darkness is irrelevant and the lamp of the nature of knowledge/wisdom blossoms. The twelve *bhāvanās* are the path of liberation; they are extremely useful in worldly life too. In calming mental agitation/uneasiness due to separation of desired or beloved ones and joining of undesirable ones, the twelve *bhāvanās* bestow tolerance and fortitude in times of calamity/adversity, detachment from sense-pleasures and passions, keep one devoted to *dharma* (righteousness and piety), and enfeeble infatuation (*moha*) and the fear of death.

Pleasure and pain, which constantly result from sense-object interactions, are transitory.

Enumeration of Anuprekṣās

The three authors — Sivarya (*Mūlārādhanā* or *Bhagavatī Ārādhanā* 1715), Vaṭṭakera in *Mūlācāra* (VIII.2) and Kundakunda (*BA* 2) — have a similar order of enumeration:

1. *adhruva*
2. *aśaraṇa*
3. *ekatva*
4. *anyatva*
5. *saṁsāra*
6. *loka*
7. *aśuci*
8. *āśrava*
9. *saṁvara*
10. *nirjarā*
11. *dharma*, and
12. *bodhi.*

While the order of enumeration is the same in all the three works, the only difference is that while in Kundakunda's *Bārasa Aṇuvekkhā* and *Bhagavatī Ārādhanā*, the term *aśuci* is used for the seventh *anuprekṣā*, *Mūlācāra* uses *aśubha* in its place.

Aśubha in *Mūlācāra* is said to be *sarva duḥkharūpa* (wholly, entirely or totally of the nature, form, aspect or mode of misery). In explanation of *aśubha anuprekṣā*, it is stated:

> There is exclusively *aśubha* alone in hells. In subhuman (animals and birds, etc. *tiryañca*), states/conditions, there are fastening or use of fetters (*bandhana*) and obstructing, blockading or hindering (*rodhana*), etc. In the human condition, there are diseases and sorrow and mourning (*śoka*), etc. And in heaven there is *aśubha* relating to the mind. — *Mūlācāra*, V.722

In *Tattvārthasūtra*, Umāsvāmi or Umāsvāti's order of enumeration of *anuprekṣās* is as follows:

1. *anitya*	7. *āsrava*
2. *aśaraṇa*	8. *saṁvara*
3. *saṁsāra*	9. *nirjarā*
4. *ekatva*	10. *loka*
5. *anatva*	11. *bodhi-durlabhatva,* and
6. *aśuci*	12. *dharma.*

The list of twelve *anuprekṣās* as enunciated in *Tattvārthasūtra* IX.7 has become more or less standard for subsequent writers in Hindi who adopt it with very minor changes in the order, possibly because of metrical needs, etc.

The order of enumeration of the twelve contemplations (*bhāvanās*) in *Tattvārthasūtra* IX.7 differs from *Bārasa Aṇuvekkhā*, *Mūlācāra* and *Bhagavatī Ārādhanā* at three places and not merely a solitary instance. First, places after *aśaraṇa*, instead of *ekatva-anyatva*, *Tattvārthasūtra* mentions *saṁsāra bhāvanā* and places *ekatva-anyatva* after *saṁsāra bhāvanā*.

Second, instead of mentioning *loka bhāvanā* after *saṁsāra bhāvanā*, *Tattvārthasūtra* places *loka bhāvanā* after *nirjarā*.

Third, instead of mentioning *dharma bhāvanā* before *bodhi-durlabha*, it has been placed at the end, i.e. as the twelfth *bhāvanā*. The order of enumeration of twelve contemplations in *Kārttikeyānuprekṣā* is the same as in *Tattvārthasūtra*.

Apart from the difference in the order of enumeration, the difference between Kundakunda's *Bārasa Aṇuvekkhā* and *Tattvārthasūtra* is that the term *anitya* is used in *Tattvārthasūtra* IX.7 in place of *adhruva* used in *Bārasa Aṇuvekkhā*. Though *adhruva* and *anitya* are similar as their meanings, they are impermanent, transitory or temporary (not eternal (*adhnīva*)) and non-permanent/impermanent (*anitya*). However, the subtle difference or distinction between *adhruva* and *anitya* is pointed out by Amrtachandra in his commentary of *Samayasāra* 74, which states:

> The influx of *karmas* bound with the Self [which is eternal] is non-eternal or in constant (*adhruva*), impermanent, transient, temporary (*anitya*) and incapable of providing refuge (*aśaraṇa*). The inflow of *karmas* is misery itself and also its traditional result is misery. Knowing this, one abstains or refrains from them.

Amrtachandra's commentary on *Samayasāra* 74 points out the difference between *adhruva* and *anitya* in the following words:

> Like the movement (*vega*) of epilepsy (*mṛgī*) disease, which increases swiftly and decreases or falls, hence the inflow of *karmas* (*āsrava*) is *adhruva*. But the Self is only of the nature of consciousness and eternal or constant only. *Anitya* like the movement (*vega*) of fever in which cold/coldness and heat, or hotness or burning sensation (*dāha*), arise successively or in sequence (*krama*).

In their commentary on *Samayasāra* 74, Muni Veersagara, following Jayasena, describes the subtle difference as follows:

> The psychic states (*bhāva*) of anger, etc. which are the conditions of the inflow (*āsrava*) of *karmas* are *adhruva* (in constant), and extremely or excessively (*atīva*) momentary, temporary, transitory or fleeting (*kṣaṇika*), like the sparkle or flash of electricity (in clouded sky). The pure nature of the Self is *dhruva* (stable, constant, permanent).

And like the movement of speed of the fever, which is sometimes coldness (*sīta*) and sometimes hot (*uṣṇa*), the anger, etc. *āsrava bhāva* with respect to being inconsistent (*adhruvata*) do not remain stable, lasting, enduring or steadfast (*sthira*), do not have stability. In this way, they are impermanent, transient or temporary (*anitya*), perishable, transitory (*vinaśvara*). But the splendid conscious, pure nature of the Self alone is perpetual, eternal (*nitya*).

In *Maraṇa-Samādhi* (pp. 135ff.), one of the Painnaya texts, the twelve *bhāvanās* are thus enumerated:

1. *anitya*
2. *aśaraṇa*
3. *ekatva*
4. *anyatva*
5. *saṁsāra*
6. *aśubha*
7. *loka*
8. *āsrava*
9. *saṁvara*
10. *nirjarā*
11. *uttama guṇa,* and
12. *bodhi-durlabha.*

The objective of these *bhāvanās* is to inculcate *vairāgya* or the spirit of detachment and renunciation; and they are explained in detail in some seventy verses (*Mar* 569-688).

The arrangement and prescription of the twelve contemplations are for the purpose of conquering and restraining the restless tendencies of the senses and the mind and for the development of the Self. By these contemplations, the bondage of *karmas* is enfeebled (*Uttarādhyayanasūtra* 29.22).

When auspicious thoughts arise, the influx of inauspicious thoughts is closed step-by-step. The contemplations are therefore the means of restraining *karmas*. Those who are desirous of liberation and purity of the mind should continue to ponder over and contemplate upon these contemplations for *saṁvega* (enthusiasm for righteousness and piety, detachment, firmness of moral self-restraints and the calmness of the mind (*praśama*) (*Jñā* 2.6).

The contemplation of the twelve *bhāvanās* enables a person to become equanimous whereby the subsidence of passions like of anger takes place and the manifestation of *samyaktva* (right belief or enlightened worldview) occurs (*Yogaśāstra* 4.111).

A Comparative Study of Various Anuprekṣās

Though small in size, *Bārasa Aṇuvekkhā* of Kundakunda is an independent treatise on *anuprekṣās* in Prakr̥t; and *Mūlācāra* (verses 693–768) VIII of Vaṭṭakera, *Bhagavatī Ārādhanā* of Sivarya (verses 1715–1875) and *Maraṇa-Samādhi* (verses 569–638), contain substantial exposition of *anuprekṣās*. Moreover, *Tattvārthasūtra* IX.7 and some of its commentaries have served as a pattern for the format of discussion of these topics. *Kārttikeyānuprekṣā* is possibly the longest sacred text dealing solely with twelvefold reflections. Naturally, it deserves to be compared and contrasted with similar works noted above, with regard to its various aspects.

Some of the *gāthās* in his works have close agreement, either in thought or in expression[4]:

KA 678, 21	*BA* 4-5; *Bha* 1717-1718, 1725	*KA* 78	*Bha* 1752
KA 26-28	*BA* 8-9; *Mūlācāra* 7; *Bha* 1743	*KA* 82	*BA* 23
KA 30-31	*BA* 11, 13; *Bha* 1746	*KA* 83	*BA* 43
KA 56	*Bha* 1801	*KA* 89	*BA* 47; *Bha* 1825
KA 63	*Mūlācāra* 27; *Bha* 1802	*KA* 101	*Bha* 1829 (?)
KA 64-65	*Mūlācāra* 26; *Bha* 1799-1800	*KA* 104	*BA* 67
KA 66	*BA* 24-29; *Bha* 1773f.	*KA* 305-306	*BA* 69
KA 68	*Bha* 1775; *Mūlācāra* 594	*KA* 393	*BA* 70

It is true that there would be much common thought and expression when authors, who have brought up in the same tradition, are dealing with similar subjects. But the above parallels

[4] A.N. Upadhye's Introduction to *Kārttikeyānuprekṣā*, p. 24.

are something more than that. One certainly gets the impression that *Kārttikeyānuprekṣā* is indebted to *Bārasa Aṇuvekkhā* for some of its ideas and expressions.

Like *Bārasa Aṇuvekkhā, Kārttikeyānuprekṣā* is addressed to both monks and householders, with greater concern for the latter. However, *Bhagavatī Ārādhanā*, Mūlācāra and *Maraṇa-Samādhi* have primarily the ascetic community in view. In this context, A.N. Upadhye states:[5]

First, *Kārttikeyānuprekṣā* lays greater stress on the fickle character of Lakṣmī who spreads very great infatuation for laymen, and other points are incidentally touched upon.

Second, *Bhagavatī Ārādhanā* stresses that there is no escape from kārmic consequences while *Bārasa Aṇuvekkhā, Mūlācāra* and *Maraṇa-Samādhi*, along with *Kārttikeyānuprekṣā*, have death in view from which there is no escape. According to *Mūlācāra* and *Maraṇa-Samādhi, Jina-Dharma* is the shelter while *Bārasa Aṇuvekkhā, Bhagavatī Ārādhanā* and *Kārttikeyānuprekṣā* recommend shelter in the *ātman*, comprising *darśana, jñāna* and *caritra* (with *tapa*, added in *Bārasa Aṇuvekkhā* and *Bhagavatī Ārādhanā*).

Third, *Kārttikeyānuprekṣā* elaborates the different grades of existence (*naraka, tiryanch, manuṣya* and *deva*) which are hinted in *Mūlācāra, Bhagavatī Ārādhanā* and *Maraṇa-Samādhi* and through which the soul wanders due to *mithyātva* and without attending to the words of Jina. Besides this elaboration, the discussion about the fivefold *saṁsāra*, mentioned in *Bārasa Aṇuvekkhā, Bhagavati Ārādhanā* as well as *Mūlācāra*, comes like an appendix in *Kārttikeyānuprekṣā*. To relinquish the infatuation for *saṁsāra, Mūlācāra* wants it to be realized as worthless, *Bārasa Aṇuvekkhā* prescribes the *niścaya naya* and escape from *karmas, Maraṇa-Samādhi* recommends the practice of religion and *Kārttikeyānuprekṣā* appeals for self-meditation.

Fourth, the opening *gāthās* of *Kārttikeyānuprekṣā* come like an

---

[5] A.N. Upadhye's Introduction to *Kārttikeyānuprekṣā*, p. 60.

explanation of *Bārasa Aṇuvekkhā*, *Mūlācāra* and *Maraṇa-Samādhi*. *Kārttikeyānuprekṣā* prescribes the tenfold *dharma* as the only aid. According to *Bhagavatī Ārādhanā*, this consists of three jewels (*ratnatraya*). The same position is fervently endorsed by *Bārasa Aṇuvekkhā*.

Fifth, the relatives, etc. why even the body, are all extraneous; so one must meditate on the *ātman*. This spritualistic tone is not sufficiently developed in *Bhagavatī Ārādhanā* and *Maraṇa-Samādhi* as well as other Jaina texts.

Sixth, like *Bārasa Aṇuvekkhā*, *Kārttikeyānuprekṣā* primarily exposes the impure character of this mortal body; one should not be attached to the body, but should concentrate oneself on the nature of *ātman*. *Mūlācāra* does not ignore this aspect, but like *Bhagavatī Ārādhanā* and *Maraṇa-Samādhi* terms this topic as *aśubha anuprekṣā*: *artha* and *kāma* (sex) are *aśubha*, while *dharma* is *śubha*. It is under the discussion about *kāma* that the filthy nature of the body is explained in *Mūlācāra* and *Bhagavatī Ārādhanā*.

Seventh, *Kārttikeyānuprekṣā* and *Bārasa Aṇuvekkhā* follow some other sources as well. *Bārasa Aṇuvekkhā* and *Bhagavatī Ārādhanā* have the same pattern of enumeration of the causes of *āsrava*, while *Mūlācāra*, *Maraṇa-Samādhi* (and partly *Bhagavatī Ārādhanā*) have some other common ideas. It is only *Bārasa Aṇuvekkhā* that introduces the *niścaya* point of view.

Eighth, *Bārasa Aṇuvekkhā* introduces you to the doctrine of three *upayogas* and insists on the meditation of the *ātman* from the *niścaya* or *paramārtha* point of view. *Mūlācāra*, *Maraṇa-Samādhi* and to a certain extent *Bhagavatī Ārādhanā* too have a similar pattern of ideas that the doors of kārmic influx should be stopped, and then follows *saṁvara*, or the stoppage of kārmic influx. *Kārttikeyānuprekṣā* has an innovative pattern which is partly in agreement with *Bhagavatī Ārādhanā*.

Ninth, *Bārasa Aṇuvekkhā* has two *gāthās*, if not only one, for *nirjarā*, which is a further step after the stoppage of *karmas*. The second *gāthā* of *Bārasa Aṇuvekkhā* is common with *Kārttikeyānuprekṣā*. In all these texts, *tapas* (penances) are emphasized as the chief instrument of *nirjarā*, which is twofold. What is suggested in *Mūlācāra* seems to be elaborated in *Kārttikeyānuprekṣā*, the exposition in which is less technical. Penance is like fire which burns the grass of kārmic seed of *saṁsāra*.

Tenth, the exposition in *Bārasa Aṇuvekkhā* is simple: the different *upayogas* drive the soul to different *lokas*. *Mūlācāra* and *Maraṇa-Samādhi* make suggestions about different kinds of *jīvas* and their miseries and *Kārttikeyānuprekṣā* has elaborated on the same to the maximum. It is interesting to note that what *Bhagavatī Ārādhanā* includes under *loka* (1799–1800) is included under *saṁsāra* in *Kārttikeyānuprekṣā* (61-65). However, the line of demarcation between these two topics is somewhat shaky. Discussion about *loka* is really a wide topic, naturally *Kārttikeyānuprekṣā* therefore includes the exposition of many subjects like *jīva* and *jñāna*, the nature and the three kinds of *jīvas*, various substances and their nature, varieties and function of knowledge, various *nayas*, etc.

Eleventh, the *niścaya* point of view helps one to distinguish *ātman* from everything else. This is correct knowledge, true enlightenment, which is rather difficult to obtain. This is very precisely stated in *Bārasa Aṇuvekkhā*. *Kārttikeyānuprekṣā* describes the series of rarities (which are hinted in *Mūlācāra*, *Bhagavatī Ārādhanā* and *Maraṇa-Samādhi*) and how the religious enlightenment is the rarest and possible only in human birth. One should therefore devote oneself to the realization of *ātman*, consisting of *darśana*, *jñāna* and *caritra*.

Twelfth, *Bārasa Aṇuvekkhā* describes the twofold *karmas* of the eleven stages for the householder and tenfold for the monk; the former are merely enumerated and the latter are explained in detail. From the real point of view, the pure *ātman* should be reflected upon. *Mūlācāra* glorifies *dharma* as preached by Jina and expounds the tenfold *dharma* for the monk. *Bhagavatī Ārādhanā* and *Maraṇa-Samādhi* glorify religion and just hint some detail. What *Bārasa Aṇuvekkhā* has done in a nutshell, *Kārttikeyānuprekṣā* has elaborated to the utmost: the twofold religion is explained in all its details. The twelve *pratimās* are expounded by providing exhaustive details about the *aṇu-*, *guṇa-* and *śikṣā-vratas*, and then follows the exposition of the tenfold *dharma* in considerable detail.[6]

Then *dharma* is defined; the characteristics of a man of faith are given; and, lastly, *dharma* is glorified. Then follows the description of twelve penances which lead to the destruction of *karmas*, with a concluding discourse on *dhyāna* of four kinds.

Directly or indirectly, *Kārttikeyānuprekṣā* has inherited a good deal from these Prākr̥t sources, but in every case *Kārttikeyānuprekṣā* presents a lucid exposition of the topics in a general manner and a detailed discussion of the topics is difficult to enumerate.[7]

Svami Kumar seems to have drawn on some additional sources as well. It is interesting that the enumeration of the twelve *anuprekṣās* adopted in *Kārttikeyānuprekṣā* is different from that found in *Bārasa Aṇuvekkhā*, *Mūlācāra* and *Bhagavatī Ārādhanā* (which concur among themselves) but agree with the one found in *Tattvārthasūtra* of Umāsvāti. Second, at a number of places, especially of a technical nature, *Kārttikeyānuprekṣā* reminds one of *Tattvārthasūtra*, as well as its commentary, viz. *Sarvārthasiddhi* of Pūjyapāda. Some context may be noted by way of illustration:

1. *Kārttikeyānuprekṣā* 88ff. reminds one of *Tattvārthasūtra* VI.1f., and some words in verse 88, the commentary of Pūjyapāda (*ātmā pradeśa parispando yogaḥ*), and
2. *Kārttikeyānuprekṣā* 95ff. is an exposition closely following *Tattvārthasūtra* IX.14, along with *Sarvārthasiddhi*.[8]

---

6 A.N. Upadhye's Introduction to *Kārttikeyānuprekṣā*, pp. 60-62.

7 Ibid., p. 62.

8 Ibid.

In this way, in almost all places where we have enumerated, the influence of *Tattvārthasūtra* is apparent. Of the two earliest commentaries on *Tattvārthasūtra*, viz. *Bhāṣya* and *Sarvārthasiddhi* (on IX.7), both of which have common ideas and expressions, it is the latter that has influenced *Kārttikeyānuprekṣā* more than the former in a number of ways:

1. The simile of *jala-budbuda* (*KA* 21) is found in *Bārasa Aṇuvekkhā* 5, in *Bhagavatī Ārādhanā* 1717 and also in *Sarvārthasiddhi* but not in the *Bhāṣya* in this context.

2. The simile of lion for death (*KA* 24) is pretty old, found in the canonical passages and in the *Bhāṣya*, but *Sarvārthasiddhi* has the simile of a tiger as in the *Mahābhārata* passage noted above.

3. *Kārttikeyānuprekṣā* seems to work out the details in the *Bhāṣya* and *Sarvārthasiddhi*, fivefold *saṁsāra*, mentioned in *Sarvārthasiddhi*, goes back to Kundakunda from whose *Bārasa Aṇuvekkhā* Pūjyapāda quotes the necessary *gāthās* as already noted.

4. *Sarvārthasiddhi* stresses *dharma* as the *sahāya* and *Kārttikeyānuprekṣā* explains it by *dhammo daha lakkhaṇo have suyaṇo*.

5. That the *ātman* is separate from the body is the basic theme.

6. *Kārttikeyānuprekṣā* follows *Sarvārthasiddhi* more than the *Bhāṣya* which is more elaborate. Neither of the commentaries introduces *aśubha* in terms of *dharma, artha* and *kāma*.

7-8. The *Bhāṣya* is more elaborate and gives some mythological illustrations, etc. in dealing with *āsrava*. *Kārttikeyānuprekṣā* follows *Tattvārthasūtra*, shown above, in the exposition of *āsrava*.

9. The twofold *nirjarā* is mentioned in the commentary and *Kārttikeyānuprekṣā* develops it in the case of the soul moving along the path of spiritual evolution.

10. Taking hints from the commentary, *Kārttikeyānuprekṣā* has made this section a veritable compendium of *kāraṇānuyoga* and *dravyānuyoga*. The threefold division of *ātman* reminds one of a similar discussion in *Mokkhapāhuḍa*, *Samādhiśataka*, *Paramappa-payasu*, etc. Some of the definitions of *nayas* (e.g. *saṁgraha*, *śabda*) remind one of *Sarvārthasiddhi* I.33. Svami Kumar shows here and there the spirit of a Naiyāyika.
11. Though some of the similes are slightly modified, the trend of the discussion in *Kārttikeyānuprekṣā* is a full development of what is found in *Sarvārthasiddhi*.
12. *Kārttikeyānuprekṣā* presents a systematic and thorough exposition of twofold *dharma*, etc. for which the material is available in plenty in *Tattvārthasūtra* and its commentaries in various contexts.[9]

Thus, Svami Kumar inherits a good deal from Kundakunda, Sivarya, Vaṭṭakera, etc. and enriched his exposition by profusely drawing upon *Tattvārthasūtra* and its accessory literature.[10]

A Compendium of Jaina Dogmatics[11]

Most of the topics included under *anuprekṣās* are of such didactic import which could be discussed without overloading the exposition, say in the manner of Subhachandra in some *anuprekṣās* in his *Jñānārṇava*, with dogmatic details and technical enumerations of a more or less fixed pattern. However, Svami Kumar is essentially a learned author, steeped in Jaina principles; naturally, though he deals with these topics like a moralist poet, his discourses are replete with manifold details whereby *Kārttikeyānuprekṣā* has become a veritable compendium of Jainism. Some outstanding contexts of topical discussion are listed below:

---

9 A.N. Upadhye's Introduction to *Kārttikeyānuprekṣā*, p. 63.

10 Ibid. p. 63.

11 This section is based on A.N. Upadhye's Introduction to *Kārttikeyānuprekṣā*, pp. 60-62.

Description of hellish, subhuman, human and divine grades of existence (*KA* 34-61);

five kinds of hellish miseries (*KA* 34-35);

saṁsāra of five kinds (*KA* 66-72);

two grades of *kaṣāyas* (*KA* 90-92);

definition of the causes of *saṁvara* (*KA* 96-99);

two kinds of *nirjarā* (*KA* 100);

nirjarā on the ladder of *guṇasthānas* (*KA* 106-108);

loka and its extent (*KA* 118-121);

jīvas: *ekendriya* varieties (*KA* 122-127);

varieties of those having more *indriyas* (*KA* 128-142);

details about living beings outside of world (*KA* 143-175);

size of the *jīva* and its relation with knowledge (*KA* 176-187);

jīva, as *kartā* and *bhoktā* (*KA* 188-191);

three kinds of *jīva* (*KA* 192-200);

jīva and *karma* (*KA* 201-204);

pudgala varieties (*KA* 205-211);

dharma, *adharma*, *ākāśa* and *kāla* (*KA* 212-223);

anekānta character of *vāstu-dravya*, *guṇa* and *paryāya*, which is endowed with origination, permanence and destruction (*KA* 224-246);

jñāna and *jñeya* (*KA* 247-256);

five kinds of *jñāna* (*KA* 257-262);

nayas and the definitions (*KA* 263-278);

sagara-dharma, its twelve stages and their individual elaboration (*KA* 305, etc.);

samyak dṛṣṭi and its characteristics (*KA* 307, etc.);

vratas, *aṇuvratas* (*KA* 331-340);

guṇa-vratas (with five varieties of *anarthadana*) (*KA* 341-351);

śikṣā-vratas (*KA* 352-369);

anāgāra-dharma and its ten varieties (*KA* 393-403);

hiṁsā (*KA* 405f.);

puṇya (*KA* 410f.); *samyaktva* and its eight characteristics;

dharma glorified (*KA* 426-437);

tapas and its twelve types (*KA* 438f.); and

four kinds of *dhyāna* (*KA* 473f.).

PART ONE

Twelve Reflections

Jaina scriptures have singled out twelve contemplations or reflections (anuprekṣās or bhāvanās). These contemplations, as mentioned in the order of Kundakunda's Bārasa Aṇuvekkhā, are discussed in the following chapters.

1

Adhruva or Anitya (Impermanence or Transitoriness)

Everything in the world is changing every moment. Nothing is permanent except the inner soul. In other words, everything is subject to change or is transitory. All material possessions, heavenly or human beings, the attachment to their kith and kin, father, mother or son, are ephemeral. All substances, including the soul substance (*jīva dravya*), are indestructible. However, their conditions or modifications are subject to constant change. Contemplation on the transitoriness of body and all worldly objects leads to detachment from these superficial and extraneous allurements. It is, therefore, essential to insulate the mind or free oneself from these distractions of attachments and focus on the transcendental, pure nature of the Self, which is eternal.

Even though one is well aware that life, youth, body, wealth, etc. as well as family, relatives, status, etc. are impermanent (*anitya*), one nevertheless hankers after pleasures, wealth, a charming body and so on. By being lustful towards them, a person commits sinful deeds and consequently suffers misery for his inauspicious acts. The Self alone is indestructible. Since all things of the worldly life are impermanent, one should consider it futile to lament over their loss and lose one's mental peace.

One can make use of the *anitya bhāvanā* by maintaining that just as wealth and property leave us, calamity, misfortune and adversity (*vipatti*), will also go away. Hence, one should have the courage, patience, endurance or steadfastness (*dhairya*) in *vipatti* and separation of desired or favourite things, including beloved ones. One should make use of the material things of happiness without attachment (Nyayavijaya 1935: 103).

Anitya (transitoriness) is regarded as the foremost among the twelve contemplations (*bhāvanās*) which are prescribed by Jainas as a desirable religious practice. *Anitya* means transient, ever-changing, transitory and impermanent. Change is one of the few constants in life; or rather the only constant in life is change. Everything is in the process of change and evolution. To stop change is to cease living. Without change, there is no growth. Change adds to newness and freshness in life. Without change, life would be dull and monotonous. In fact, one can neither know nor realize the value of health unless one falls sick and one does not really experience happiness unless one has gone through hardships and misery.

Contemplation of *anitya bhāvanā* instills in us a sense of detachment, equanimity, self-reliance (*puruṣārtha*), self-restraint (*saṁyama*), and control of passions (*kaṣāyas*) and emotions. Contemplation on the impermanence of things makes us reflect on our inner Self, to search for the changeless reality behind the ever-changing, the quest for seeing and experiencing the real "I", which is different from the "I" of body and senses.

Everyone, including kings or princes, has to die, turn by turn; no one can protect them from death (Bhudhar Das's *bhāvanā*). All worldly dreams and all worldly expectations are false. The body, youth and life are unsteady, unstable or fickle (*asthira*) and ephemeral (*kṣaṇa-bhaṅgura*) (Yugalji's *bhāvanā*).

The physical body is inert, perishable and impermanent. The eternal "I" (consciousness), that both pre-exists and survives the body, is eternal. There is continuity of the Being, the eternal Self.

Thus, the *anitya* (transitoriness of the physical body and other external objects) draws our attention to the permanent "I", the changeless beneath the changes; this is how Chitrabhanu (1980: 1-15) designates the *anitya* contemplation. In this way, *anitya* contemplation emphasizes that we should identify ourselves with the eternal "I" (the Self), rather than with the transitory inert, animate matter, the physical body.

Unless a changeless base remains at the back of a change, the latter cannot be recognized at all. In the absence of such a base, recognition of the changes taking place constantly at the bodily and mental levels would not be possible at all. Thus, change and changelessness go together. They cannot but coexist.

Though *adhruva* and *anitya* have similar meanings conveying the transitoriness/impermanence of things/objects, the subtle difference between the two is pointed out by Amrtachandra in his commentary on *Samayasāra* 74 (see *supra*).

The *anitya bhāvanā* of Jainism seems similar to *anicchā* in Buddhism, wherein everything is impermanent, nothing is permanent. In Jainism, however, the soul or the Self is eternal/permanent. Moreover, according to Buddhism, the duration of life of a thing is exceedingly brief, lasting only while a thought lasts. As soon as a thought has ceased, the thing is said to have ceased. In Jainism, on the other hand, nothing new is created, nothing is destroyed; modifications only appear and disappear.

The group of body, sense objects and consumption/enjoyment or sexual intercourse are all of the nature of a short-lived bubble of water (Pūjyapāda 1960: 324, para 799).

In his commentary *Tattvārtha-Vārttika* (also known as *Tattvārtha-Rājavārttika* on verse IX.7 of *Tattvārthasūtra*, Akalaṅka states:

> The Self, which grasps matter (*pudgala*), substance (*dravya*), due to its attachment, etc. psychic states: these *upaṭṭa pudgal dravya* and *anupaṭṭa pudgal* are all permanent from the substantive

perspective (*dravya dṛṣṭi*) but from the modification point of view (*paryāya dṛṣṭi*) are impermanent due to constant changes in their modes.

J.L. Jaini in his translation of *Tattvārthasūtra* (1956: 178) explains:

> Of the matter assimilated as *karma* by the soul, that which is accepted (or grasped) by the soul is *upaṭṭa*. The rest is *anupaṭṭa* matter which is not taken in by the soul.

In this context, Akalaṅka (1993: 770) observes:

> The physical body, enjoyment of sense obejcts, etc. are transitory like a water bubble. Whatever joining together (*saṁyoga*) were there in the pregnancy condition, are not present today. The deluded soul misapprehends them as permanent due to ignorance or perverted knowledge (*ajñāna*). Apart from the conscious attentiveness of knowledge and intuition or perception, other objects are not eternal (*dhruva*). One should contemplate in this manner the transitoriness of the objects of the world. Due to such contemplation, there will be no mental grief in the separation (*viyoga*) of these objects.

In his commentary on *Tattvārtha-Śloka-Vārttika* on *Tattvārthasūtra* IX.7 on *anitya* contemplation, Vidyanandi (commentator Manikchand) states that to think about transitoriness (*anityapana*) is *anitya* contemplation. Thinking of the twelve reflections and repeatedly pondering over them are *anuprekṣās* (Kaundeya 1969: 157, v. 16).

The thought that all worldly objects are transient and fleeting leads to a feeling of non-attachment towards them. The renunciation of worldly objects arises from such non-attachment (Dharma Raja 1990: 3).

In this world, the position and pelf (money, wealth), contacts and correspondence, physical gifts and worldly accessories are all transitory (*Mar* 574-577). In this context, A.N. Upadhye states:

> The śramaṇic, or what is called ascetic, poetry is essentially characterized by that basic pessimism and consequent *ivṛtti*

which originates from the notion of transitoriness (*anityatā*) and is expressed in various ways.

Life, youth, grandeur, majesty or power (*vaibhava*), happiness and residing together with the mother–father and relations and attachment of them are particular place, posture, celestial being, evil spirit or demon and human beings are all transitory (*Mūlācāra* 695). One should contemplate that collected materials or implements (*sāmagrī*) senses, beauty, intellect, youth, life, power or strength, brightness (*teja*), home or residence, sleeping, sitting posture and dealings, etc. are all transitory (*anitya*) and ephemeral (*kṣaṇa-bhaṅgura*) (*Mūlācāra* 696). Death will overtake everyone, no one can escape from it.

Jñānārṇava by Acharya Shubhachandra (1975) in Sanskrit describes *anitya bhāvanā* in these words:

> Hey foolish soul (*mūḍha*)! You are destroying the three worlds by your affection in the pleasures arising out of the senses which are destructible in a moment. Why don't you see that? —*Jñā* 8
>
> Hey soul! Understand that the body is surrounded by diseases and youth or young age is surrounded by old age.
>
> Also know that the prosperity of the grandeur or majesty (*aiśvarya*) is destructible and life is nearing death. —*Jñā* 10
>
> The sense enjoyments (*bhoga*) in the world are like a snake's expanded hood (*phana*) which causes death. —*Jñā* 13
>
> Son, wife, relatives, wealth, body, etc. leave you, and whatever remains, will also necessarily depart. Then why does the soul grieve over them in vain for their cause. —*Jñā* 17
>
> Hey soul! The acquisitions (*parigraha*) necessarily leave or depart after giving burning sensation (*dāha*) and anguish or grief (*santāpa*) in the hearts of people. How can these *parigraha* be capable of your affection? —*Jñā* 24
>
> The past colour, strength, charm and beauty do not come again. This living being continues to expect them in vain. —*Jñā* 38

> The great sages have said that the families and relatives, strength, kingdom, ornaments, wealth, etc. are destructible like the collection of covering of clouds. This ignorant and foolish person has the intellect of their being permanent in vain. —*Jñā* 41

Bhagavatī Ārādhanā by Acharya Sivarya (1990) in Prākr̥t describes *adhruva anuprekṣā* as follows:

> The world along with celestial, human and subhuman (*tiryañca*) beings are destructible as a water bubble. Accordingly, the three worlds (lower, upper and middle) are said to be destructible. All the supernatural powers (*r̥ddhi*) are also destructible.
>
> — *Bha* 1711
>
> All the pleasures are happiness (*sukha*) of human, subhuman or celestial beings, arising out of the desired, cherished or favourite (*iṣṭa*) objects of the five senses in the mind are unsteady and destructible like a water bubble, i.e. *adhruva*. — *Bha* 1712
>
> The master and servant, son, brother, etc. are all impermanent (*anitya*). — *Bha* 1713
>
> The youth or young age of human beings is unstable or changeable. — *Bha* 1716
>
> On the onset of the condition of old age, the beauty, auspicious nature of loveliness (*subhagatā*), youth, knowledge, and penance are diminished or decayed. Old age is the mother of dejection or meekness (*dīnatā*), foster-mother (*dhāya*) of scolding, reproach or disrespect (*tiraskāra*), concept or tele-bearer (*dūtī*) of death, and favourite confidant of a female friend (*sakhī*) of fear.
>
> — *Bha* 1719

The nature of substance is its evolution as a single principle in states composed of the three "moments" of origination or coming into existence (*utpāda*), annihilation, perishing, decay or going out of existence (*vyaya*) and persistence or permanence (*dhrauvya*) (*TS* V.30). In other words, the substance remains the same, but its conditions or modes (*paryāya*) always changes or is transitory. The substance is also said to possess attributes or qualities (*guṇa*) and modifications or modes (*paryāya*) (*TS* V.38). The attributes coexist with substance while modifications succeed each other.

Pravacanasāra 95 defines substance as:

> That which, whilst it does not forsake its innate nature, is characterized by origination, annihilation and stability or persistence and which possesses or is endowed with qualities and modifications, is called a substance.

Awareness of the transitory nature of sensual pleasures and passions like anger enable one to avoid clinging to objects of a transitory nature and motivates one to practise equanimity and self-control. As a result, one attains the goal of peace, happiness, freedom and self-realization.

How *paryāya* (change or modifications) in the material objects affects the power (psychic dispositions) attributes of persons because of their intense attachment to them is aptly described by Acharya Samantabhadra as follows:

> Persons desirous of a pot, a crown and gold become sad, happy and indifferent at the destruction (of the pot) origination (of the crown) and persistence (of gold) on account of their causes.

The psychological states of sadness and happiness and indifference, which are generated in the Self, originate in material objects existing in the external world. Thus, the process of origination, destruction and continuity in material objects causes changes in the psychic states or dispositions as well.

Paryāya (transitoriness of things) is an important concept in Jaina philosophy. *Anitya* (transitoriness) is considered to be the foremost amongst twelve contemplations (*bhāvanās*) which are prescribed for Jainas as a desirable religious practice. *Anitya* means transient, ever-changing, transitory and impermanent. Change is one of the few constants in life; or rather the only constant in life is change. Everything is in a process of change and evolution. To stop change is to cease living. Without change, there is no growth.

Change is considered as the only constant in life. But philosophers like Parmenides, Immanuel Kant and modern Idealists deny the objectivity of change and consider change as an illusion or an appearance due to our special mode of perception.

Change adds to newness and freshness in life. Without change, life will be dull and monotonous. In fact, one can neither know nor realize the value of health unless one falls sick and one does not really experience happiness unless one has gone through hardships and misery.

Contemplation of *anitya bhāvanā* instills in us a sense of detachment, equanimity, self-reliance (*puruṣārtha*), self-restraint (*saṁyama*) and control of passions (*kaṣāyas*) as well as emotions. Contemplation on the impermanence of things makes us reflect on our Self, to search for the changeless reality behind the ever-changing, the quest for seeing and experiencing the real "I", which is different from the "I" of the body and senses and is their substratum.

The concept of *paryāya* is extremely important. First, it helps in understanding the real nature of existence. Second, it forms the basis of the dynamic process of development and revolution. Third, it facilitates growth and adds newness to life. Fourth, *paryāya* forms the genesis of the Jaina doctrine of *anekānta* which reconciles the apparent contradictions between continuity and change, the one and the many, unity and diversity, etc. Fifth, *paryāya* signifies that the conscious substance (*jīva*) may and does develop *vibhāva paryāyas* while retaining its innate nature (*svarūpa*) of intrinsic purity, thereby providing the basis for self-realization, i.e. regaining the *svabhāva* or the state of pure consciousness. Finally, *paryāya* instills a sense of non-attachment, calmness in adverse circumstances, equanimity, self-restraint and control of desires, acquisitions and passions.

Writing about the *bhāvanā* of transitoriness, Acharya Mahaprajna (2010: 23-24, 26) states:

> This body, youth, the glory and the riches — all is transitory. Life itself is transitory. When the fact of transitoriness is kept in view, all pride is of itself dissolved. One who does not realize the fact of transitoriness is very much liable to anger. But a person in whose consciousness it is firmly established that all union is transitory and that material objects are perishable is not perturbed at the loss of material goods. . . . Attachment to the body is the root of all other attachments. If one can get rid of one's attachment to the body, the infatuation of other material objects begins to dissolve itself. . . . Whatever exists in the world is all transitory. No relationship is lasting. All unions end in separation.

"Enjoyment, misery, luxury, wealth, power and poverty, even life itself, are evanescent", Swami Vivekananda says. He adds:

> There are two things, the looker on and the thing looked upon — it will appear always that the universe is one of change, continuously changing all the time. But the reality is that there is both change and changelesslessness in this universe. — 1902: 347

Mahatma Gandhi also recited a poem by Shrimad Rajchandra, which says:

> Wealth is like lightning, fame is like a colour fading. Life is like a wave in the sea. Sensual desires, like the rainbow we see. All is temporary. . . . Why revel in pleasures [that] are momentary?
> — Cited in Mehta 2017

2

Aśaraṇa (Helplessness or Lack of Action)

No power can save anyone from death, which is unavoidable. Constant reflection on this reality leads to non-attachment to the body, equanimity of mind and fearlessness, and a feeling that the transcendental, pure nature of the Self, which is devoid of the bondage of *karmas* and their fruition as also the very existence of *karmas* in the soul (i.e. the pure nature of the Self, is distinct or apart, free from the defilement, impurity and limitations of *karmas* is the only protection, refuge or shelter itself from birth, old age, death, disease and fear (*BA* 11).

In a world beset with old age, distress, death, etc. man has to suffer pain and anguish. Only the Self and its conscious exertions at moral and spiritual discipline are his only true refuge (*śaraṇa*).

Meditation on unprotectedness or helplessness (*aśaraṇa*), seeking some protection from some other persons helps us to see that other people and things as well are themselves helpless. How can they help you when they are themselves helpless? This reflection gives a new insight — not to be dependent on others, but to realize that the real or true help comes from within, our own consciousness, our true Self, which is our protection (*śaraṇa*), our invisible refuge. As soon as one knows of this protection, one starts lifting oneself by engaging oneself in moral and spiritual advancement and following the path of liberation, consisting of enlightened worldview, knowledge and conduct. Our true Self is the greatest protection.

All happiness that depends on others is bound to disappear sooner or later. It is temporary, momentary and it is illusory. Only that joy is yours which wells up within your own being. It is our very nature to be joyous; here there is no need to depend on anyone else. Your happiness is within you. Lord Buddha tells Ānanda, go along having the Self as a lamp, the Self as a refuge and none other refuge; having *dhamma* (*dharma*) as a lamp, *dhamma* as a refuge and none other refuge. *Saṁyutta Nikāya* III.142-143 states: "Let him cast off all fetters, let him make of Self a refuge", as the Buddha himself has done.

Jaina scriptures state:

> Let true knowledge, i.e. enlightened knowledge, be my refuge; let true vision, i.e. enlightened worldview, be my refuge; let true conduct, i.e. enlightened conduct, be my refuge; and may Lord Mahāvīra be my refuge.

From the external, other-referential point of view (*vyavahāra naya*), the Omniscient Lord, Arihanta, the liberated souls (*siddhas*), the saints (*sādhus*), who are following the path of liberation and the *dharma*, the law promulgated by the Omniscient Lord (Kevalī) is the refuge and from the internal, self-referential point of view (*niścaya naya*), one's own Self is the refuge.

The soul is unprotected from the fruition of *karmas*, i.e. death, etc. (Jaini 1956). There is no protection for the transmigratory soul in the middle of miseries or sufferings of birth, old age, death, disease, etc. Only *dharma* is the shelter or refuge (*śaraṇa*) (Pūjyapāda 1992: 324-325, para 800).

In his commentary *Tattvārtha-Rājavārttika* on *Tattvārthasūtra* IX.7 pertaining to *aśaraṇa bhāvanā*, Akalaṅka (1993: 770) points out:

> Protection (*śaraṇa*) is of two kinds: worldly and other-worldly. Each one of these is of three kinds: conscious soul (*jīva*), non-conscious and inanimate matter (*ajīva*) and mixed (*miśra*). King or God, celestial being (*devatā*) are worldly *jīva* protection. The fort, etc. are *ajīva* protection and village, city, etc. are *miśra śaraṇa*. The five revered souls including Omniscient Lord is other-worldly *śaraṇa*; their images, etc. are *ajīva śaraṇa*; and the saints with the apparatus, materials of *dharma* (*dharma upakaraṇa*) are *miśra śaraṇa*.
>
> For the souls affected by birth, old age, disease, death, separation of dear and beloved ones, joining together of unloved, disliked, unfriendly ones, loss, poverty, etc. there is no *śaraṇa* (protection). This sturdy and strong body is only helpful in taking food, not in the time of suffering. The wealth, collected, amassed or hoarded, does not go beyond (human) mode (*paryāyāntara*).
>
> The friends, who are companions or attendants in happiness and suffering, cannot protect one from death. The nearby relatives also cannot protect from disease. If there is any means of protection, it is *dharma* of excellent conduct; this alone can help to get over the ocean of misfortunes and adversities of the world. Even the kinds of gods or celestial beings (Indra), etc. cannot protect one from the clutches of death. Therefore, *dharma* is the only protection to save us from the worldly addictions to calamities or reprehensible habits (*vyasanas*). None of the friends, wealth, etc. is *śaraṇa*.
>
> The current of this kind of thinking is *aśaraṇa* (unprotectedness) contemplation. In this way, there does not remain the feeling of mineness (*mamatva*) in worldly concerns on the onset of fear and mental agitation or passions by the contemplation that "I am *aśaraṇa*", and one's mind is drawn towards the words uttered by the Omniscient Lord.

In his commentary on *Tattvārtha-Śloka-Vārttika* on *Tattvārthasūtra* IX.7 on *aśaraṇa* contemplation, Vidyanandi (commentator Manikchand) states that to thinking, reflecting or pondering (*cintana*) that there is no protection of any one is *aśaraṇa anuprekṣā*.

Only *dharma* (righteousness and piety) preached by the Omniscient Lord (Jinendra Deva) is the protection or refuge (*śaraṇa*) (Rajchandra 1988: 102). Instead of having any covetousness of someone else's protection, one should be self-dependent by accepting the protection of only the glorious divine Lord and *dharma* of the nature of compassion, self-restraint, etc. (Nyayavijaya 1935: 104).

Though a man recognizes that life, youth, body, wealth, family, relatives, status, etc. are impermanent (*anitya*), still he hankers after pleasures, wealth, a charming body, etc. being lustful towards them, he commits sinful deeds and suffers miseries as a result of his own inauspicious acts. However, the Self alone is indestructible. Since all things of the worldly life are impermanent, one should think that it is futile to lament over the loss of those and to lose our mental peace.

One can make use of the *anitya bhāvanā* by thinking that just as wealth and property leaves us, calamity, misfortune, adversity (*vipatti*) will also go away. Hence, one should have the courage, patience, endurance or steadfastness (*dhairya*) in *vipatti* and separation of desired or favourite things, including beloved ones. One should make use of the material things of happiness without attachment (Nyayavijaya 1935: 103).

Know that birth is accompanied by death; youth is succeeded by old age, wealth is perishable. Thus, one should reflect that everything is transient (*Samanasutta* 507).

Whatever with which you are infatuated, that life and local beauty are transient like a flash of electricity. Oh King! why do you not understand what is useful or beneficial in the other world? (*Uttarādhyayansūtra* 18.13).

Anitya (transitoriness) is considered to be the foremost of the twelve contemplations (*bhāvanās*) which are prescribed for Jainas as a desirable religious practice. *Anitya* means transient, ever-changing, transitory and impermanent. Change is one of the few constants in life or rather the only constant is change. Everything is in the process of change and growing. To stop change is to cease living. Without change there is no growth. Change adds to newness and freshness in life, without change life will be dull and monotonous. In fact, one can neither know nor realize the value of health unless one falls sick and one does not really experience happiness unless one has gone through hardships and misery.

Contemplation of *anitya bhāvanā* instils in us a sense of detachment, equanimity, self-reliance (*puruṣārtha*), self-restraint (*saṁyama*), and control of passions (*kaṣāya*) and emotions. Contemplation on the impermanence of things makes us reflect on our inner Self, to search for the changeless reality behind the ever-changing, the quest for seeing and experiencing the real "I", other than the "I" of body and senses.

The physical body is inert, perishable and impermanent. The eternal "I, consciousness", that pre-exists and survives the body, is eternal. There is continuity of the Being, the eternal Self.

The kings, princes, etc. all have to die on their turn; no one can protect them from death (Bhudhar Das's *Bhāvanā*). All the dreams of the world and all the expectations in the world are false; the body, youth and life are unsteady, unstable or fickle (*asthira*) and ephemeral (*kṣaṇa-bhaṅgura*) (Yugalji's *bhāvanā*).

Thus, *anitya* (transitoriness of physical body and other external objects) draws our attention to the permanent "I", the changeless beneath the changes, as Chitrabhanu (1980: 1-15) designates *anitya* contemplation. In this way, *anitya* contemplation emphasizes that we should identify ourselves with the eternal "I", the Self, rather than identifying ourselves with the transitory inert, animate matter, the physical body.

Unless something changeless remains at the back of a change, the latter cannot be recognized at all. In the absence of such a base, recognition of the changes taking place constantly at the bodily and mental levels would not be possible at all. Thus, change and changelessness go together. They cannot but coexist.

Though *adhruva* and *anitya* have similar meanings conveying the transitoriness or impermanence of things or objects, the subtle difference between the two is pointed out by Amrtachandra in his commentary on *Samayasāra* 74 (see *supra*).

Anitya bhāvanā of Jainism seems similar to the Buddhist *anicchā*. In Buddhism, everything is impermanent, nothing is permanent. In Jainism, however, the soul or the Self is eternal/permanent. Moreover, according to Buddhism, the duration of life of a thing is exceedingly brief, lasting only while a thought lasts. As soon as a thought has ceased, the thing is said to have ceased. In the Jaina view, however, nothing new is created, nothing is destroyed, only modifications appear and disappear.

The utter helplessness of every living being is due to the fact that nothing can afford protection from death, which is unavoidable. It is in the contemplation of the real nature of the Self, which is eternal, that one can find peace in the state of helplessness. Constant meditation on this reality results in equanimity of mind and feeling of fearlessness (Dharma Raja 1990: 3).

When one is pestered by birth, old age and death, the only shelter is the Jina-*śāsana*. Even with all the military equipment, no king has been able to conquer death. Neither miracles nor medicines, neither friends nor relatives, not even gods, can save a man from death; and none else can share its agonies (*Mar* 578-583).

In this context, A.N. Upadhye observes:

> The *ātman* is his own shelter, an architect of his fortunes and misfortunes; and none else can save him from the consequences of his *karmas*. The great Tīrthaṅkaras have already shown the path by their own example. This theme is closely linked with the *karma* doctrine which leaves no margin for divine intervention in human affairs. A touching exposition of this *anāthatā* or *asatānatva* is found in *Uttarādhyayanasūtra* XX in which this idea is very nicely driven home to King Śreṇika.

Since the enlightened worldview, enlightened knowledge, enlightened conduct and enlightened austerities inhere in the Self, the Self alone is my protection.

A horse, an elephant, a chariot, a human being, power, a vehicle, *mantra*, medicine, knowledge, moral conduct and relations — these all are not the protectors from the fear of death (*Mūlācāra* 697). Only the rules of disciplines of Jina (Jina-*śāsana*) and *dharma* expounded by Lord Jina are the only protectors (*Mūlācāra* 698-699).

In its exposition of *aśaraṇa bhāvanā*, *Bhagavatī Ārādhanā* states:

> One has to experience birth, old age, death, disease, anxiety, fear and anguish (*vedanā*), etc. sufferings, on the coming into operation or rise (*udaya*) of *karmas*, of which there is no counteraction or antidote. — *Bha* 1729

> Neither knowledge nor learning (*vidyā*), nor *mantra* nor any medicine, nor one's strength, nor courage or vigour (*vīrya*), nor horses, nor elephants, nor chariots, nor warriors, nor incantation, bribery, threat and guile (*sāma, dāma, daṇḍa, bheda*), etc. means (the traditional means for a person (king) to attain his purposes), are the protections or refuge (*śaraṇa*) on the coming into operation or rise (*udaya*) of *karmas*. — *Bha* 1734

> On the supernatural beings, who are possessed of knowledge and learning (*vidyādhara*), strong and powerful persons (*baladeva*), a mighty or supreme king, an emperor of a wide region (*cakravartī*) and the king of celestial beings (Indra), etc. very powerful personages (*mahābalī*) and great, valiant, bold and mighty persons (*mahāparākramī*) are also not the refuge (*śaraṇa*) of anyone. They also cannot protect. — *Bha* 1738

> On the coming into operation or rise (*udaya*) of *karmas* of which there is no counteraction or antidote (pain feeling or anguish-producing *karmas*, *asata vedanīya*, etc. *karmas*), only the enlightened worldview or right belief, enlightened knowledge and enlightened conduct, which are the cause of the destruction of *karmas*, are the only protectors and refuge (*śaraṇa*). — *Bha* 1741

Speaking of the *āśaraṇa bhāvanā*, *Jñānārṇava* states:

> When the time (*kāla*), i.e. death comes, no one is the refuge (*śaraṇa*). The time (*kāla*) devours a child, person, rich and poor, the valiant or a hero (*śūravīra*) is also a coward. In this way, it devours all the living beings alike. —*Jñā* 11

> The *kāla* swallows everyone having a merciless or cruel intellect. Only by taking refuge of one's knowledge and one's own (transcendental, pure) nature (*rūpa*) can there be protection from *kāla*. —*Jñā* 19

Briefly, all beings experience according to one's capacity and one is the causal agent or doer (*kartā*) or destroyer (*hartā*) of anyone. From the internal, self-referential point of view (*niścaya dṛṣṭi*), one's own Self is the only refuge (*śaraṇa*). And from the external, other-referential view or perspective (*vyavahāra dṛṣṭi*), the five most revered dignitaries (Omniscient Lord, Arahanta, etc. *pañca parameṣṭhi*) alone is the refuge (*śaraṇa*), because they are the cause of real non-attachment (*vītarāgatā*). Therefore, leaving or giving up the refuge of all other (*anya*), one should think only of the aforesaid two protections or refuge (*śaraṇa*).

In brief, the five most reverent souls (*pañca parameṣṭhi*) is the refuge, the *dharma* propounded by the Omniscient Lord is the refuge; the triple jewels of enlightened worldview, knowledge and conduct, is the refuge; excellent forgiveness, etc. ten *dharmas* are the refuge; and the Self itself is its own refuge.

Describing *aśaraṇa bhāvanā*, Acharya Mahaprajna (2010: 32) observes:

> The truth of all times is that a man can definitely rely only on his own valour and exertion. In fact, shelter or refuge lies only in one's own endeavour, nowhere else. On the basis of this ultimate truth, not to repose too much or exclusive trust in other people's protection, constitutes *bhāvanā* of not seeking refuge outside oneself. The man who is permitted by this *bhāvanā*, develops a

> strong sense of responsibility and has equanimity is not disturbed even when others betray him. . . . That which is alien can provide no refuge.

I give up (all forms of) possessiveness (and attachment) knowingly of deceit, delusion and remove the three *śalyas* (thorn or blemish), *nidāna*, i.e. desire for future sense pleasures from my mind, speech and body. The three restraints (*guptī*) of mind, speech and body, in five carefulness (*samiti*) (in walking, speaking, eating, putting and handling things and cleanliness) are my protection and refuge (*Samanasutta* 510).

The wise men should think that mother, father, daughter-in-law, brother and son — none of them, while experiencing the miseries of the *karmas*, are able to provide refuge to me (*Uttarādhyayanasūtra* 6.3).

3

Ekatva (Being Alone or Solitariness)

According to *ekatva bhāvanā*, one is alone/all alone in the world and suffers the pains and sorrows.

Each soul is born alone, dies alone and alone experiences the consequences of his/her actions. In *ekatva bhāvanā*, one contemplates that I am one, alone, solitary (*ekkoham*), that nothing whatever or nothing of any other is mine (*nimmamo* or *nirmama* in Sanskrit), that I am pure (*śuddho*), that I am endowed with the characteristics of knowledge and intuition, and that only unity or oneness (*ekatva*) with the pure Self (*śuddha aiyatta*) is worth acquiring (*upādeya*) and to be aspired for. The self-restrained person should contemplate on this reflection in this way (*BA* 20[1]).

Reflections on *ekatva bhāvanā* instils a sense of responsibility since the Self alone has to bear the consequences of its actions.

In *Niyamasāra* 101, Kundakunda states:

> The embodied, mundane soul dies alone, is born alone and if the soul dies alone, it alone realizes its own pure and perfect Self (after being liberated from *karmas*).

---

1 This verse is somewhat similar to *Samayasāra* 38 and 73.

One should contemplate as such. You alone are the cause of attainment of self-realization. Therefore, the one who yearns to become free from all sorrows must seek the Self, embark on an inner journey and be self-focused.

When you experience "I am", Chitrabhanu (1980: 39) observes:

> You are living in your [own] consciousness [alone]. There is no duality. As soon as you say "I want" desire begins. From desire comes the object. . . . Out of the two "I" and "want", a third thing comes "the world". This trinity is born from duality. The world out there is born every time you separate from the subject, your centre, "I". As soon as you are out of your consciousness, duality is there, the world is there.

Ekatva (being alone) means to realize ultimately, "I am", not "I want". It means to break from the concept of duality and be oneself. When you bring the whole world into "being", life merges into one flow. Then there is no manifestation of otherness, only oneness (*ekatva*). The idea behind this meditation [of *ekatva*] to make an individual strong on his own . . . [and not to depend on others] (ibid.).

Contemplations on this *bhāvanā* leads to non-attachment due to having knowledge of the nature of the Self.

I am alone (*ekākī*), all the souls appear/come in the world united or having oneness (*ekatva*) (with body and *karmas*); I had thought that body, wealth, etc. are mine, but they also leave me alone (Yugalji's *Bhāvanā*).

Ekatva bhāvanā is not for being selfish, to be self-dependent, and able and awaken one's own power of the Self (Nyayavijaya 1935: 106).

The external, social or other-referential aspects of *ekatva* (oneness) are the gospel (*mantra)* for social engineering. It is a solution for all ills and crimes. A lifestyle based on *ekatva* and all actions corresponding to it shall be natural, scientific and truthful.

Universal brotherhood and humanism are its worldly symbols. The present world needs humanism or humanness more than ever.

This is because our (present-day) relations seem to be oriented not by humanness, but by considerations of caste, creed, colour, nationality or other denominations. There is religious fanaticism, communalism, regionalism, casteism, and even linguistic chauvinism. The implications of such divisions are rampant hatred, ill-will, violence and worse terrorism that has become a global problem.

To be humane or being human is to be kind, benevolent, tender and merciful. Thus, the sooner the humanness is adopted, the greater the chance of it ushering in a golden period of peace and stability (Singh 2016).

I am alone the doer of my actions and the enjoyer of the fruits of them (Jaini 1956: 149). I am alone to experience the great miseries consequent upon the recurrence of birth, old age and death; no one is mine and other; I alone am born and die alone. None of my relations can remove my miseries (ibid.: 325-326, para 802).

In his commentary on *Tattvārtha-Rājavārttika* on *Tattvārthasūtra* IX.7, Akalaṅka (1993: 711) states:

> Both *ekatva* (one, being alone, solitary, unity or oneness) and variety or diversity (*anekatva*) are of four kinds with reference to substance (*dravya*), place (*kṣetra*), time (*kāla*) and character or disposition (*bhāva*). *Dravya ekatva* is in each living entity, etc. substance. The space-point (*pradeśa*), checked by one minutest atom (*paramāṇu*) of space is *kṣetra ekatva*. One moment of time (*samaya*) is *kāla ekatva* on the path of liberation is definitely *bhāva ekatva*. In the same way, there are different kinds of *anekatva* also. Neither one nor many (*aneka*) is definite. From a general (*sāmānya*) perspective, one (*eka*) by the particular (*viśeṣa*) perspective become many (*aneka*).
>
> The person obtaining or acquiring for sure *ekatva* (oneness) with enlightened knowledge, by giving up external and internal

possessiveness (*parigraha*). One's *mokṣa-mārga* (path of liberation of the nature of *yathākhyāta* conduct (ideal and passionless conduct) is *bhāva ekatva*. For acquiring that I alone have to make efforts, neither anyone is my own (*sva*), nor anyone is other (*para*). I alone am born and I alone die. Neither any living being is my own (*sva-jana*), nor any living being is other (*para-jana*), can remove the miseries or sufferings of disease, old age, death, etc. Relatives and friends do not go beyond the cremation or burial ground.

Dharma alone is the companion forever. Thinking in this manner is *ekatva anuprekṣā*. By contemplation of this, one does not have attachment to *sva-jana* and aversion in regard to *para-jana* and by acquiring non-possessiveness (*aparigraha*) one engages in effort for attaining liberation.

In his commentary on *Tattvārtha-Śloka-Vārttika* on *Tattvārthasūtra* IX.7 on *ekatva* contemplation, Vidyanandi (1969, vol. 7: 159) (commentator Manikchand) states:

> To take birth, to obtain old age, to die, again to take birth, to be of old age, to die — in such numerous psychical movements or recurrences (*avratī*), the Self alone continues to experience great pain and suffering; in that experience, there is no one to be looked or hoped for or to be expected (*apekṣanīya*). One's own people (*sva-jana*), other persons (*para-jana*) is there who can be of assistance or helpful (*sahāyaka*); the Self alone experiences the fruits or consequences of meritorious or demeritorious (*puṇya-pāpa*) (*karmas*); he alone attains liberation; looking about for any *sahāyaka* is useless; there can be no *sahāyaka*; such reasoning (*tarkaṇā*) is *ekatva anuprekṣā*.

Each and every soul has its individuality. Every soul comes alone to occupy its body. It also departs from its body — all alone, at the moment of death. Therefore, the Self alone can destroy its *karmas* in order to emancipate itself from the mortal coil.

Others do not accompany one to the next world. One has to suffer all alone for one's *karmas*. It is futile to weep for others without understanding one's own plight (*Mar* 584-588).

A.N. Upadhye points out:

> The themes of *ekatva* and *anyatva* go together. The *ātman* is essentially lonely [it should be alone] or single throughout this transmigratory journey.

One alone departs being afflicted or oppressed from disease and under the subjection of death in the middle of one's own relations and attendants, dependents and family. One alone becomes miserable, weeps and befalls or endures death. No one else goes with him (*Mūlācāra* 700).

This soul alone binds auspicious and inauspicious *karmas*. One alone transmigrates in this world, one alone is born, and one alone dies – one should contemplate of *ekatva* in this manner (*Mulācāra* 701).

Being Alone Is not Being Lonely or Feeling Lonely

In discussing *ekatva anuprekṣā/bhāvanā*, many commentators have mistakenly used the term "loneliness" or "lonely". These include J.L. Jaini (1956: 149, v. I.7), Vilas Sangave (1990: iii), M.K. Dharma Raja (1990: 2), *Maraṇa-Samādhi* and A.N. Upadhye (see *supra*). It is absolutely necessary to clarify that being alone is not being lonely or feeling lonely.

There is a vast difference between being alone and being lonely or feeling lonely, between aloneness and loneliness. Loneliness means that you miss the presence of the other or that you feel the absence of the other. To be alone means that being by oneself is enough. Loneliness is painful and hence we hope to get happiness from other and also feel pleasure in the company of other. We make our world because loneliness hurts. We try to fill this loneliness by being attached to persons and things, which are transitory, and in case of separation or loss thereof, we feel pain and anguish. Aloneness means that you are happy to be with yourself. Your world, your whole world is in you. There is nothing lacking. You are complete, you are whole, your happiness is within you. From aloneness comes non-attachment. And when there is no attachment, mind does not waver; it becomes stable.

Recognizing the value of solitude or being alone, William Deresiewicz (2009: B6) observes:

> [Though] solitude was not always stigmatized; in earlier times, the ability to be alone was recognized as a necessary part of the religious experience, or a prerequisite to appreciate nature . . . it is becoming increasingly difficult to be alone . . . in the modern age.

With the spread of telephone and television technologies including computers, which is creating "a culture of connectivity and connections", Deresiewicz worries that "we are losing the ability for introspection — no real excellence, personal or social, artistic, philosophical, scientific or moral, [or spiritual] can arise without solitude". In fact, one should contemplate that in the mindless pursuit of power, ego or material riches, what has one gained and, more importantly, what has one really lost (Deresiewicz 2009: B6). For instance, righting itself is a solitary activity.

In this context, Ishan Chaudhury (2015) states:

> Being alone, gathering one's thoughts or even soaking in the air may seem as doing nothing. But put to good use, such time provides the fuel for bursts of qualitiative action. We must learn to inculcate the habit of being in such an inactive state in order to rise above the mediocre when "active" in the traditionally accepted sense.

Thinking that "I" (my soul is distinct from the body), one should not be frightened or perplexed by the pleasures or the pain of the body and not have attachment and infatuation of the body (Nyayavijaya 1935: 106).

Describing *ekatva bhāvanā*, *Jñānārṇava* states:

> In this world, the Self alone experiences the fruits of consequences of past *karmas*, where the pleasurable and painful, and in all ways, the Self alone acquires the other body from the earlier/previous body in all the conditions of existence (*gati*). —*Jñā* 2

No one is a friend or companion of this living being in joining together (*saṁyoga*) or separation (*viyoga*), in birth and death and in experiencing sufferings or pleasures. The Self alone experiences (all that). —*Jñā* 4

Whenever this soul does any bad or good deed or action for the sake of a purpose of son, friend, wife, etc. he alone experiences the consequences in hellish, etc. conditions of existence. There also, no one, son, friend, etc. is the companion in experiencing the consequences of the fruition of *karmas* (*karmaphala*). —*Jñā* 5

The connection of the world (*saṁsāra*) is due to infatuation (*moha*); and if *moha* vanishes, then why does the Self as one (*eka*) attain liberation?, i.e. one attains liberation. —*Jñā* 10

Bhagavatī Ārādhanā describes *ekatva anuprekṣā* as follows:

The soul indulges in sinful acts for the sake of a relative or friend (*bandhu*) or kinsman (*bāndhava*) or one's own body, and for nurturing or maintaining *bāndhava* and one's own body, the Self alone experiences their fruits or consequences in hellish, etc. (conditions of existence, *gati*). — *Bha* 1742

Bandhu-bāndhava, wealth and body, etc. acquisitions (*parigraha*) are not of anyone. When the soul goes to other world (*paraloka*), then no one goes with it. The Self alone goes; this is *ekatva bhāvanā*. — *Bha* 1745

Replying to the question that if these *bandhu*, etc. are not going with (*sahāyaka*), who goes with the Self, it is stated: "The Self's enlightened conduct, i.e. *dharma* of the nature of triple jewels (enlightened world view or right belief, enlightened knowledge and enlightened conduct together) is *sahāyaka* in *paraloka*.

— *Bha* 1747

Commenting on *Bhagavatī Ārādhanā* 1747, Aparajit Suri states:

The person, who keeps, maintains or preserves *ratnatraya dharma* while going to a bad condition of existence (*durgati*), that *dharma* places that person in an auspicious (*śubha*) place or condition. The *ratnatraya dharma* is the cause of *abhyudaya*, i.e. prosperity

> and excellent happiness in the world as also in the next world as well as *niḥśreyas*, i.e. liberation (*mokṣa*). One should practise again and again that "no other is my *sahayak*".
>
> — Quoted in Sivarya 1990

Such contemplation is to be done constantly.

In brief, one alone becomes deceased and dies; one alone bears the unbearable or intolerable sufferings of hell. In reality, excellent forgiveness, etc. ten *dharmas* alone are the Self's own intimate relations, friends or guides.

Being alone means you are not dependent on others. The moment you depend on someone else, it leads to fear, which, in turn, creates all kinds of illusions and problems. Because we have leaned on others, we feel confused, we are afraid, we do not know what to do, think or act.

The aloneness of the Self surpasses all empirical terms and generally determine and often clearly define, any other phenomenon in the related field of experiences.

Describing the *bhāvanā* of solitariness (being alone), Acharya Mahaprajna states:

> A man, who firmly realizes that the soul is alone, the individual is alone, is not perplexed when no cooperation is forthcoming because his consciousness is fully permeated by the *bhāvanā* of aloneness. . . . [One should] remember the eternal truth that man is essentially alone. . . . Attachment arises in duality; in the absence of duality, it dissolves. It is an Upaniṣadic saying — "What delusion or grief can come to a man who keeps alone." . . . The only way to experience aloneness is to accept the truth that all coming together is accidental. The body, clothes, shelter are all transitory. Passions like anger, etc. and diseases are . . . not innate but conditional.
>
> — 2010: 39-41

> I am one; alone; no one is mine and I am also of no one else.
>
> — *Ācārāṅgasūtra* 1.8.6

> No one can share the sufferings of others. Every living being is born alone and dies alone. — *Sūtrakṛtāṅgasūtra* 2.1.13

Man alone experiences sufferings; friends, son, one's own people like a brother, relations, etc. no one can share that. Because *karma* follows only the doer (*kartā*) of that *karma*, only he has to experience the fruits thereof (*Uttarādhyayanasūtra* 13.23).

Man has to experience the fruits of one's own *karmas* alone.

4

Anyatva Bhāvanā (Otherness from the Body)

THE otherness of the pure nature of the Self from all other, including body (no-*karma*), material or physical *karma* (*dravya-karma*) and impure psychic dispositions (*bhāva-karma*) conditioned by material *karma*, other states, conditions or modes of the Self and other substances. The mother, father, brother, son, wife, etc. bear no relationship to the Self; they all exist, motivated by their own sake (*BA* 21). Since the body, etc. are distinct from the Self, one should contemplate that they are other (*anya*) from the Self which is endowed with knowledge and intuition. *Samayasāra* is replete with the concept of *ekatva-vibhakta*, i.e. contemplations of *ekatva* and *anyatva*.

Reflections on the fact of distinctness of the soul or consciousness from the perishable body, other material objects and possessions and relations lead one to focus one's attention (*upayoga*) on the eternal sentient (*cetanā*) Self and its essential nature.

Anyatva (otherness), Chitrabhanu (1980: 54-55) observes,

> means that which is other than your essence or the Self. It helps you to see two things: (1) *anya*, where you have mistakenly identified yourself or mixed yourself up; and (2) *sva*, your real Self. It is a process of separation [otherness]. You are not that with which you have identified.

> Your real Self cannot be identified with anything. It is unique.... If you have created identity with something, and that something is taken away from you, you experience great pain....
>
> In reflecting on *anyatva*, start with your own body and say, "The body other (*anya*) from what I am. The body is *anya*, or other. I am *sva* or the Self". Don't confuse one with the other. See them for what they are.

Thus, one can understand the value and significance and the rarity of enlightened worldview (*samyak darśana*), which means ascertaining (and then having conviction in) the true nature of things (the Self and the non-Self, *sva*, one's real Self, and *anya* or *para* (other) as they really are.

The world, my relations and friends, wealth and even my body and mind are not mine; they are all distinct from my real Self (Jaini 1956: 149). Though there is unity or oneness (*abheda*) between the Self and the body, there is a difference/distinctness in regard to their characteristsics. The body is transient, "I" am eternal. The body has a beginning and an end and "I" (the Self) am without beginning and end. In this manner, by being confined or equipped with the resolution or solution of the problem of the mind, the desire or ambition (*spṛhā*) in body, etc. does not arise. One obtains liberation due to the pre-eminence of non-attachment through the contemplation of the knowledge of spiritual principles (*tattva-jñāna*) (*SAS* 802). One experiences discriminative insight (*bheda-jñāna*) between the body and the soul.

In his commentary on *Tattvārtha-Rājavārttika* on the *Tattvārthasūtra* IX.7 concerning *anyatva anuprekṣā*, Akalaṅka (1993, vol. 2: 771-772) states:

> *Anyatva* (otherness) as also of four kinds of differences (*bheda*) depending on (1) name (*nāma*); (2) representation (*sthāpanā*); (3) privation or substance (*dravya*); and (4) present condition (*bhāva*) (*TS* I.5). The Self (*ātmā*) or a living being (*jīva* is *nāma* difference, distinction or particularity (*bheda*). The wooden image of Lord

> Mahāvīra is *sthāpanā bheda*. The soul substance, non-soul (*ajīva*) substance, is *dravya bheda* (or a president-elect may well be called the president is *dravya bheda*); and in only one soul the differences or distinctions of child, youth, human being, celestial being, etc. modification (*paryāya*) *bheda* is *bhāva bheda*.
>
> Though there is no difference between the body and the Self with respect to bondage, yet there is a difference from the perspective of characteristics. By the practices of conduct, etc. the skilled or deft person with a natural knowledge, etc. situated in infinite worth-acquiring qualities is said to be liberation, which is extremely different or distinct from the body, is *mukti* (liberation) or *śivapada anyatva*.
>
> For attaining the supreme *anyatva*, one should contemplate in this manner: the body is one-sensed, I am beyond senses; the body is ignorant, I am a knowing (person); the body is impermanent, I am permanent; the body is with beginning and end, I am beginningless and infinite; I have acquired lakhs of bodies, I am a conscious being, quite different or distinct from them; when I am distinct even from the body, then what to talk of external worldly objects or passions? Contemplation like that is *anyatva anuprekṣā*. Due to this contemplation, one does not have any desire for the body, etc. and one begins to make efforts for attaining liberation.

In his commentary *Tattvārtha-Śloka-Vārttika* on *Tattvārthasūtra* IX.7 pertaining to *anyatva anuprekṣā*, Vidyanandi (commentator Manikchand) states:

> Due to the Self and the body being of different or distinct characteristics, to think of the Self as different from the body and to discuss the difference of their characteristics is *anyatva anuprekṣā*. — Akalaṅka 1993, vol. 7: 159

While contemplating of *anyatva bhāvanā*, if one does not have discriminative insight and knowledge (*bheda-jñāna*), then his contemplation of that is of no use.

The world, my relatives and friends, my body and mind, they are all distinct from my real Self (Sangave 1990: iv).

Each individual soul is separate/distinct from every other soul and every other object. The soul and the body are entirely distinct from each other. Whatever is considered as belonging to oneself is not so. Because the real Self has nothing to do either with any other being or object. In other words, each individual soul is an entity by itself with its own identity distinct from others (Dharma Raja 1990: 3).

The body and relatives are all distinct from the Self (*Mar* 589). In this context, A.N. Upadhye observes:

> One has to realize one's responsibility and oneself as separate [it should be distinct or different] from everything else, from the subtle *karmas* to gross body and other possessions and relatives. That the soul and body are different is the central theme of the discussion between King Paesi and the monk Kesi in *Rāyapasenaijjam*.

Mother–father, relatives, etc. are other, different or distinct from my Self. They are together with me in this universe, but they do not go with me in the other universe/world. When the body, etc. is other [not mine], again the other external objects are obviously other (*anya*). The Self is of the nature of knowledge. In this manner, one should contemplate of otherness (*Mūlācāra* 702-704).

In the discussion of *anyatva anuprekṣā*, many persons have mistakenly used the term "separate" or "separateness" (*pṛthak* in Hindi), which is not the same as *anyatva* (otherness). For instance, many scholars including Lal Bahadur Shastri, not aware of the actual difference between separate (*pṛthak*) and otherness (*anyatva*), used the word "separate" in place of other (*anya*). The Self is not separate from matter or material *karma*, the other substance, though it is different or distinct from it. *Pṛthakatva* (separateness), Kundakunda points out in *Pravacanasāra* 106, is "occupying of [a] different place, while *anyatva* is non-identity (*a-tad-bhava*) [it is not the same]".

The physical body in the embodied existence of human birth,

though other (*anya*), different (*bhinna*) or distinct (*vibhakta*) from the conscious Self, as the two (body and soul) have their own characteristics, the body is not separate (*pr̥thak*) from the soul.

Jñānārṇava describes *anyatva bhāvanā* in these words:

> If one looks from the perspective of bondage of *karmas*, the Self is of the nature of bondage and of the same form or appearance (*ekarūpa*) and if one looks at from the perspective of their natures (*svabhāva*), the Self is consciousness and bliss (*cidānanda*), having distinctive characteristics from body, etc. and is different or distinct from other substance (*para dravya*), pure. —*Jñā* 1
>
> From the perspective of bondage, the conscious being (*cetanā*) and the non-conscious inert matter (*acetanā*) are similar; in reality, however they are different from each other, there is no oneness (*ekapanā*). From the beginningless time, there is synthesis, mixing or union between the two of the nature of immersion in one place (*eka kṣetra-avagaha*), but in reality they are different things. —*Jñā* 2
>
> When the Self is extremely different or distinct from the body, then how can there be sameness, identity or unity (*ekatā*) with external family or relatives, because they directly look different. —*Jñā* 7
>
> You should always contemplate in all ways that in this world, son, friend, wife, etc. are other (*anya*) things/entities and of the nature (*anya-svabhāva*); never contemplate that there is oneness (*ekapanā*). —*Jñā* 9

The *anyatva anuprekṣā* is described in *Bhagavatī Ārādhanā* 1749 as follows:

> One feels sorrow by seeing other souls, other relatives, etc. who are different from one's own Self, such as a person suffering or affliction, but this ignorant soul does not feel concern and anxiety though surrounded by many bodily, mental, etc. sufferings.

In this infinite world, of the Self, wandering in many conditions of existence (*gati*), due to one's deluded view, etc. *karmas*, which is own person (*sva-jana*) (no person is one's own). It is only because of infatuation or attachment that one thinks that this person is my brother, father, son, sister, servant or master. The reality is that they are all other (*Jñā* 1750). They are other (*anya*) than me and I am other than they. The contemplation of *anyatva* with reference to one's own (*sva*) and other (*para*) is *anyatva anuprekṣā*.

That "I" (the Self) is permanent and the body is transitory; I am a conscious entity and the body is non-conscious. When there is otherness (*anyatva*) or distinctness between the body and "I" or "me", then why there will not be *anyatva* with other things or objects?, i.e. there will be *anyatva* with other objects. To contemplate in this way is *anyatva anuprekṣā*.

Describing this *bhāvanā*, Acharya Mahaprajna (2010: 48) observes:

> With the awakening of the *bhāvanā* of otherness, many complexes are dissolved. . . . A man is freed of tensions and complexes . . . created by a person through the identification of himself with his body.

My soul endowed with knowledge and intuition or faith is alone permanently mine; all others, i.e. the body and the states of attachment, etc. have the characteristic of joining together (*saṁyoga*), my relationship with them is only that of *saṁyoga*; they are other than me (*Samanasutta* 516).

This body is other from one's soul, I am other, brother and relations are also other from me. Knowing this, a skilful person should not be attached to them (*Samanasutta* 519).

The lust and enjoyment of sense-pleasures are other and I am other. Then why should I have attachment in other things (*Sūtrakṛtāṅga* 2.1.13). Wife, son, friend and relations are only fellow beings of a living person. No one goes along with them at the time of death (*Uttarādhyayanasūtra* 18.14).

5

Saṁsāra
(Mundaneness, Transmigration)

The transmigratory existence of every soul in the cycle of births and deaths and wandering in the world in the four conditions of existence (*gati*) of heavenly, hellish, subhuman (animals, etc.) and human beings is replete with birth, old age or senility, death, disease and fear, and is fraught with union and separation, gain and loss, pleasure and sorrow, as also honour and dishonour (*BA* 36). Therefore, one should view life realistically and turn to contemplation on the pure nature of the Self and to thoughts of self-purification as the surest and sole means to get rid of the miseries of existence and attain salvation.

Reflection on the fact of distinctness of the soul or consciousness from the perishable body, other material objects and possessions and relations lead one to focus one's attention (*upayoga*) on the eternal sentient (*cetanā*) Self and its essential nature.

The soul moves in the cycle of existences and cannot attain true happiness till it is out of it (Jaini 1956: 149). The acquisition of another existence for the soul due to the maturity of *karma*s is *saṁsāra*. Contemplating about the nature of *saṁsāra* is *saṁsāra anuprekṣā* (Pūjyapāda 1944: 325, para 801).

The rich and poor in this *saṁsāra* are all unhappy. One should be content with what he has and not be jealous of others having more property. One should think that many of our thoughts are of our own making (Nyayavijaya 1935: 104-105).

In his commentary *Tattvārtha-Rājavārttika* on *Tattvārthasūtra* IX.7 pertaining to *saṁsāra anuprekṣā*, Akalaṅka (1993) states:

> Obtaining of inner or inter modes/modifications (*paryāya-antara*) by the Self, due to substance (*dravya*), etc. acting as a supportive factor (*nimitta*), is said to be *saṁsāra*. The Self has four conditions: (1) *saṁsāra*, i.e. worldly existence of births and deaths; (2) *asaṁsāra*, i.e. absence of *saṁsāra*; (3) non-*saṁsāra*, i.e. little (*iṣat*) and *sāra*; and (4) that which is extraordinary from these three conditions.
>
> The transmigration or wanderings in four conditions (*gatis*) of existence (hellish, subhuman (animal, birds, etc.), human and celestial being), having many wombs or births/rebirths (*yoni*), which is quite painful, is *saṁsāra*.
>
> Not taking of birth again, attainment of liberation (the position of bliss — *śivapada*) or state/position of supreme happiness is *asaṁsāra*.
>
> *Iṣat saṁsāra* or non-*saṁsāra* is the condition of *jīvanmukta*, i.e. liberation in the embodied existence of the Omniscient Lord Arihanta, Tīrthaṅkara (Jina), who is embodied (*paramātmā*, in which there is total cessation of any kind of attachment, passions of ignorance, etc. though the body and the activities of mind, speech and body (*yoga*) continue to function (for that reason, he is called *sayoga-kevalī*). In that condition, there is no wandering in the worldly existence, and the Self has not yet attained liberation [without body and *yoga*, i.e. the condition of *ayoga-kevalī*].

The fourth condition of the Self, which is extraordinary (from the above-mentioned), three conditions of the Self are that of *ayoga-kevalī* (the state of disembodied *siddhas*). These liberated souls are devoid of vibrations or actions of the body (*śarīra parispanda*) in the space-points of the Self (*ātma-pradeśa*) of the *ayoga-kevalī* or *siddhas*. So long as there is movement (*calana*) in the *ātma-pradeśa* even when there is no *śarīra-parispanda*, till then there is *saṁsāra*.

From the perspective of the mundane soul, *saṁsāra* is beginningless and without end, i.e. infinite (*anādi ananta*). With respect to those who can be liberated (*bhavya*), it (*saṁsāra*) is beginningless (*anādi*) but with extirpation (*uccheda*). Non-*saṁsāra* is with beginning and with end (*sari santa*). *Asaṁsāra* is also with beginning and with end (*sadi santa*).

The substantive *dravya-saṁsāra* is of four kinds due to the difference regarding *karmas*, no-*karmas*, *vastu* (thing or object) and *viṣayāśraya* (dependence on senses). Akalaṅka then goes on to describe in detail the other four kinds of *saṁsāra*: place, *kṣetra-saṁsāra* (two kinds); time, *kāla-saṁsāra* (two kinds); worldly existence, *bhava-saṁsāra* (thirty-two kinds); character, *bhava-saṁsāra* (two kinds) and their different kinds.

Concluding his discussion on *saṁsāra anuprekṣā*, Akalaṅka (1993: 770-771) remarks:

> In this crowded, dense and disordered (*saṅkula*) *saṁsāra* of many thousands of birds due to the mounted upon the instrument or appliance of *karmas* (*karma-yantra*), the soul wanders or transmigration as sometimes being father, it becomes brother, son or grandson, being mother it becomes wife or daughter.
>
> Contemplation on the nature of *saṁsāra* in this manner is *saṁsāra anuprekṣā*. Contemplating in this way, due to becoming fearful and mental agitation from the miseries and sufferings, freedom from worldly concerns and desires takes place and the soul endeavours for the destruction of the mundane worldly existence (*saṁsāra*).

In his commentary on *Tattvārtha-Śloka-Vārttika on Tattvārthasūtra* IX.7 pertaining to *saṁsāra anuprekṣā*, Vidyanandi (1969, vol. 7: 159) (commentator Manikchand) states:

> Obtaining of numerous other (*anya*) cycles of births or transmigratory existences (*bhavas*) of the Self due to substance

> (*dravya*), place (*kṣetra*), time (*kāla*), etc. acting as supportive factors (*nimittas*) – the detailed consideration of that is *saṁsāra anuprekṣā.*

The soul moves in sorrowful conditions and in the cycle of births and deaths and cannot attain true happiness till it is cut off therefrom (Sangave 1990: iv).

Each soul has been ceaselessly transmigrating in the cyle of life, death and rebirth in all varieties of existence. This relentless cycle is fraught with sorrow and anxiety. One should, therefore, turn to reflection on emancipating oneself from the remorseless continuity of this condition of bondage (Dharma Raja 1990: 4).

When the mind is deluded and not knowing the correct path, the *ātman* wanders in *saṁsāra*, in various births, suffering physical pains and mental agonies. Birth, death, privations, etc. are to be faced all along: the same soul plays different roles in different parts without following the *dharma* (*Mar* 590-600).

In this context, A.N. Upadhye states:

> Many descriptions of the endless *saṁsāra* with its privations and miseries in the four grades of life are found in the canon. *Sūyagadam* describes the miseries in hell in one of its chapters, I.5.1-2; and Miyaputta convinces his parents that ascetic life is really covetable when one remembers the various miseries one has to experience in different lives.

The soul, being imbued with delusion and not seeing the path of liberation (of enlightened worldview, knowledge and conduct) described by Lord Jina, transmigrates in the terrible and wicked *saṁsāra*, bound by extremely dense with the climbing or creeping plant of the nature of infatuation (*Mūlācāra* 705). Transmigration or change in the cycle of births and deaths is *saṁsāra*. It is of four kinds relating to substance (*dravya*), place (*kṣetra*), time (*kāla*) and state or psychic dispositions (*bhāvas*). It is joined or connected with the four types of existence (*gatis*) of hellish, human, subhuman and celestial (*Mūlācāra* 706).

In other Jaina scriptures, *saṁsāra* is said to be of five kinds.

Saṁsāra (transmigration) occurs due to the psychic states (*bhāvas*) of coming into operation or rise of *karmas*, the subsidential, the subsidential-cum-destructive, etc. *bhāvas*. The hellish, human, subhuman and celestial beings undergo transmigration (*saṁsāra*) due to being imbued with the eight kinds of *karma*. The *saṁsāra* is in the dispositions (*bhavas*) of delusion, lack of self-restraint (*asaṁyama*), anger, etc. passions and vibratory activities of mind, speech and body. This *saṁsāra* is beginningless and endless for the liberable soul (*bhavya*) and beginningless and with end for the soul is not likely to be liberated (*abhavya*). This transmigration is of one kind in respect of transmigration in general; it is also of two kinds, three kinds, four kinds, five kinds, six kinds, etc. (*Mūlācāra* 707).

During transmigration, there is fear of old age and death, separation (*viyoga*) of desirable and cherished ones, joining of (*saṁyoga*) undesirable ones, and great pain, anguish and suffering (*vedanā*) arising from diseases — these are all terrible miseries (ibid. 708).

The soul experiences thousands of sufferings by being born and dead in hell, human, subhuman and celestial existences (ibid. 709). In fact, experiences of enjoyments during the celestial or human existences result in giving suffering innumerable times in hellish and subhuman existences (ibid. 710). I have experienced *saṁyoga–viyoga*, gain or loss, happiness and misery, honour and dishonour — all these (ibid. 711). In this manner, by knowing the constancy (*sthiratā*) various kinds of miseries in *saṁsāra*, one should contemplate that it (*saṁsāra*) is without essential content, insubstantial and worthless (*nissāra*) (ibid. 712).

Jñānārṇava describes *saṁsāra bhāvanā* as follows:

> In the great cyclical movement (*āvartta*) of the four conditions of existence and the ocean of the nature of *saṁsāra* replete with sufferings, the wretched, meek, or friend, helpless living being wanders continuously uninterrupted. —*Jñā* 1

The living beings die and are born passing through the mobile and immobile bodies bound with their own fetters of *karmas*.

— *Jñā* 2

In this *saṁsāra*, the mother of a living being becomes daughter after dying and the daughter because mother after dying; and again the same woman becomes your daughter after dying. In this manner, the father becomes son after dying and again the same person becomes son of son. Thus, change continues to take place. — *Jñā* 16

In all the four conditions of existence (hellish, subhuman, human and celestial), individual beings experience many kinds of sufferings. In other words, they do not have happiness anywhere. — *Jñā* 17

Describing *saṁsāra anuprekṣā*, *Bhagavatī Ārādhanā* states:

One enters the great forest of *saṁsāra* due to the mind being infatuated by deluded views. The soul is afflicted by numerous miseries or sufferings in *saṁsāra* due to not having faith and not knowing the meanings of the words or utterings of the Omniscient Lord (Jina). — *Bha* 1763

In this ocean of *saṁsāra*, there are crocodiles, etc. cruel, fierce and terrible creatures in the form of the faults of violence, etc. and there are many fish of the character of two kinds of living beings, immobile and mobile. The acquisition of a new body, old age, death are the states of living beings, which are of five kinds (viz. one-sensed, two-sensed, three-sensed, four-sensed and five-sensed beings having many intermediate kinds. — *Bha* 1765

There is no place or region where the living being has not been born and died infinite times in the past. — *Bha* 1770

Then *Bhagavatī Ārādhanā* describes that the mundane souls wander in five kinds of *parivartana* (cycle of wanderings):

(1) *bhava-saṁsāra* or *bhāva parivartana* (incarnation or the modes of living beings cycle) in four conditions of worldly existence (*gati*); (2) *dravya-saṁsāra* or *dravya parivartana* (*dravya*, substance) or matter (*pudgal*) cycle); (3) *kṣetra-saṁsāra* (space cycle); (4) *kāla*

saṁsāra (time cycle); and (5) *bhāva-saṁsāra* (thought cycle).[1]

The ignorant soul, affected by hunger, thirst and other sufferings, enters in the mouth of the snake of the nature of *saṁsāra*, which is the supportive factor (*nimitta*) of great sufferings (*Bha* 1778).

Describing the *bhāvanā* of *saṁsāra*, Acharya Mahaprajna (2010: 36-37) states:

> In the *bhāvanā* of transmigration . . . [one] perceives and feels thus: How long have I been roaming about in this world? There is no form of existence in which I have not taken birth. . . . He perceives various kinds of suffering in all forms of existence. He wants to break away from this bondage of endless transmigration. Attachment and aversion are the principal causes of transmigration. . . . Attachment and aversion create delusion. Delusion obstructs knowledge and intuition.

A soul endowed with the three jewels (*ratnatraya*) (of enlightened worldview, knowledge and conduct) constitutes an excellent causeway? One can cross the transmigratory cycle of births and deaths with the help of the divine boat of the three jewels (*ratnatraya*) (*Samanasutta* 514).

Birth is misery, old age is misery, disease is misery and death is misery. This transmigratory world (*saṁsāra*) is of the nature of completely or entirely full of misery, in which the living beings of *saṁsāra* are undergoing trouble, suffering anguish, pain or affliction (*kleśa*) (*Uttarādhyayanasūtra* 19.16).

What is that activity (*karma*) to which I do not go to the condition of existence in *saṁsāra*, which is predominantly replete with misfortune and misery (*Uttarādhyayanasūtra* 8.1)?

---

[1] For details, see *TS* II.10. Also see *Sarvārthasiddhi* commentary on *Tattvārthasūtra* of Pūjyapāda and *Tattvārtha-Rāja-Vārttika* commentary on *Tattvarthasūtra* of Akalaṅka on that aphorism.

6

Loka (The Nature of the Universe)

THE universe is a compendium of souls and other substances (*BA* 39). All the substances existing in the universe are uncreated, eternal and indestructible. But they do undergo changes and assume different shapes, forms or modes. Belief in divine intervention in this process as in individual emancipation is, therefore, a myth. The thought-activities of worldly souls can be broadly classified as evil or inauspicious (*aśubha*), auspicious (*śubha*) and pure (*śuddha*) (*BA* 42). Contemplation of these aspects of the universe leads to clarity of vision. It fosters distaste for worldly life or sorrow and anxiety and strengthens the resolve to realize the true nature of the pure Self.

Loka is that in which six substances are found.

Reflection upon the nature of the universe, which is subject to multiple states of origination, decay, continuity, evolution and dissolution, leads to enlightened vision (*samyak darśana*).

The universe is very extensive; our value in that is a like an atom. Of what we can be proud of? We should make use of this *bhāvanā* to manifest the qualities of humility, etc. (Nyayavijaya 1935: 108-109).

To contemplate upon the nature of the universe is *loka anuprekṣā* (Pūjyapāda 1992: 328, para 808).

In his commentary *Tattvārtha-Rājavārttika* on *Tattvārthasūtra* X.7 with respect to *loka anuprekṣā*, Akalaṅka (1993: 773) observes:

> In the infinite space without living beings and material objects (*alokākāśa*), the universe (*loka*) is of the shape or form of a person (*puruṣakāra*). To contemplate about the nature of universe is *loka anuprekṣā*. By contemplation of this *anuprekṣā*, the purification of the knowledge of the principles of life (*tattva-jñāna*) takes place, and attachment and aversion from the mind are removed.

In his commentary *Tattvārtha-Śloka-Vārttika* on *Tattvārthasūtra* IX.7 pertaining to *loka anuprekṣā*, Vidyanandi (1969, vol. 7: 157, commentator Manikchand) states that to think about or ponder over in regard to what the universe (*loka*) is made or formed of is *loka anuprekṣā*.

The nature of the universe and its constituent elements and the fact of life regarding the continuous transmigration of the soul for want of enlightened worldview, knowledge and conduct (Sangave 1990: iv).

The cardinal fact about the universe is that it has existed all the time. And it is un-created and eternal. The universe operates on its own law. Belief in divine intervention in this process as an individual emancipation is, therefore, a myth (Sangave 1990: iv).

There is no happiness in this world, in the various grades of existence. Birth, death, disease, impure body, separation and mental disturbances: all these leave no room for happiness (*Mar* 605-610).

In this context, A.N. Upadhye observes:

> A gradation list of the rarities is often met within the canon (*Uttarādhyayana* X). Starting from *nigoda*, the soul is on a march of spiritual progress through various grades of living beings. Then to be born as a human being at a suitable place, in a good family, with perfect and healthy body and the requisite opportunities for religious enlightenment is something that is rare. If the *loka anuprekṣā* inculcated the feeling of immense space, this *anuprekṣā*

of *bodhi durlabha* makes one realize the feeling of endless time which in course of series of births produces the impression of the rarity of human birth and of religious enlightenment.

In reality, *loka* is of one kind, two kinds, three kinds and many kinds. In this way, one should contemplate about the good disposition or feeling of the *loka* through substance and modes (*Mūlācāra* 713). The universe is of one kind in general. It is of two kinds: upper *loka* and lower *loka*. It is of three kinds due to the character of origination, destruction and stability/continuity. It is of four kinds considering the forms of existence (four *gatis*). It is of five kinds in respect of five *astikāyas*. It is of six kinds due to the nature of the six substances. It is of seven kinds with respect to seven principles (*tattvas*). It is of eight kinds in respect of thought-constructions (*vikalpas*) of eight kinds of *karmas*, etc. It is thus of many kinds. In this way, one should contemplate about the existence of *loka* with respect to the difference of substances and the difference of various modes.

Certainly/definitely, this is genuine, natural and not artificial, without beginning and end, by its nature permanent and also filled with living beings and inanimate objects (*Mūlācāra* 714). Contemplation on *aśuci* has two benefits: (1) it removes the fraud of casteism and untouchability; and (2) the attachment to pleasures is reduced. Though the body is impure, one should not be careless about it for it is the means of practising *dharma* (Nyayavijaya 1935: 107).

Instead of having disgust towards the impure body, one should have affection for the *samyak darśana*, etc. qualities hidden in the body.

Where there are principles of motion, principles of rest and space, in the same way, the going and coming of a living being or soul (*jīva*) and inanimate matter (*pudgala*), there is *loka*, beyond that there is infinite space (*Mūlācāra* 715). In this *loka*, the soul experiences pleasure and pain made/formed through one's own *karmas*, and again and again, one is born and dead in the terrible/fearful infinite existence or world (*Mūlācāra* 717).

The description of *loka bhāvanā* in *Jñānārṇava* is as follows:

> *Loka* is that space, in which there are conscious living beings and inanimate material objects; outside of that space, there is only (infinite) space alone, which is called *aloka* or *alokākāśa*, without living beings and material objects. — *Jñā* 1
>
> This *loka* is not created by anybody and is not held, maintained and preserved by anyone. It is held or established in space even without any support. — *Jñā* 3
>
> Though this *loka* is beginningless and endless (*anādi nidhana*), self-proved (*svayaṁsiddha*) and indestructible and there is no God, ruler or master and no destroyer; still it is filled or replete with living beings, etc. things. — *Jñā* 4

Bhagavatī Ārādhanā describes *loka anuprekṣā* in these words:

> One who is mother in this birth, (she) is wife in the incarnation or birth; and by becoming wife again becomes mother. In this way, all relations in this world (*saṁsāra*) are changeable. — *Bha* 1793
>
> In this universe (*loka*) and other universe (*para-loka*), even relatives, a brother or friend (*bandhu*) becomes an enemy of persons. In this *loka* and *para-loka* even mother eats the meat of her own son, what is that wretchedness, hardship, suffering or affliction (*kaṣṭa*) more than this? — *Bha* 1798
>
> Even the enemy, who is the cause of numerous sufferings, becomes again a favourite *bandhu*, i.e. relative, brother or friend. In this way, close relationship of friendship and enmity are changeable. — *Bha* 1799
>
> By contemplation of the condition of the universe, arises detachment from worldly concerns and desires (*vairāgya*). Blessed, luckily or virtuous are the persons who have liberated themselves from the conditions of the universe. — *Bha* 1805
>
> Unsteady or inconstant (*cañcala*) like electricity in the sky, weak, frail or impotent (*durbala*) like frost, foam or lather (*phena*), seized, devoured or affected (*grasta*) by diseases and affected by death – seeing this kind of universe (*loka*), how can the intelligent or wise person have affection (*anurāga*) with that. — *Bha* 1806

7

Aśuci (Impurity of the Physical Body)

THE physical body is consisted of blood, flesh, urine, excreta, etc.; it is foul smelling, impure, skin coated, impermanent, inert, inanimate matter and subject to disintegration (*BA* 45). The soul is distinct from the body. It is devoid of *karmas*, is the abode of infinite bliss and is pure. This ought to be contemplated all the while (*BA* 46). Constant contemplation along these lines weans the mind away from all afflictions of attachment to the allurements of the physical body and is an effective aid to the realization of the pure nature of the Self. Therefore, "I am not the body" is a positive and useful reflection. I am not the body, not the mind; nor voice, nor cause of these: neither the doer of action, nor getting it done by others, nor consenting/approving the same (*Pravacanasāra* 160).

Reflection on this *bhāvanā* leads to renunciation of attachment to the body and concentration on the intrinsic purity of the Self. By giving up false pride of the body, which is a house of filth and urine, disease and old age, we should make use of it for the attainment of liberation (Rajchandra 1988: 111). Contemplation on *aśuci* has two benefits: (1) it removes the fraud of casteism and untouchability; and (2) the attachment to pleasures is reduced. Though the body is impure, we should not be careless about it for it is the means of practising *dharma* (Nyayavijaya 1935: 107).

Contemplation on *aśuci bhāvanā* should lead to the termination of sense attachments to the body.

The body is impure and dirty. Purity is of two kinds: of the soul itself, and of the body and other things (Jaini 1956: 149). The body is the womb or source of extremely impure objects. By disregarding the body and thereby becoming unobstructed or untroubled, one should contemplate for the crossing over of the ocean of births (Pūjyapāda 1992: 326, para 804).

In his commentary *Tattvārtha-Rājavārttika* on *Tattvārthasūtra* IX.7 pertaining to *aśuci anuprekṣā*, Akalaṅka (1993: 772) states:

> Purity (*śucitva*) is of two kinds: worldly and other-worldly. Washing the blemish of the dirt of *karmas*, the situation of the dwelling of the Self in the Self alone is other-worldly purity. Its means are enlightened worldview or right belief (*samyak darśana*) and the saints endowed with the triple jewels and placed thereby in the region of liberation, etc. since it is the means of liberation.
>
> Time (*kāla*), fire, ashes, earth or clay, dung, water, knowledge and being without disgust, devoid of remorse and aversion — these are eight kinds of worldly purity famous in the world.
>
> None of the means can purify the body because it is extremely impure. The primary causes of the body are seminal fluid (*vīrya*) and menstrual discharge (*raja*), which are extremely impure. The secondary cause is the state-of-evolution or transformation of food, etc.
>
> The mouthful of food eaten becomes thin and impure as phlegm or mucus in reaching the digestive system; then arriving at the gallbladder is transformed into acidity; thereafter by arriving at the wind bile and divided by wind, it is divided in the form of residue and bodily secretion (*rasa*). The residue portion is transformed into the form of urine, excrement or mucus (*mala*), sweat, etc. in the altered form of *mala* and the bodily secretion is transformed into the form of blood, flesh, fat, bone, marrow and semen. All these conditions are extremely impure.

> The place of all these is the body, which is like a dirty home. There is no means of removing this impurity. Its impurity is not removed even by bathing, anointing or smearing, sunlight, rubbing, fragrance or scent, garland, etc. Like burning matter, it transforms the objects coming in its contact like itself. Due to its contact, water, etc. objects themselves become impure.
>
> Enlightened worldview, etc. contemplated again and again reveal extreme purity of the Self. Thinking in this manner is the impurity (*aśuci*) contemplation (*bhāvanā*). Memorizing and reflecting in this way leads to detachment from the body and by being unobstructed or untroubled, the mind becomes ready for crossing the ocean of births.

In his commentary on *Tattvārthasūtra* IX.7 regarding *śuci* contemplation, Vidyanandi (1969, vol. 7: 159, commentator Manikchand) states:

> The menstrual discharge (*raja*), seminal fluid (*vīrya*), etc. are inauspicious (*aśubha*); the activities of the body such as experimental mucus (*mala*), urine, are also impure; to think and ponder over these kinds of types of impurity is *aśucitva anuprekṣā*. — Commentary on *TS* V.16

The physical body is filthy and impure. The charm or attractiveness associated with it is superficial and illusionary. The soul is distinct from the physical body. The feeling of attachment to the unclean and impure body is a delusion and must be discarded.

In *Maraṇa-Samādhi*, there is inauspicious (*aśubha*) reflection (*bhāvanā*) in place of *aśuci*. In that regard, it is stated that *dharma* "alone is *śubha*, auspicious or beneficial, while wealth and pleasures lead one ultimately to misery" (*Mar* 601-604).

Commenting on *aśubha* in *Maraṇa-Samādhi*, A.N. Upadhye observes:

> The contents under *aśubha* deserve special thought, and the impurity of the body is not even referred to in *Maraṇa-Samādhi*. It

> is interesting that *uttame ya guṇe* is to be understood for *dharma*, possibly through the ten *dharmas*, which are, as a rule, qualified by the term *uttama* (excellent). Some handy similes are introduced here and there. An over-greedy person suffers like a fish which has swallowed the hook. — *Mar* 615
>
> Five *indriyas* prove dangerous like serpents handed unaided by charms, etc. (*Mar* 618). A soul subject of kārmic influx is like a leaky boat (*Mar* 618).
>
> Knowledge, meditation and penances bring under control sense-pleasures and passions like reins of the horses (*Mar* 621).
>
> The penances destroy the seed of *saṁsāra* just as fire burns a lump of grass (*Mar* 621).

Describing *aśuci*, A.N. Upadhye states:

> That the body is impure, pleasures thereof are futile and delusive, and the *ātman* alone is worth pursuing: this is a favourite theme of the canon.

Describing the nature of *aśubha anuprekṣā* (in place of *aśuci*), Vaṭṭakera in *Mūlācāra* states:

> There is exclusively *aśubha* alone in hells. In subhuman (animals and birds, etc. *triyañca*) states/conditions, there are fastening or use of fetters (*bandhana*) and obstructing, blockading or hindering (*rodhana*), etc. In the human condition, there are diseases and sorrow and mourning (*śoka*), etc. And in heaven there is *aśubha* relating to the mind. — *Mar* 600-604

Artha (gold, etc.) is the basis of all futile, senseless, injurious acts (*anartha*). There is an obvious connection thereof (i.e. wealth) with labour, suffering, enmity, fear, sorrow, quarrel/strife, attachment, aversion and infatuation — these are inauspicious things (*Mūlācāra* 723). All these are called *aśubha*.

Women, clothes, gold, etc. are considered only *artha*. Sexual pleasure, etc. of sensual pleasures (*kāmasukha*) are also *aśubha*. The pleasures of five sense objects are said to be *kāmasukha*. From these, there are always punishment/penalty, death, deception, fear; these are short-lived and worthless (*nissāra*). The body, being filthy, dirty and impure, is also *aśubha*. In other places (in treatises like *Tattvārthasūtra*) it is called *aśuci*. *Artha*, sense pleasures and the body, etc. are all *aśubha* (*Mūlācāra* 727).

Jñānārṇava describes *aśuci bhāvanā* in these words:

> The body of the living beings is by nature decaying, is reprehensible, blameworthy, contemptible or vile (*nindya*). Similarly, it is filled/replete with bodily humour (phlegm, bile, etc.) or secretions (*dhātu*) and near to or resembling *dhātu*, i.e. *upadhātu*. And it is born or originated from the semen, etc. seed. For this reason, it is a place of remorse, aversion or disgust (*glāni*). —*Jñā* 1

> This body, surrounded by blood, flesh and fat, is decaying; it is a skeḷeton of bones and bound with nerves, has bad smell. No place of the body can be praised. —*Jñā* 2

> The body itself is dirty and from the mixture or contact (*saṁsarga*) thereof, even the most excellent objects of things, such as camphor (*kapūra*), saffron (*kesara*) and sandalwood (*candana*) are made dirty. —*Jñā* 12

In *Bhagavatī Ārādhanā*, *aśuci bhāvanā* is replaced by *bhāvanā* (inauspicious thoughts). Its description of *aśubha anuprekṣā* is as follows:

> Wealth or the assets (*artha*), sexual desire of the object of desire (*kāma*) and the body of all the human beings is inauspicious (*aśubha*). *Dharma* (righteousness and piety), which alone is the only one source of all the happiness and well-being, is auspicious or virtuous (*śubha*). —*Bha* 1807

> Wealth is the foundation or root of all injuries, losses or misfortunes (*anarthas*) and of faults in this world and the other world (*para-loka*). It is a cause of great fears and is the bolt or impediment (*argala*) in the path of liberation. —*Bha* 1808

Speaking of inauspiciousness of *kāma* (sex), *Bhagavati-Ārādhanā* states:

> The sensual or sensuous desires and enjoyments (*kāma-bhogas*) are dirty and are produced by the joining of other's body; it is the cause of the fall of human beings; it makes one insignificant and unworthy in the eyes of people; it is for a short period; and it is the cause for sufferings in both worlds; also it is not easy.
> — *Bha* 1809

Describing the inauspiciousness or impurity of the body, it is stated in *Bhagavatī-Ārādhanā*:

> This body is produced or brought about by a skeleton of bones, it is bound with blood vessels, it is smeared, stained or sullied (*lipt*) by the earth of the flesh, and it is replete or full of many impure things. In this way, this impure body is disgusting. — *Bha* 1810
>
> Water does not make the body pure; it becomes dirty by the contact of the body. — *Bha* 1812

Replying to the question that if the body is impure, who or what is pure, *Bhagavatī Ārādhanā* states:

> Righteousness and piety (*dharma*) are pure; those who are endowed with *dharma*, even the celestial beings bow to them. By the practice of *dharma*, the bodies of the saints become pure.
> — *Bha* 1814

By contemplating on *aśuci*, if one is still attached to one's own or others' body, then that contemplation is a mockery.

Describing *aśuci bhāvanā*, Acharya Mahaprajna (2010: 56-57) states:

> It is necessary for a *sādhaka* [aspirant for moral and spiritual development] to have a right view of the body. The body is the root of attachment. All the people are tied up with the body. If the attachment to the body is not dissolved, there can be no progress in *sādhanā* [practice]. The *bhāvanā* of uncleanliness loses

> this bondage and ultimately dissolves it. . . . Although the body is impure, unclean, it is also the temple of God. After having viewed the uncleanliness, and after shedding off all attachment [to it], the *sādhaka* should also observe the holy pure . . . soul within.

This body is transient, full of impurity, is born from impure objects. It is the receptacle of bodily misery and afflictions, i.e. replete with sufferings, and anguish or discomfort (*Uttarādhyayanasūtra* 19.13). This human body is worthless and vain (*asāra*); it is the house of malady and disease; it is afflicted with life and death. I do not get happiness even for a moment in this *asāra* human body (*Uttrādhyayanasūtra* 19.15).

8

Āsrava (Inflow/Influx) of Karmas

DUE to the carelessness of the mind, words and deeds, there is an inflow of *karmas*, which keeps a person in bondage.

The four *pratyayas* of delusion, lack of moral discipline, passions (*kaṣāya*) like anger, pride, greed and deceit are the causes of the influx of *karmas* (*BA* 47). The influx of *karmas* and the consequent bondage of *karmas* are the causes of transmigratory existence of births and deaths (*BA* 58) and that of innumerable suffering (*BA* 56). One should always contemplate on the pure nature of the Self as it is devoid of both kinds of inflow of *karmas* (wholesome and unwholesome).

Reflection on this *bhāvanā* draws attention to harmful effects of passions and indulgence in sense-gratification for health, happiness and social well-being.

The twelve kinds of lack of moral self-restraints, sixteen passions (*kaṣāya*), nine quasi-passions, five kinds of delusion, fifteen kinds of activities of mind, speech and body (*yoga*) are the gates facilitating the influx of *karmas* (Rajchandra 1988: 118). Pondering over harmful effects of pleasures of senses arising from attachment thereto and the causes of suffering and the kārmic bondage is *āsrava bhāvanā* (Nyayavijaya 1935: 108).

In the context of *karmas*, the inflow (*āsrava*), stoppage (*saṁvara*) and shedding (*nirjarā*) of *karmas* are discussed with reference to their qualities of usefulness and faults (*guṇa-doṣa*) as Akalaṅka says. The inflow (*āsrava*) and the consequent bondage (*bandha*) of *karmas*, which takes place by the coming into operation, rise or fruition (*udaya*), the *audāyika* state (*bhava*) of the Self, is imbued with only faults. *Saṁvara* and *nirjarā* are however useful and beneficial since they are the cause of liberation.

The inflow and the bondage of good, auspicious (*śubha*) of meritorious (*puṇya*) *karmas* apart from representing bondage is nevertheless helpful in customarily attaining liberation.

The stoppage (*saṁvara*) and shedding (*nirjarā*) of *karmas*, which are primarily the result of subsidence (*upaśama*), subsidence-cum-destruction (*kṣayopaśama*) and destruction (*kṣāyika*) *bhāva* respectively, are the means of liberation.

The transcendental, pure nature of real "I" (the Self) is non-relational or independent of *karmas* (*karma-nirapekṣa*) consciousness-as-such (*pāriṇāmika bhāva*), which is of a *nirupādhi* character (unconnected to or free from kārmic adjuncts or encumbrances (*upādhi*) and is *niṣkriya* (inactive) of the five thought-characteristics (*bhāvas*) (*TS* II.1). *Miśra*, i.e. subsidence-cum-destruction (*kṣayopaśama*), subsidential (*aupaśamika*) and destructive (*kṣāyika*), are the causes of liberation. The fruition (*audāyika*) is the cause of bondage and *pāriṇāmika niṣkriya* is neither the cause of bondage nor the cause of liberation (*PKS* 56 JS).

The inflow of *karmas* is the cause of one's mundane existence and, among others, it is the product of passions (Jaini 1956: 149). *Āsrava* is the cause of sufferings in the world and the next world. The passions, etc. also give rise to killing/slaying, bondage, dishonour/disgrace and sufferings like affliction, anguish, strife (*kleśa*), and also make us wander in many forms of existences (Pūjyapāda 1944: 327, para 805).

In his commentary *Tattvārtha-Rāja-Vārttika* on *Tattvārthasūtra* IX.7 pertaining to *āsrava saṁvara* and *nirjarā anuprekṣā*, Akalaṅka points out that these are discussed in the contemplations with reference to thinking their qualities or usefulness in force (*guṇa-doṣa*).

As regards *āsrava*, Akalaṅka states:

> *Āsrava* is connected with harm or injury in this worldly existence and also in the other-world. The madness or frenzy of the senses, etc. is sharp like the flow of the great river.

Then Akalaṅka describes how an intoxicated and being frenzy-with-sex (*mast*) elephant, i.e. sense of touch falls in the pit and suffers intense sufferings at the hands of human beings; the birds fall prey to many misfortunes and adversities due to the sense of taste; the snake endures destruction due to the sense of smell; the flies fall prey to the ocean of adversities due to the sense of sight and deer fall prey to many misfortunes by being caught in the net due to their sense of sound.

The Self thus wanders in numerous births being inundated with or immersed in many kinds of sufferings in the other world. In this manner, by thinking of the faults of the inflow of *karmas* (*āsrava*), the intellect of auspiciousness in excellent forgiveness, etc. *dharma* continues to remain (Akalaṅka 1993: 772).

In his commentary *Tattvārtha-Śloka-Vārttika* on *āsrava karmas*, Vidyānandi (1969, vol. 7: 159, commentator Manikchand), states:

> To have concern, anxiety or apprehension (*cintā*) about the continuing inflow (*āsrava*) of *karmas* is *āsrava anuprekṣā*. One should think about or ponder over the faults of *āsrava*.

All mental activity leads to the influx of kārmic matter. Delusion, anger, pride, envy, deceit and greed generate *karmas*. Their inflow is responsible for the continued mundane existence (Dharma Raja 1990: 4).

Attachment, aversion, negligence, sensual temptation, greed, fivefold sin — all these lead to the inflow of *karmas* into the soul like water into a leaky boat (*Mar* 611-618).

The soul which is sinking in extremely terrible, frightful or awesome worldly existence as a result of being joined with abundant, plentiful or ample fish of the character of suffering and fear, which are the supportive factors (*nimitta*) in the influx of *karmas* (*Mūlācāra* 729). The Jaina texts speak of seven kinds of fear:

1. death;
2. ailment, pain and suffering;
3. loss of reputation, dishonour and shame;
4. injury to wife and children;
5. loss of wealth;
6. helplessness or accidents; and
7. anxiety about the other world.

Attachment, aversion, infatuation of the senses, the four instincts or animate feeling (*saṁjñā*) (these are four primary instincts), viz. fear, food, sex, copulation or mating (*maithuna*) and possessive or acquisitive instinct (*parigraha*), vulnerability or honour (*gaurava*) and passions and also the vibratory activities of mind, speech and body — there is an influx of *karmas* due to all these (*Mūlācāra* 730). Non-violence, etc. (i.e. non-violence, untruthfulness, stealing, unchastity and *parigraha*) are the doorways of entrance of five sinful *karmas* (*Mūlācāra* 738).

Delusion or deluded view (*mithyātva*), vowlessness, lack of moral self-restraints or non-abstinence (*avirati*), carelessness (*pramāda*), passions (*kaṣāya*) like anger and the activities of the mind, speech and body (*yoga*) are said to be the causal conditions (*hetu*) of the [influx (*āsrava*) and consequent] bondage of *karmas* by Umāswāmi in *Tattvārthasūtra* VIII.1 and *Dravya Saṁgraha* 30. Bondage is always preceded by the *āsrava* of the five causal conditions, excluding *yoga*.

All the others occur due to the coming into operation or rise (*udaya*) of deluded *karmas* (*mohanīya karmas*).

In reality, the activities of the body, speech and mind (*yoga*) (*TS* VI.1) alone are the supportive factors (*nimitta*) of the influx (*āsrava*) of *karmas*. Therefore, *yoga* alone is said to be *āsrava* (*TS* VI.2).

In *Bārasa Aṇuvekkhā* 47, the states-of-evolution (*pariṇāma*) of delusion (*mithyātva*), lack of moral conduct [violence, untruth, stealing, unchastity and possessiveness (*parigraha*)], passions (*kaṣāya*) like anger and the activities of the mind, speech and body (*yoga*) are said to be the gates of *āsrava*, i.e. the inflow of *karmas*. These are five, four and three kinds respectively (*BA* 47). In other words, the *pariṇāma* of the Self of *mithyātva*, etc. is *āsrava*. However, in verse II.33 of *Praśamarati Prakaraṇa*, the same Umāsvāmi has also stated that attachment (*rāga*) is the main cause of the influx (*āsrava*) and consequent bondage of *karmas*, delusion, etc. are said to be the multitude of attachment. In other words, *mithyātva*, etc. arise only due to attachment. Therefore, attachment (*rāga*) alone is the basic cause of the bondage of *karmas*.

In verse 150 of *Samayasāra*, specifically stated that attachment binds the *karmas* (*ratto bandadi kammaṇo*). In *Samayasāra* 177, attachment, aversion and infatuation (*moha*) are declared to be *āsrava bhāva*, i.e. the psychic states which cause influx of *karmas* and that without these, *āsrava bhāva*, *bhāva pratyaya*, *dravya pratyaya*, i.e. the influencing factors (*prayāya*) of delusion, etc. are the states-of-evolution (*pariṇāma*) of material *karma* and hence called *dravya* (physical) *pratyaya*. They do not become the causal condition (*hetu*) of the bondage of *karmas* (*SS* 177). Delusion, etc. are due to attachment, aversion, etc. (*SS* 164-165).

Jayasena categorically states that on the coming into operation or rise (*udaya*) of the *dravya pratyaya*, when the Self, leaving its [*nirupādhi*] pure nature evolves into attachment, etc. [impure] psychic states, then bondage takes place, not by the *udaya* of *karmas* (*SS* 164-165 JS). If the bondage of *karmas*, he adds, takes place by the coming into operation or rise (*udaya*) of *karmas* (*karma udaya*), then there will always be *saṁsāra*, i.e. transmigration of souls in the cycle of births and deaths because *karma* or *udaya* always exists in the case of mundane souls (*saṁsārī jīva*) (*SS* 164-165 JS).

Pravacanasāra 84 states:

> Various kinds of bondage take place, when the soul evolves into infatuation, attachment and aversion, therefore they are to be destroyed.

Pravacanasāra 83 observes:

> The deluded state of the soul with reference to substance, etc. is called infatuation (*moha*); covered with this, the soul is perplexed and develops attachment and aversion.

It further (180) states:

> Bondage takes place when the soul evolves into attachment, aversion, infatuation (*moha*). [Of these] *moha* and aversion are inauspicious and attachment is auspicious as also inauspicious.

In *Tattvārthasūtra* VI.1-2, *yoga* (the activities of body, speech and mind) is described as the channel of the influx or inflow (*āsrava*) of kārmic matter into the soul. The causal conditions (*hetu*) of the influx (*āsrava*) and consequent bondage of *karmas* are said to be the deluded view (*mithyā-darśana* or *mithyātva*) of five kinds, viz. one-sided view of things (*ekānta*); perverse belief (*viparīta*); doubt or scepticism (*saṁśaya*); veneration of all goods (*vinaya*) and wrong belief caused by ignorance (*ajñāna*); twelve kinds of vowlessness or non-abstinence (*avirati*), viz. lack of compassion for six classes of living beings (five immobile and mobile), lack of restraint of five senses and mind; gossip or talk (four kinds) concerning food, women, politics and scandal or theft, etc.; five senses; four passions (*kaṣāya*) of anger, pride, deceit and greed; affection (*sneha*) and sleep; twenty-five kinds of passions of anger, etc. of the most intense (*anantānubandhi*), intense (*apratyākhyāna*), moderate (*pratyākhyāna*) and mind (*sañjvalana*) (4 × 4 = 16) plus nine quasi-passions (*no-kaṣāya*) of scornful laughter (*hāsya*), liking or relish (*rati*), dislike or hatred (*arati*), grief or sorrow (*śoka*), fear (*bhaya*), disgust or abhorrence (*jugupsā*) and three kinds of sexual desire, fifty-seven kinds of influx (*āsrava*) and consequent bondage of *karmas*. And if the three activities of mind, speech and body (*yoga*) are included, the total becomes sixty.

The explanation or exposition of *āsrava bhāvanā* in *Jñānārṇava* is as follows:

> The vibratory activities of body, speech and mind (*yoga*) are the channels of the inflow of kārmic matter into the soul (*āsrava*).
>
> – *TS* VI.1-2; *Jñā* 1
>
> *Yama*, i.e. non-violence, etc. moral self-restraints or vows, *praśama* (calmness of mind due to the subsidence of anger, etc. passions), *nirveda* (detachment from the worldly desires of affection of *dharma*), the thinking or pondering over of the life principles (*tattva*), etc. — if one has dependence of support of these, and mounted on the four contemplations of amity or friendship (*maitrī*), appreciation of the good qualities of others (*pramoda*), compassion or pity (*karuṇā*) and indifference or equanimity towards the perverted beings (*madhyastha*), only that mind produces auspicious or virtuous *āsrava*. —*Jñā* 3
>
> Inflamed by the fire of anger, etc. passions and bewildered, confused or troubled (*vyākula*) by the sense objects — such a mind collects or accumulates the mundane, worldly existence of relating to births. —*Jñā* 4

There are seven causes of sinful *āsrava* (*Jñā* 9):

1. deluded view;
2. anger, etc.;
3. the companions of sexual desire, etc.;
4. the objects of five senses;
5. negligence or laxity, such as reprehensible gossip (*vikatha*);

6. the vibratory activities of mind, speech and body (*yoga*) (*TS* VII.1); and
7. the bad concentration or meditations of mourning or painful concentration (*raudra*) (*TS* IX.28).

Bhagavatī Ārādhanā describes *āsrava karmas* in these words:

In the ocean of births and deaths, which is united or combined with the wave of the nature of different kinds of faults and which is filled or replete with aquatic creatures of the nature of sufferings. *Āsrava* is the cause of the wandering in the ocean (*Bha* 1815). The cause of wandering in this *saṁsāra* ocean is no doubt *karma*, but *āsrava* is otherwise the cause of *karmas*.

Just as the body smeared with oil invites dust, so also the Self is smeared or sullied with the oil of deluded views (*mithyātva*), etc. (i.e. lack of moral self-restraints (*asaṁyama*) and passions (*kaṣāya*) like anger, the space-points of the soul are attached with the kārmic material particles. *Āsrava*, i.e. the states-of-evolution of the Self, is the cause in the evolution of the Self as of the character of *karmas*. — *Bha* 1817

Mithyātva, *asaṁyama*, *kaṣāya* and *yoga* (the vibratory activities of the mind, speech and body) are *āsravas*. Of these, *mithyātva* is the absence of faith or conviction of bewilderment and confusion (*vimoha*) in the life principles of categories (*padārthas*) as uttered by the Omniscient Lord (Arihanta). — *Bha* 1819

The five faults of violence, truthfulness, theft, unchastity and possessiveness are called *asaṁyama*. The four passions of anger, pride, greed and deceit are having the sense of attachment and aversion. — *Bha* 1820

The sensuous desires, pride in being endowed with a mind (*saṁjñī*) and attachment, aversion are to be reproached because due to these faults even the person endowed with enlightened worldview (*samyak-dr̥ṣṭi*) engages himself in sinful activities.
— *Bha* 1822

Compassion (*anukampā*) and pure conscious attentiveness (*śuddha upayoga*) on the doors of the inflow (*āsrava*) of auspicious or virtuous (*śubha* or *puṇya*) *karmas*. And the states-of-evolution (*pariṇāma*) contrary or opposite of these (i.e. compassion in pure conscious attentiveness) are the doors of the inflow (*āsrava*) of sinful (*pāpa*) *karmas*. — *Bha* 1828

Describing the *āsrava bhāvanā*, Acharya Mahaprajna (2010: 65, 70) observes:

> Every moment of attachment and aversion is the movement of attraction [influx] of *karma* or the bondage of *karman*. . . . Attachment and aversion are the two principal flaws. Attachment breeds deceit, and greed and aversion give birth to anger and pride. . . . In a time of intensest [most intense] passion [of anger, etc.], a man cannot practise even partial abstinence. In a time of intense passion, complete abstinence is not possible.

Delusion (*mithyātva*), the lack of moral restraints or vowlessness (*avirati*), passions like anger, and the activities of the mind, speech and body (*yoga*) — these are *āsravas* (*Jai Dhavalā* 1.9.54). When a person's attachment is excellent, there is an inclination of compassion (*anukampā*) inside, and there is no sinful, wicked or impure psychic dispositions, these there is influx (*āsrava*) of meritorious or virtuous traits in that person (*Pañcāstikāyasāra* 135).

9

Saṁvara
(Stoppage of the Influx of Karmas)

One should control one's mind, speech and deeds to stop the inflow of *karmas*.

One should always contemplate on the pure nature of the Self as it is devoid of both kinds of the inflow of *karmas* (wholesome and unwholesome). *Saṁvara* is the inhibition of the influx of *karmas*. One should inhibit the inflow of *karmas* by moral and spiritual discipline of the five self-restraints of non-violence, etc. *Saṁvara* helps to contemplate on the beneficial effect of moral and spiritual discipline in the restraint of the senses and the mind.

Saṁvara (stoppage) of the inflow of *karmas* is practised through the observance of moral and spiritual discipline consisting of five abstentions or vows, fivefold carefulness (*samiti*), threefold self-control (*guptī*), ten moral values (*dharma*), etc. (*TS* IX.1 and IX.2). Austerities or penances (*tapa*) are the causes of both shedding of (*nirjarā*) as well as the stoppage (*saṁvara*) of *karmas* (*TS* IX.3).

For the liberation of the Self, shedding and eradication or destruction of the already accumulated *karmas* are not enough, because if the coming in or inflow (*āsrava*) of *karmas* is not stopped, new *karmas* will get accumulated. Therefore, along with *nirjarā*, *saṁvara* is also essential.

The stoppage of the sources or gates of sin is *saṁvara bhāvanā* (Rajchandra 1988: 118). Contemplation of the stoppage of the causes of suffering and kārmic bondage is *saṁvara bhāvanā*. Also pondering over the good qualities and virtues in order to stop at the door of wicked or immoral is *saṁvara bhāvanā* (Nyayavijaya 1935: 108).

The inhibition of the inflow of *karmas* does not restrict or obstruct the well-being of the Self. In this manner, the thinking of the qualities and benefits of *saṁvara* is *saṁvara anuprekṣā*. By pondering over in this manner, the soul is continuously ready for *saṁvara* and by this one obtains liberation (*mokṣa*) (*SAS*, para 806).

In his commentary *Tattvārtha-Rāja-Vārttika* on *Tattvārthasūtra* (*TS* IX.7) regarding *saṁvara anuprekṣā*, Akalaṅka (1993: 772-773) states:

> The Self, that is united with *saṁvara* like the tortoise contracting its limbs, does not have the force of the inflow of *karmas* (*āsrava*). As in the large boat in the great or mighty ocean if there is any hole or opening and it is not closed, then the destruction of those dependent on the boat is inevitable or bound to occur due to the gradually incoming of water, and by closing the hole, one reaches one's desired destination peacefully. In the same way, due to the closing of the door of the coming of the *karmas*, there can be no obstacle, limitation or restriction in the auspicious, virtuous or meritorious outcome. Contemplation of the qualities or usefulness of *saṁvara* is *saṁvara anuprekṣā*. As a result of such thinking, the human being remains energetic in regard to *saṁvara*.

In his commentary *Tattvārtha-Śloka-Vārttika* regarding *saṁvara anuprekṣā*, Vidyanandi (commentator Manikchand) points out (1969, vol. 7: 159):

> To think about and ponder over the good thought of the stoppage of the inflow of *karmas* is *saṁvara anuprekṣā*. One should do a good recollection or meditation of the qualities or virtues of *saṁvara*.

The inflow of *karmas* must be stopped by cultivating this very virtue

(Sangave 1990: iv). Non-attachment helps in stopping the inflow of *karmas*. Abstinence from undesirable activities in adherence to moral and spiritual pursuits ensures the arrest of the influx of kārmic material (Sangave 1990: iv).

The eradication of passions, subjugation of the senses, restraints over the mind, speech and body through knowledge, meditation and penances rescue the soul from kārmic influx (*Mar* 619-624).

One should inhibit senses, passions, the four primary instincts, vulnerability (*gaurava*), attachment, etc. as they are the cause of influx of *karmas* (*Mūlācāra* 740). The senses, passions and faults are restrained by austerities, knowledge and modesty or humility (*Mūlācāra* 742).

The inflow or coming in of *karmas* due to delusion, lack of self-restraint, passions and the activities of mind, speech and body (*yoga*) are restrained (*nigraha*) and prevented or prohibited (*nirodha*) (*Mūlācāra* 744).

The fruit of *saṁvara* is liberation. Therefore, one should contemplate on *saṁvara anuprekṣā* (*Mūlācāra* 745).

Saṁvara bhāvanā is described in *Jñānārṇava* as follows:

> The stopping of all inflows (*āsrava*) of *karmas* is proclaimed or declared as *saṁvara*. It is of two kinds: *dravya-saṁvara* and *bhāva-saṁvara*. —*Jñā* 1
>
> Those engaged in austerities (including meditation, *dhyāna*), which wash away sins, the severing or breaking the taking or acceptance of kārmic matter (*karma pudgala*) is declared or uttered as physical (*dravya*) *saṁvara*. —*Jñā* 2
>
> That which acts as the supportive factor (*nimitta*) for wandering in the cycle of births (*saṁsāra*), the cessation or stopping of the activities of acceptance of *karma* is to be known from the scriptures as psychic (*bhāva*) *saṁvara*. —*Jñā* 3
>
> By forgiveness, humility, straightforwardness and renunciation, the passions of anger, pride, deceit and greed are in sequence overcome as they are contrary to or opposite of them. —*Jñā* 6

The self-restrained persons (*yogī*) remove or refute attachment and aversion by equanimity and they remove or refute deluded view, etc. psychic states by being disinterested or indifferent (*nirmama*) to sense objects and other things and enlightened worldview or right belief. —*Jñā* 7

Those self-restrained (*saṁyamī*) persons, devoid of doubts, who are prepared or ready for *saṁvara*, remove or refute the poison of absence or lack of moral self-restraints by the nectar of ambrosia (*sudhā*) of self-restraints (*saṁyama*). —*Jñā* 9

The mighty tree of *saṁvara* of which all the five self-regulations or carefulness (*samiti*) in walking, speaking, eating, handling things and cleanliness are its root, *saṁyama* of the equanimous state of mind (*sāmayika*) is its trunk, calmness of mind due to substance of passions (*praśama bhāva*) are its big branches, excellent forgiveness, etc. ten *dharma* are its flowers and contemplation of twelve reflections are its fruits. —*Jñā* 12

Bhagavatī Ārādhanā discusses *saṁvara anuprekṣā* with respect to *saṁvara* of deluded view, passions, and *pramāda* consisting of *vikatha* (reprehensible gossip), passions and sense objects and thereafter describes *guptī* (self-restraints of the mind, speech and body), *samiti* (carefulness in walking, etc.) and conquest of hardships or sufferings (*pariṣaha-jaya*).

Deluded, the door (*dvāra*) of inflow (*āsrava*) (of *karmas*) is stopped or blocked by enlightened worldview (*saṁyaktva*) or right faith or belief. And the door of *āsrava* of violence, etc. is blocked by a bolt for fastening the door of moral self-restraints or vows of non-violence, etc. —*Bha* 1829

The passions of anger, pride, deceit and greed are to be conquered by forgiveness, humility, straightforwardness and contentment respectively. —*Bha* 1830

The wicked forces of senses, which are engaged or occupied in sense objects, are controlled by the knowledge of self-control or restraints (*dama*). —*Bha* 1831

The negligence or laxity (*pramāda*) of reprehensible gossip (*vikatha*) is prevented or stopped by truthful speech. Study (*svādhyāya*), meditation (*dhyāna*) and single-minded or one-pointed concentration (*ekāgratā*) are the opposite of *vikatha.*

Forgiveness, humility, straightforwardness and contentment are opposite of passions of anger, pride, deceit and greed respectively.

The contemplation of knowledge, due to which one remains in the place or region and devoid of objects of sense pleasures (*indriya viṣaya*), pleasantness and unpleasantness in sense objects, leads to attachment and aversion, one-point concentration of mind, not remembering the faults of attachment and aversion caused by sense objects, and not having respect in obtaining of sense objects, are opposite of *pramāda* of sense objects. — *Bha* 1833

The army of enemies of *karma* cannot destroy the city of moral self-control (*saṁyama*) due to *guptī* (self-restraints of mind, speech and body (*Bha* 1834). For that reason, *guptī* is said to be the cause of *saṁvara.*

Mounted on the firm boat of self-regulations or carefulness (*samiti*) one crosses the ocean of *saṁsāra* untouched by crocodiles and fishes of sin, destroying the six kinds of living beings (these are five kinds of immobile beings (viz. earth-bodied, water-bodied, fire-bodied, wind-bodied and plant-bodied) and mobile beings. — *Bha* 1835

Even though afflicted of the collection or aggregate of hardships and sufferings (*pariṣaha*), a person not leaving or giving up the enlightened worldview, one should continue to remember the life principles (*tattva*). — *Bha* 1838

The stoppage of the inflow of kārmic matter into the soul is called *saṁvara* (*TS* IX.1). The means or causal conditions of *saṁvara* (*TS* IX.2) are:

1. three kinds of restraints (*guptī*) of mind, speech and body (*TS* IX.4);
2. five kinds of carefulness (*samiti*) (*TS* IX.5) in walking, speaking

(*bhāṣa*), eating, receiving, lifting, putting in handling things and cleanliness;

3. ten kinds of righteousness and piety (*dharma*), viz. forgiveness, humility, straightforwardness, contentment, truth, moral self-restraint, renunciation, non-inquisitiveness (*akiñcana*), chastity and austerities (*TS* IX.6);
4. twelve kinds of contemplations to be meditated upon again and again (*anuprekṣā*) (*TS* IX.7) of transitoriness, unprotectiveness, transmigration in the cycle of births and deaths (*saṁsāra*), being alone, otherness, impurity of the body, influx of *karmas*, stoppage of *karmas*, shedding of *karmas*, the nature of the universe, rarity of enlightenment, and *dharma* of triple jewels of enlightened worldview, knowledge and conduct, which together are the path of liberation;
5. twenty-two kinds of tolerance and endurance of sufferings so as to remain steadfast on the righteous path of liberation (*pariṣaha-jaya*) (*TS* IX.9), viz. hunger, thirst, cold, heat, insect bites, nakedness, disinterest in likes and dislikes, women, walking too much, not to disturb the posture of meditation in face of danger, resting on hard earth, abuse, beating or murder, begging, failure to get alms, disease, contact with thorny shrubs, discomfort from dirt or dust, indifferent to respect and disrespect, conceit of knowledge, ignorance or lack of knowledge, and slack belief or lack of attaining enlightened worldview; and
6. five kinds of right or enlightened conduct (*TS* IX.18), including pure and absolute non-injury, all but entire freedom from passions, and ideal and passionless conduct – a total of fifty-seven kinds of *saṁvara*.

Of these, *guptī* is the right or proper restraint, or subjugation or stoppage of the perverse activities of mind, speech and body (*yoga*) (*TS* IX.4). *Samiti* (carefulness) is the stoppage of carelessness (*pramāda*), of the ten kinds of *dharma*, the first four are the means of conquering and restraining of the four passions (*kaṣāyas*), controlling of conquering anger by forgiveness, pride by humility, deceit by straightforwardness and greed by *śauca*; and quasi-passions. The next five vows (*vrata*) are the means of stopping of or desisting from five sins of violence (*saṁyama*), untruth (*asatya*), stealing (*asteya*), chastity (*brahmacarya*) and possessiveness or acquisitiveness (*akiñcana*), i.e. non-abstinence (*avirati*), of *karmas* as also of *saṁvara*. *Anuprekṣās* are the means of resisting or stopping of five kinds of delusion (*mithyātva*) and other negative thoughts and calming of passions.

The twenty-two *pariṣaha-jayas* are meant to remain steady in the path of *dharma* of liberation and to tolerate with equanimity the adverse situations faced in the path of *dharma* and are helpful in *saṁvara*.

The five kinds of conduct are useful in attaining one's well-being (*hita*) and for preventing of that which is not right, useful or for the well-being of a person.

Thus, the six means of *saṁvara* are used in the stoppage of *mithyātva*, etc. five causal conditions of the influx of *karmas*.

10

Nirjarā (Dissociation or Shedding of Karmas)

THE *karmas* should be dissociated from the Self through austerities (*tapa*) before they come to fruition.

In order to attain liberation, *saṁvara* alone is not enough. One has also to eradicate the already accumulated kārmic matter through the process of *nirjarā*. The word *nirjarā* is derived from the Sanskrit verbal root *jṛ* which means to wear down, to rub to pieces, to crush, etc. Thus, falling away of all *karmas* attached to the Self is called *nirjarā*, which is of two types: the first is due to ripening (*vipākaja*) and the second is due to process other than ripening (*avipākaja*) (Akalaṅka 1993: 488 cited in Shiv Kumar 2000: 100). If the *karma* ripens by itself, i.e. wears down on its own in due course of time, it is called *vipāka nirjarā*; but if it is plucked unripe and then ripened by an artificial device it is known as *avipāka nirjarā* (ibid.). The process and activities of the Self whereby the effect of kārmic coating on the texture of the Self is neutralized resulting in their falling away from the Self are called *nirjarā* (ibid.).

Nirjarā consists of the observance of austerities (*tapas*), both external and internal which are an effective means of inhibiting (*saṁvara*) as well as wearing off (*nirjarā*) of *karma* (*TS* IX.3). When austerities are part of an enlightened conduct, they not only wear off *karmas* already bound to the soul but also prevent the further accumulation of *karmas*. The term *tapas* includes any form of self-discipline which purifies the Self and thereby leads to liberation.

According to Pūjyapāda, the causes of inhibition have been specified in order to exclude practices and rituals such as religious pilgrimage to holy places, sacred ablution (bathing in holy waters), deluded ordination, offering one's head to the deity as a gift, worship of gods and demi-gods in order to win their favour and so on. Such practices and rituals are inspired by attachment, hatred and delusion, which attract rather than inhibit *karma* (*TS* IX.3).

Destruction of the *karmas* through twelve kinds of austerities (six external and six internal) (see *supra*) is *nirjarā bhāvanā* (Rajchandra 1988: 118). Contemplating on the destruction of source of suffering in misfortune and the longing or desire of causing suffering is *nirjarā bhāvanā* (Nyayavijaya 2000: 108).

Reflection on *nirjarā bhāvanā* enables us to make conscious efforts to remove impurities and negativities by the various kinds of austerities (for these, see *supra*).

Kārmic matter must be shed, from or shaken out of the soul (Jaini 1956: 149). *Nirjarā* is of two kinds: that which is devoid of the use of intellect (*abuddhipūrva*) and that which is skilful based (*kuśalamūla*). That *nirjarā* which is brought into birth due to the maturity of the fourth edition of *karma* in hellish, etc. form of existence is *abuddhipūrva*. And *nirjarā* which takes place by conquering of hardships and sufferings (*pariṣaha*, see *supra*) is *kuśalamūla nirjarā*. Pondering over the benefits and faults of *nirjarā* is *nirjarā anuprekṣā* (*SAS*, para 807).

In his commentary *Tattvārtha-Rāja-Vārttika* on *Tattvārthasūtra* pertaining to *nirjarā anuprekṣā*, Akalaṅka (1993: 773) observes:

> *Nirjarā* is considered or described as ripening or maturing of pain and anguish. *Nirjarā* is of two kinds: inauspicious or unskilful devoid of intellect (*abuddhipūrva*) and that having its basis in skilful, deft

> feeling (*kuśalamūla*). In hellish, etc. conditions of existence there is *abuddhipūrva nirjarā* due to the maturity of the fruition of *karma*, which binds inauspicious (*karmas*). There is *kuśalamūla nirjarā* by conquering or overcoming the hardships or sufferings (*pariṣaha-jaya*) and austerities of penance, etc. which binds auspicious (*karmas*) or does not bind at all. In this way, contemplation of the qualities of usefulness in force is *nirjarā anuprekṣā*. To do that, one's mind becomes ready for the shedding of *karmas* (*nirjarā*).

In his commentary *Tattvārtha-Śloka-Vārttika* on *Tattvārthasūtra* IX.7 regarding *nirjarā anuprekṣā*, Vidyanandi (1969, vol. 7: 159, commentator Manikchand) states:

> To think or ponder over the nature, character or kind/type of the shedding of *karmas* is *nirjarā anuprekṣā*. One should investigate or deliberate in regard to the qualities of virtues and faults of *nirjarā*.

Kārmic matter should be destroyed from the soul by practising penance (*tapa*) (Sangave 1990: iv). Right perception, right knowledge and right conduct enable the aspirant to make spiritual progress and disentangle the Self from the attachment of *karmas*. The layer of *karmas* is dissolved and eliminated from the Self through progressive renunciation and reflection on the intrinsic virtues of the soul. *Karmas* can thus be eliminated from the Self even before they come to fruition (Dharma Raja 1990: 4-5).

Fortunate are those who have served worldly attachment, follow the path of religious life and thus destroy *karmas* (*Mar* 625-628).

Speaking of *āsrava*, *saṁvara* and *nirjarā*, A.N. Upadhye observes:

> *Āsrava*, *saṁvara* and *nirjarā* are three of the seven principles of nine categories (*padārtha*) of Jainism; they are closely linked with the *karma* doctrine; they explain *saṁsāra* on the one hand and lead the soul on to liberation on the other; and further, they form, to a very great extent, the basis of gender ethics and morality. At all suitable contexts they are discussed in the canon. Practically the whole of *Panhavagaranaim* is devoted to explain *āsrava* and *saṁvāra*.
>
> — Schubring 1935: 186

Persons who stop the influx of *karmas* are imbued with austerities of penance (see *supra*), and *nirjarā* takes place in their case. That *nirjarā* is said to be of two kinds: part or whole (*Mūlācāra* 746).

The fire of austerities, blazing or burning with virtuous or moral conduct (*śīla*), most excellent profound meditation (*samādhi*) and self-restraint (*saṁyama*) joined with the wind of most excellent knowledge, burns the seed of existence of births (*Mūlācāra* 749).

The Self obtains immeasurable, unequalled or incomparable happiness by being free from the bondage of birth, old age and death after *nirjarā* of all *karmas* takes place. Therefore, one should contemplate on *nirjarā bhāvanā* in the mind (*Mūlācāra* 751).

Jñānārṇava describes *nirjarā bhāvanā* as follows:

> Those in whom the bondage of *karmas* are worn out by the shedding (*nirjarā*) (of *karmas*), from which the decaying of the seed of the wandering in births takes place, that is called *nirjarā*.
>
> —*Jñā* 1

> *Nirjarā* is of two kinds: *sakāma nirjarā* and *akāma nirjarā*. Of these, the first takes place in those who observe self-restraints (and austerities), while *akāma nirjarā* takes place of all living beings.
>
> —*Jñā* 2

> Just as the ripening of the fruits of trees takes place of its own and they are also ripened in straw (*pal denā*), so also the *karmas* are shed off on maturity on their own and they are also shed by certain means (*upāya*) such as austerities. —*Jñā* 3

> As gold is purified by heat (fire), similarly the living beings with faults become pure through the fire of austerities. —*Jñā* 4

> The steadfast and resolute heroes, who have apprehension of the wanderings in rebirths, observe both fasting (*anaśana*), etc., six external and expiation (*prāyaścitta*), six internal kinds of austerities or penances. —*Jñā* 5-6, see *TS* IX.19-20

Though *karmas* are associated with living beings since beginningless time, they are shed off quickly by meditation (*dhyāna*), and thus the soul is purified like gold. —*Jñā* 8

The virtuous person observes both external and internal austerities, that are dependent on the Self itself (*ātmādhīna*), particularly excellent *dhyāna tapa*. By this *tapa*, one destroys the coverings of *karmas* that are collected together or amassed from a long time, there by entering the dwelling place of the supreme bliss, the ocean of omniscience. —*Jñā* 9

In *Bhagavatī Ārādhanā*, *nirjarā anuprekṣā* is described in the following words:

After stopping the inflow (*āsrava*) of *karmas* through the various means of *saṁvara*, the saint engages himself in various kinds of austerities, described in the scriptures, which are the conditions (*hetu*) of *nirjarā*. — *Bha* 1839

Without the austerities, by some were alone, one is not liberated from the *karmas*, just as the well-protected wealth is not reduced without enjoyments. — *Bha* 1840

Nirjarā is the dissociation of material *karmas* bound in previous times: it is of two kinds: *savipāka nirjarā* and *avipāka nirjarā*. — *Bha* 1841

Just as the fruits ripen in their own time and can also be ripened by certain means before time, so also in *savipāka nirjarā* the (previously bound) *karmas* are shed off on maturity after imparting their fruit and they can also be shared off by certain means, i.e. austerities (*tapa*) (*Bha* 1842), which is called *avipāka nirjarā*.

Just as the gold mixed with stone is purified or separated with ore by heating it in a great fire, so also the living being is purified of kārmic dust through the fire of the nature of austerities. — *Bha* 1847

Replying to the question/doubt as to if the soul is purified, i.e. *karmas* are destroyed by austerities (*tapa*), what is the necessity of *saṁvara*, it is stated:

> Jaina scriptures speak that without *saṁvara*, by austerities (*tapa*) alone, there is no liberation, i.e. destruction of all the *karmas*) (because new/fresh *karmas* may continue to accumulate) because if fresh water can continue to enter a pond, tank or reservoir (*tālāb*), then the *tālāb* cannot be dried up completely.
>
> —*Bha* 1848

The self-restrained (*saṁyata*) warrior, verse 1850 of *Bhagavatī Ārādhanā* adds, equipped with *saṁvara* and excellent *tapa* of meditation (*dhyāna*), by defeating the whole army of *karma* enemies in the battlefield of self-restraint, attains the unique kingdom of prosperity, happiness, lustre or splendour (the title of Goddess Lakṣmī) of the nature of liberation (*mokṣa*).

The means of shedding (*nirjarā*) of previously cumulative *karmas* are by austerities or penances (*tapas*). Without *tapa*, one cannot obtain liberation by *saṁvara* alone. In fact, *tapa* is said to be the cause of *nirjarā* as well as *saṁvara* (*TS* IX.3). Even in the absence of *saṁvara*, one cannot attain liberation by *nirjarā* alone. Both *saṁvara* and *nirjarā* are necessary for liberation.

The obstruction/restriction of desires is called *tapa*. The austerities undertaken with the object of worldly fame, respect, repuation or gain is called childish *tapa* or *tapa* of ignorant persons. In reality, by rising above the worldly desires, the exertion undertaken for the destruction of *karmas* only is *tapa*. Describing the characteristic of *tapa*, Akalaṅka states: "That which destroys *karmas* is *tapa*" (*TRV* IX.19-18). The subjugation of sensual pleasures (*viṣaya*) is *tapa* (*SAS* IX.20).

The austerities (*tapa*) are of two kinds: external and internal, of which the external austerities are the means of internal austerities. Both external and internal austerities of *tapa* is of six kinds each. The external austerities are:

1. fasting or abstention from food (*anaśana*);
2. semi-fasting, reduced diet or eating less than one's fill (*avamaudārya*);

3. voluntary limiting the range of choice or the variety and the manner of seeking food (*vṛttiparisaṁkhyāma*);
4. daily giving up one or more of six kinds of delicacies, viz. butter or ghee, milk, curd, sugar, salt and oil (*rasa-parityāga*);
5. sitting, sleeping or residing in a lonely place devoid of insects and disturbance (*vivikta-śayyāsana*); and
6. bodily discomforts (*kāya-kleśa*) (*TS* IX.19).

The internal austerities are: (1) expiation (*prāyaścitta*); (2) reverence, veneration or respect (*vinaya*); (3) service of saints or worthy people; (4) study (*svādhyāya*); (5) giving up attachment to body, etc. (*kāyotsarga*); and (6) concentration (*dhyāna*) (*TS* IX.20).

Mokṣa means liberation from the bondage of *karmas*. It is the highest objective of human endeavour. Describing the characteristic of *mokṣa*, Umāsvāmi states:

> Liberation is the freedom from all kārmic matter, owing to the absence or non-existence of the causal conditions (*hetu*) of bondage and to the shedding of all *karmas*. — *TS* X.2

The liberated souls are also called *siddhas*. The Self (*jīva*) is miserable due to the bondage of *karmas*. After liberation, man is not born again.

Saṁvara and *nirjarā* are the causes of liberation. *Saṁvara* prevents and stops the incoming of fresh/new *karmas* and *nirjarā* means the shedding of previously accumulated *karmas*. By *nirjarā*, the previously acumulated *karmas* are dissociated, but if the soul continues to bind fresh *karmas*, then one cannot get liberation. Similarly, if the incoming of fresh *karmas* is stopped but the shedding of previously accumulated *karmas* is not destroyed, then also one cannot attain liberation.

One who denounces enjoyments (of sense pleasures) even when capable of enjoyment, that person does great shedding of *karmas*. He attains the great fruit of the nature of liberation (*Bhagavatīsūtra* 7.7).

11

Dharma

Dharma is the law expounded by the Jina, the true, good path of righteousness and piety or liberation and excellent forgiveness (*kṣamā*), etc. With a view to practise *dharma*, one should engage himself in ten kinds of excellent forgiveness, etc. (*BA* 70), the moral self-restraints of non-violence, etc. (*BA* 76), self-regulations of carefulness in walking, speaking, eating, placing things and cleanliness (*BA* 76) and austerities (*BA* 77). Constant contemplation on the pure nature of the Self with equanimity is also desirable.

Reflection on this *bhāvanā* creates confidence in the mind of the aspirant and infuses strength needed to practise the path of enlightened worldview, enlightened knowledge and enlightened conduct. The alignment of these three aspects or faculties of consciousness, viz. feeling, knowing and doing, can liberate us from worldly sufferings and ensure peace, happiness and social well-being (*TS* IX.7).

The word *dharma* has multiple meanings depending on the context in which it is used. These include: conduct, duty, right, justice, virtue, morality, religion, religious merit, good work, according to a right or rule, etc. Many other meanings have been suggested, such as law (*torah* in the Judaic sense); *logos* (in Greek); "way" (in Christianity); and even *tao* (in Chinese). None of these is entirely accurate and none of them conveys the full force of the term like *dharma* does in Sanskrit. *Dharma* has no equivalent in the Western lexicon.

Dharma has the Sanskrit root, *dhṛ*, which means "that which upholds" or "that without which nothing can stand" or "that which maintains the stability and harmony of the universe". *Dharma* encompasses the natural, innate behaviour of things, duty, law, ethics and virtue. Every entity in the cosmos has its particular *dharma* – from the electron, which has the *dharma* to move in a certain manner, to the clouds, galaxies, plants, insects and, of course, man. Man's understanding of the *dharma* of inanimate things is what we now call physics (Malhotra 2006).

That *dharma* which has been expounded by Lord Jina is of the characteristic of non-violence; truth as is its basis (*ādhāra*); modesty or humility (*vinaya*) as its root; forgiveness as its strength (*bala*). It is protected by chastity (*brahmacarya*) wherein the pre-eminence is of subsidence (*upaśama*) (of *karmas*); destiny (*niyati*) is its characteristic; being devoid of or free from possessiveness (*parigraha*) is its support (*ālambana*). From the gain of these, liberation with the attainment of many kinds of prosperity and high status in this world and other-worldly prosperity (*abhyudaya*) is certain. Contemplation in this manner is *dharma anuprekṣā* (*SAS*, para 810).

In his commentary *Tattvārtha-Rāja-Vārttika* on *Tattvārthasūtra* IX.7 pertaining to *dharma anuprekṣā*, Akalaṅka states:

> The enquiry, investigation or research in regard to *mārgaṇā sthāna* (soul quests), *jīva-sthāna* or *jīva-saṁsāra* (soul classes) and *guṇa-sthāna* (stages of moral and spiritual evolution) is adequately described as *dharma* in the instructions or commands of the Omniscient Lord (Jina-*śāsana*); this is *dharma* contemplation.

The fourteen soul quests (*mārgaṇā sthāna*) are the ways in which a detailed knowledge of souls is provided: the form or mode of human, etc. condition of existence (*gati* – four kinds); senses (*indriyas* – five kinds); body (*kāya* — five kinds); vibratory activities of mind, speech and body (*yoga* — three kinds); sex (*veda* — three kinds); passions of anger, pride, greed and deceit (*kaṣāya* — four kinds); knowledge (*jñāna* — eight kinds); intuition (*darśana* — four kinds); restraint (*saṁyama* — seven kinds); thought-paints (*leśyā* — six kinds); liberableness or capacity to attain liberation from kārmic bondage (*bhavyatva*) and those who do not have such capacity (*abhavya* — two kinds); enlightened view (*saṁyaktva*); brain processes or rationality (*saṁjñitva* — two kinds); and intake for body (*āhāra* — six kinds) (i.e. a total of sixty).

The soul-classes (*jīva-sthāna* or *jīva samāsa*) are said to be fourteen in verse 72, fifty-seven in verse 73, ninety-eight in verses 79-80 and 570 in verse 78 of *Gommaṭasāra Jīva Kāṇḍa*.[1] The division of souls into 570 soul classes is meant only for clear exposition and to grasp different varieties of souls, though strictly and logically there are in reality only ninety-eight soul classes (Jaini 1990: 44-46, 53-63). These are classified primarily on the basis of the differences of bodies obtained in the four conditions (*gati*) of transmigratory existences of hell, human beings, celestial beings and subhuman, animal, birds, etc. the number of senses and those with or without mind (*saṁjñitva*), including the ability to move voluntarily from one place to other place, i.e. mobile (*trasa*) and immobile (*sthāvara*).

In the fourteen stages of spiritual development (*guṇa-sthānas*), passions play an important role. At most of these stages, the degrees of intensity of anger, pride, deceit and greed are reduced gradually. Of these, anger is the first to be reduced and so on (Marida 1990: 55). At the lowest rung of the ladder, i.e. the first *guṇa-sthāna* of complete delusion or ignorance, the four passions are at their maximum level of strength/intensity. This perverted state persists in the second and third stages as well. At the fourth stage, the tenacious or most intense passions are eradicated; the person comes to have an enlightened vision and can hope to rise further on the ladder of

---

[1] J.L. Jaini himself lists 406 soul classes.

spiritual progress. At the seventh stage, anger is either absolutely quietened or actually destroyed, while the other three passions remain in a slight degree. In the subsequent four stages (eighth to eleventh), the gross and subtle flickering passions are gradually suppressed or eliminated.

In the eighth stage, the soul makes full preparation either for the ascent on the ladder-of-subsidence (*upaśama-śreṇī*) of the form of the continuous subsidence of conduct-deluding *karmas* or for the ascent on the ladder-of-destruction (*kṣapaka-śreṇī*) of the form of the continuous process of destruction of conduct-deluding *karmas*.

In the ninth stage, one attains complete freedom from *māyā* (deceit); the quasi-passions coexist with and strengthen the passions. In the tenth stage, one is free from quasi-passions such as scornful laughter, fear, grief, disgust, etc. and all his passions, except subtle greed, are destroyed. If the eleventh stage is reached by the suppression of the subtle greed, rather than by sublimation or destruction of the passions, a fall is inevitable and the soul may fall down to the sixth, fifth, fourth, second or even to the lowest first stage. It is only when the soul reaches the twelfth stage of complete elimination of all the sixteen kinds of passions and nine quasi-passions that one is completely immune or free from any fall and is absolutely sure of liberation.

The thirteenth stage of moral and spiritual development is the stage of *sayoga-kevalī* (the Omniscient Lord with *yoga*) (the activities of the mind, speech and body) or the liberated soul in the embodied existence, *jīvan-mukta* imbued with the activities of mind, speech and body (*yoga*). He is called *arhat* (worthy of reverence, homage and worship) or Arahanta or Arihanta, i.e. one who has conquered internal enemies of attachment, etc.) and destroyed four destructive *karmas* (*ghātīya-karmas*) and knowledge-obscuring (*antarāya*) *karmas*).

An *arhat* is endowed with infinite intuition, infinite knowledge, infinite bliss and infinite vigour. He has attained enlightenment and is free from all defects; he is beyond attachment and aversion. He is totally disinterested and dispassionate and he has qualified himself for the attainment of *nirvāṇa* (liberation). The word *nirvāṇa* is common to both Buddhism and Jainism, and the Buddha as well as Mahāvīra are called *arhats*.

An *arhat* is an ideal saint. He is completely free from anger, pride, deceit and greed. He is endowed with equanimity between friends and foes, having neither attachment towards friends nor hatred or aversion towards foes. In *Pravacanasāra*, conduct is said to be *dharma*; *dharma* lies in equanimity, and equanimity means that state of the Self which is devoid of infatuation (*moha*) and emotional agitation or disturbance (*kṣobha*) (Jain, J.P. 2014: 219, *gāthā* I.7), which is caused by attachment, aversion and passions. An *arhat*, who has realized the true nature of the Self, has developed the soul's maximum potential and is established in his intrinsic nature of pure consciousness.

The fourteenth last stage of moral and spiritual development is the stage of *ayoga-kevalī* (the Omniscient Lord devoid of *yoga*) or the liberated state of the *siddhas*, who have destroyed the remaining four (of the eight material *karmas* (*TS* VIII.4), non-destructive *karmas* (*aghātīya karmas*)), which are age-determining and leading to pleasure and pain.

Concluding the discussion on *dharma*, Akalaṅka (1993: 776) observes:

> In this manner, Lord Arahanta has beautifully done the exposition of *dharma*, which is the condition (*hetu*) of liberation; thinking about this is *dharma anuprekṣā*. Due to this, affection or devotion for *dharma* takes place. In this way, due to the contemplations holding and maintaining of excellent forgivness, etc. *dharma* takes place and also of great self-restraint (*saṁyama*).

One who contemplates the *anuprekṣās* practises *dharma* such as excellent forgiveness (*kṣamā*), etc. *dharma* and is energetic and enthusiastic in regard to overcoming or conquering the hardships (*pariṣaha-jaya*). Therefore, *anuprekṣā* is described in between these two, viz. *dharma* and *pariṣaha-jaya* (*TS* IX.2).

In his commentary *Tattvārtha-Śloka-Vārttika* on *Tattvārthasūtra* IX.7 concerning *dharma anuprekṣā*, Vidyanandi (1969, vol. 7: 157, commentator Manikchand) states:

> After the excellent or good position of the best, the most excellent or the most eminent (*śreṣṭha*) (*dharma* one should think or ponder again and again that the Omniscient Lord Jinendra has done good things, that he has performed the act of determining, defining, investigating or examining (*nirūpaṇa*) of the stages of moral and spiritual development (*guṇa-sthāna*) and soul quests (*mārgaṇā*). The greatness or grandeur of the instructions of Jinendra for imperishable, permanent and durable (*akṣaya*) infinite time, infinite living beings, suffering from numerous great diseases of birth, old age, death, its *nirūpaṇa* is an impossible undertaking.

The path to liberation is through right faith, right knowledge and right conduct. Firm belief in the real nature of the soul ensures one's advance through self-realization. Steadfast reflection on the precepts of the Jinas and adherence to them leads to the goal of eternal peace (Dharma Raja 1990: 5).

The path of religion preached by the Jinas is highly beneficial. The deeper the attachment and spirit of renunciation, the nearer one goes to the goal of religious life, viz. the seat of highest bliss (*Mar* 629-631).

In this context, A.N. Upadhye states:

> *Dharma* covers the twofold religion and the consequent modes of religious life with its attendant rules of conduct and pious living, prescribed for householders and monks. *Uvāsagadasāo* describes the rules for a householder, and the life of a monk is elaborately described in *Ayaraṅga* and other texts of the canon. The term *dharma-svakhyatattva* reminds one of *sakkaya-dhamma*.[2]

---

[2] There is an interesting and elaborate explanation of *svakkatha* as an adjective of *dhamma* in Kosambi 1940: 144-145.

Excellent forgiveness (*kṣamā*) and excellent (law) *dharma* expounded by the Tīrthaṅkaras are beneficial to all living beings of the world. Individuals who have taken refuge/shelter in that *dharma* with purification of the mind are auspicious, blessed or praiseworthy (*dhanya*), virtuous, meritorious, righteous and pious (*puṇyaśālī*), and are those who have accomplished the purpose, successful or contented (*kṛtārtha*) (*Mūlācāra* 752).

Forgiveness, etc. ten kinds of *dharma* are: (1) forgiveness (*kṣamā*); (2) humility (*mārdava*); (3) straightforwardness (*ārjava*); (4) purity (*śauca*); (5) truth (*satya*); (6) self-control (*saṁyama*); (7) austerities (*tapa*); (8) renunciation (*tyāga*); (9) non-attachment or non-acquisitiveness (*akiñcanya*); and (10) chastity or sex fidelity (*brahmacarya*).

This is the order of ten *dharmas* given in *Tattvārthasūtra* IX.6. In *Mūlācāra* 754, the order of these ten *dharmas* is: *kṣamā*, *mārdava*, *ārjava*, *śauca*, *satya*, *tyāga*, *tapa*, *saṁyama*, *akiñcanya* and *brahmacarya*.

Of the order of the ten *dharmas*, as given above (on the basis of *TS* IX.6), the first four imply control or absence of four passions (anger, pride, deceit or crookedness and greed) respectively. The fifth, sixth, eighth, ninth and tenth are five vows or self-restraints of non-violence, etc. The seventh is austerities (*tapa*), which is of two kinds: external and internal.[3]

As subsidence (*upaśama*), compassion (*dayā*), forgiveness and *vairāgya* (non-attachment to worldly attractions and desires) increase in that manner that the Self undecaying, imperishable, permanent or durable (*akṣaya*) happiness of liberation is reflected or thought of (*bhāvita*) (*Mūlācāra* 755).

The description of *dharma bhāvanā* in *Jñānārṇava* is as follows:

> I bow to that *dharma* by which one is purified and liberated, which is damp or moist with compassion, and which is the tree that grants all desires (*kalpavṛkṣa*). —*Jñā* 1

---

3 See *Tattvārthasūtra* IX.19-20; for their description, see *supra*.

By practising even a part of that *dharma*, which is proclaimed in Jain *dharma* as having the self-restrained saints attain liberation.

—*Jñā* 2

Dharma protects all mobile and immobile living beings from the hardships, sufferings or miseries, and provides the whole world with the nectar or ambrosia of happiness. —*Jñā* 6

Dharma is preceptor (*guru*), friend, master and relative, and protects with affection the helpless, orphaned or wretched without reason (*Jñā* 11). Apart from *dharma*, there is no other protection.

Dharma goes with human beings to the other world (*para-loka*) protects him, and by taking him out of the mud and mire (*paṅka*) of the (mundane existence of) births, puts him in the path of liberation. —*Jñā* 15

Like *dharma*, there is no other means of attaining all kinds of prosperity and high status in the world (*abyudaya*); it is the root of the tree of happiness and bliss (*ānanda*); is beneficial, worth worshipping and giving liberation. —*Jñā* 16

Dharma is said to be of ten kinds, viz. forgiveness, humility, purity (*śauca*), straightforwardness (*ārjava*), truth, self-restraint (*saṁyama*), chastity or sex-fidelity, austerities (*tapa*), renunciation (*tyāga*) and non-attachment or non-acquisitiveness (*akiñcanya*).

—*Jñā* 20

Hey Self! If leaving hell is extremely desired or cherished (*iṣṭa*) or if you want to attain the supreme power, wealth and abundance of the Lord of Celestial Kingdom, and if the supreme *puruṣārtha* (human effort) of liberation is earnestly desired or devoutly wished (*prārthanīya*), then what more to say, practise *dharma*.

—*Jñā* 23

Bhagavatī Ārādhanā describes *dharma anuprekṣā* in these words:

The Self, who maintains or preserves *dharma*, capable of effecting abundance of happiness in right earnest and with dedication, attains worldly happiness and well-being as also the happiness of liberation. —*Bha* 1851

Dharma is venerable, to be worshipped (*pūjya*), is worthy of trust of all, the favourite of all and is honourable or celebrated (*yaśasvī*). One can observe *dharma* happily or with ease. — *Bha* 1852

The excellent *dharma* is the cause of all the well-being in human and celestial regions, and in the end happiness of liberation (*mokṣa*). — *Bha* 1853

For the people, who are stuck, caught or snared in the enjoyments of the world imbued with attachment and aversion, interest or inclination towards non-attachment (*vītarāga*) *dharma*, which is devoid of taste or relish. — *Bha* 1856

He, whose conduct, which stops or blocks the door of incoming of *karmas*, that are capable of bringing the mseries or sufferings of the world, is devoid of faults or faultless, his birth in human mode is successful. — *Bha* 1857

As a person's detachment or disinterest in sensual pleasures or worldly concerns (*nirveda*), renunciation from the attachment of the world (*vairāgya*), compassion (*dayā*) and restraining of mind is increased in the same manner; liberation (*mokṣa*) is brought near. — *Bha* 1858

Victory of the *dharmacakra* (wheel of the law), i.e. teachings of the Omniscient Lord, Jina, of which enlightened worldview, or right belief, is the hub or centre (*nābhi*), the Jina's utterings or teachings having twelve components/parts (*dvādaśāṅga* scripture) is the spoke, the moral self-restraints or vows (*vrata*) are rim (*nemi*) and the current of austerities is second rim. — *Bha* 1859

The intrinsic nature of an object or a living being is said to be *dharma* by Kundakunda. In *Tattvārthasūtra* IX.6, Umāsvāmi has stated that virtues like forgiveness are said to be *dharma*. Samantabhadra has described the triple jewels of enlightened worldview, enlightened knowledge and enlightened conduct as *dharma*. And in many places, non-violence or protection of living beings from any injury or harm is said to be *dharma*.

In this regard, *Pravacanasāra* 7 states:

> Conduct is *dharma*. *Dharma* is defined as equanimity. And equanimity is said to be a state-of-evolution of the soul free from infatuation (*moha*) and mental agitation, excitement or fret (*kṣobha*).
>
> Jain, J.P. 2014: 219

I have this, I do not have this, I have to do this, I have not to do this, remaining thinking all that, the thief of fate or death takes away the vitalities or bio-energies (*prāṇa*). Then, why is there negligence (*pramāda*) in engaging in *dharma* (*Uttarādhyayanasūtra* 14.15)?

12

Bodhi-durlabha (Rarity of Enlightenment)

Bodhi-durlabha (rarity of enlightenment) leads to wisdom or true insight of the reality of things and of the right path of liberation.

The true insight of the enlightened worldview and knowledge is the most difficult thing to be attained. Since all the impure psychic dispositions are the result of the coming into operation, rise or fruition of (material) *karmas*, they are to be abandoned (*BA* 84).

Four things are rare in this universe, viz. *manuṣyatva* (human birth and inclination towards self-effort), *śruti* (study), *śraddhā* (conviction) and *saṁyama* (self-restraint). Reflection on this *bhāvanā* instils in us a sense of urgency and determination not to waste human birth, the time at our disposal, our energies and resources in transitory worldly pleasures but to gird up our loins to make efforts to control our passions, eliminate laxity, procrastination, lethargy (*pramāda*), to practise moral and spiritual discipline and attain enlightenment.

All the advantages and gains are easy to get in the world, but obtaining truth is difficult. Human birth, good education and good company are also difficult (Nyayavijaya 1935: 109).

The importance and significance of the true insight (*bodhi*) of the reality of things, both the Self and the non-Self, is quite obvious from the fact that it is due to the absence of, which is the cause of the inflow (*āsrava*) and the consequent bondage (*bandha*) of *karmas*, the Self (ignorant of the true nature of the Self) identified itself with other (*para*) (*SS* 92), *karmas* and no-*karmas* and the *pratyaya* (*SS* 51), deluded view (*mithyātva*), lack of moral self-restraints or non-abstinence (*avirati*), anger, etc. passions (*kaṣāyas*) and the vibratory activities of the mind, speech and body (*yoga*) (*SS* 109).

The enlightened soul, who knows and is fully aware of the particular, special or exceptional distinction (*viśeṣa*) *antara* (*SS* 69 and 71) [discriminative insight and wisdom (*bheda-vijñāna* or *bheda-jñāna*) (*SS* 69 JN and *SS* 71 JS)], the Self (*appaṇam*), does not become the doer (*kartā*) or the causal agent of various *karmas* (*SS* 93).

Samayasāra 93 emphasizes the importance of discriminative insight and wisdom (*bheda-vijñāna*) or *prajñā* (proper understanding of the reality of things, knowledge, intelligence or discriminative wisdom) facilitates acquisition of true insight with the reality of things (*bodhi*). *Prajñā* differentiates and cuts off the Self and the kārmic bondage by their own intrinsic and distinctive properties, attributes, characteristics/features (*SS* 294-295). Thus, the Self obtains liberation from *karmas* (*SS* 293) and realizes its own transcendental pure nature (*SS* 295).

Just as the Self is divided or rendered distinct (*vibhakta*) (from *karmas*) by *prajñā*, so also by the very same *prajñā*, the Self is realized (*SS* 296). The true insight of the reality of the nature of "I", the Self as *ceda* or *cetāyita* (conscious entity) (*SS* 297), *draṣṭā* (the interested observers or seer) (*SS* 298) and *jñātā* (knower) (*SS* 299) is apprehended by *prajñā* (*SS* 297-299). Whatever mental states remain (besides) are all to be known to be other (*para*) than "mine" (*SS* 297-299), i.e. the reality of "I".

In view of what is stated above, getting or obtaining of discriminative insight or wisdom, which is a means of getting *bodhi*, the true insight into the reality of things as they are, is very difficult and rare.

It is difficult to attain the right belief, knowledge and conduct (Jaini 1956: 149). In this universe, it is difficult to get birth in human mode (*paryāya*). It is still difficult to again get birth in the human mode after one has fallen from it. After one gets human birth, it is further difficult to get country, good lineage, proper senses and health. Getting all these if one does not get right, the human birth is useless, vain (*vyartha*). After getting, indulging or delighting in pleasures of sense objects (*viśva-sukha*) makes it fruitless, useless or unproductive. Hardly ever or perhaps (*kadācita*) one is unattached to *viṣaya-sukha*, still getting the inclination towards austerities, propagation of *dharma* and involuntary death with common happiness is very difficult. To think that by having these only the gain of enlightenment (*bodhilābha*) the successful is the rarity of enlightenment or true inside of the reality of things in right path of liberation (*bodhi-durlabha anuprekṣā*). In thinking in this manner and obtaining enlightenment (*bodhi*), the Self never has negligence (*pramāda*) (Pūjyapāda 1992: 328, para 809).

In his commentary *Tattvārtha-Rāja-Vārttika* on *Tattvārthasūtra* IX.7 pertaining to *bodhi-durlabha anuprekṣā*, Akalaṅka (1993: 773) states:

> To get or obtain the mode of mobile (*trasa*) living being (in the world existence) is extremely difficult and to get or get *bodhi* gain (*bodhilābha*) (enlightenment, wisdom or true insight of the reality of things and the right path of liberation) is extremely difficult; this thought is *bodhi-durlabha anuprekṣā*.
>
> One can realize the importance, significance and rarity of being a mobile soul when compared with the *nigoda* and immobile *sthāvara* living beings, which are infinite. *Nigoda* is the lowest form of life, micro-organism, the minute living being, the general/ common (*sādhāraṇa*) vegetable kingdom (below animal life) in which one physical body contains infinite souls, having a very short span of life. The infinite immobile (*sthāvara*) souls are of five kinds: earth-bodied, water-bodied, fire-bodied, air-bodied, and plant-bodied one-sensed living beings. Thus, one can understand the rarity of being a mobile living being.

Even within the mobile souls, there are many, who are deprived of a part, especially a limb, maimed or disabled, i.e. having disabled senses (*vikalendriya*). Therefore, to be five-sensed (living being) is likewise difficult.

Even within the five-sensed souls, there are innumerable animals and birds, etc. Therefore, as compared to being in their modes (*paryāya*), to get the mode of a human being is difficult or rare like a jewel (*ratna*).

After the destruction of the human mode, to get it (the mode of a human being) again is difficult.

Even if one obtains a human mode, to obtain birth and residence in good or excellent country (*su-deśa*) in the innumerable human ocean, devoid of discrimination between good or beneficial and harmful thoughts (*hita-ahita vicāra*) is difficult.

Even if one obtains human birth in a good and excellent country, getting/obtaining good family (*su-kula*) is extremely difficult. Due to birth in a good family/lineage, the tradition (*paramparā*) of good character, virtuous nature and moral or decent conduct (*śīla*), modesty, courtesy or humility (*vinaya*), and good or virtuous conduct or behaviour is obtained.

In that, what is mentioned in the preceding paragraph, a long span of life, strength of senses, good looks or handsomeness (*rūpa*) and health, etc. are more and more (*uttarottara*) difficult.

Even when one gets all these, if one does not obtain the true, good or worthy path of righteousness and piety or true path of liberation (*sat-dharma*), then like the mouth devoid of eyes, all that is useless.

Even after getting the difficult to get *dharma*, to spend time in sensual pleasures is like burning of sandalwood for ashes or cinders (*bhasma*). Thus, being unattached to sense pleasures (*viṣaya-virakta*) is difficult.

Even after being *viṣaya-virakta*, *samādhi* (profound meditation or absorption) of the nature or character of thought (*bhāvanā*)

> of austerities or penances, the propagation of *dharma* and dying peacefully, calmness or equanimity, without sorrow, grief or anguish (*sukha-maraṇa*) is extremely difficult or rare.
>
> From this kind of *samādhi* alone, the gain of *bodhi* (*bodhilābha*) can be successful. Contemplation in this manner is *bodhi-durlabha anuprekṣā*. By obtaining this *bodhi*, the Self, by having control of passions and elimination of laxity, procrastination, lethargy or negligence (*apramāda*), remains engaged in the well-being or welfare of oneself.

In his commentary *Tattvārtha-Śloka-Vārttika* on *Tattvārthasūtra* IX.7 on *bodhi-durlabha anuprekṣā*, Vidyanandi (1969, vol. 7: 157, 159 comm. on *TS* V.16, commentator Manikchand), states:

> Enlightened knowledge (*samyak-jñāna*) is difficult. One gets the gain of good or excellent *dharma* of the nature or character of triple jewels (enlightened view, knowledge and conduct) discriminative insight or wisdom (*bheda-vijñāna*) and the experience of one's own Self, etc. with great difficulty, trouble, inconvenience, labour, effort, hardship or suffering (*kaṣṭa*); by putting trust or faith in this way to think that to get *bheda-vijñāna* is difficult, is *bodhi-durlabha anuprekṣā*.

Birth as humans is rare compared to the number of creatures who are denied this opportunity. For it is only as a human being that one can follow the path towards final liberation (*mokṣa*). An aspirant must make the utmost use of his life as a human being by engaging himself in self-purifying activities. The enlightened *ācāryas* thus delineate the twelve reflections in a sequence that enable the seeker to divert his thoughts away from external worldly distractions and to concentrate on his own innate pure Self (Dharma Raja 1990: 5).

While wandering in this worldly wilderness, there are so many tempations that it is very difficult to find the correct and advantageous position and therefrom reach religious enlightenment given out by the Jinas (*Mar* 632-638).

In this context, A.N. Upadhye points out:

> A gradation list of the rarities is often met with in the canon (*Uttarādhyayanasūtra* XXXVI). Starting from *nigoda*, the soul is on a march of spiritual progress thorough various grades of living beings. Then to be born as a human being at a suitable place, in a good family, with a perfect and healthy body and with requisite opportunities for religious enlightenment is something that is rare. If the *loka-anuprekṣā* inculcated the feeling of immense space, this *anuprekṣā* of *bodhi-durlabha* makes one realize the feeling of endless time which in course of series of births produces the impression of the rarity of human birth and of religious enlightenment.

Birth as a human being in this infinite world is difficult (*Mūlācāra* 757). Birth and residence in a good and excellent country and good family or lineage (*kula*), having good appearance, features or beauty (*rūpa*), a long span of life and long life, health, power or strength (*bala*), humility, hearing the lectures on *dharma* (*dharma-śravaṇa*), the intellect of grasping or obtaining (*grahaṇa buddhi*) and good memorizing and not forgetting in future (*dharma*) — all these are also successively and increasingly difficult (*Mūlācāra* 758).

Even after obtaining all the things mentioned above, it is not easy to have true insight (*bodhi*) in the law (*dharma*) propounded by Jina (Jina-*śāsana*) (*Mūlācāra* 759). If this *bodhi* is once separated, obtaining it again is definitely not easy. Hence, any negligence (*pramāda*) is not correct (*Mūlācāra* 760).

When the Self after obtaining enlightened worldview (*samyaktva*) of subsidence (*upaśama*), destructive (*kṣāyika*) and destructive-cum-subsidence (*kṣayopaśamika*) kinds is endowed with austerities and self-restraints (*saṁyama*), then he obtains imperishable or permanent (*akṣaya*) happiness (*Mūlācāra* 762).

Therefore, I also contemplate on the Self in that manner through conviction or faith (*śraddhā*), enthusiasm or apprehension of the miseries of the world (*saṁvega*), strength and humility so that that *bodhi* continues to remain for long time (*cira kāla*) (*Mūlācāra* 763).

One knows/understands the soul (*jīva*), inanimate matter (*pudgala*), etc. six substances (*dravya*) as also nine basic principles (*tattvas*) or categories (*padārtha*). In this manner, one should contemplate and be attentive to *bodhi* having thousands of qualities (*Mūlācāra* 764).

In describing *bodhi-durlabha bhāvanā*, *Jñānārṇava* explains that getting an enlightened worldview or right belief beginning from the lowest form of life (the micro-organism (*nigoda*)) is more and more difficult. It observes:

> It is extremely difficult for the soul, continuously afflicted by the enemy of the nature of sins, to get out of *nigoda*, which is below the hells. —*Jñā* 1

> After getting out from the *nigoda*, the soul is born in immobile (*sthāvara*) living beings (the earth-bodied, water-bodied, fire-bodied, air-bodied and plant-bodied one-sensed beings) (*TS* II.13). And due to the coming into operation or rise (*udaya*) of some virtuous or meritorious (*puṇya*) *karma*, the soul obtains mobile (*trasa*) condition of existence (*gati*). —*Jñā* 2

> At some point of time, hardly ever or perhaps (*kadācita*) one gets *trasa-gati*, to obtain a developed state or condition (*paryāptatā*) (which is meant to explain the abnormalities and deformities in living beings) in subhuman (*tiryañca*) (such as animals and birds) *gati* is possible due to the destruction not from less or insignificant (*nyūna*) *puṇya*, i.e. it is possible only due to a lot of *puṇya*. Even in that *tiryañca* state or condition, to get the five-sensed state of the rational being having a mind (*TS* II.2 and II.24) is very difficult. Rationality signifies capacity of receiving instructions, understanding, actions (*kriyā*), preaching and recitation. Moreover, a rational soul investigates before acting what ought to be done or ought not to be done; distinguishes between things as they are and as they are not in reality. A rational soul also comes

to you on being called by his name (Jaini 1956: 42). Further, even then, to get complete component parts or organs of the body (*avayava*) is much difficult. —*Jñā* 3

In this world of living beings, getting human birth and in that state or condition also being virtuous or talented (*guṇa sahita*), getting an excellent country, a good community or caste (*jāti*), family (*kula*), etc. are possible due to the destruction of more and more *karmas*. These are very difficult. —*Jñā* 4

Even after obtaining all that (as stated in *Jñā* 4), to have long life, complete materials of five-senses, pre-eminent and excellent intellect, calmness, and a mild degree of passions like anger is extremely difficult. —*Jñā* 5

Kadācita, even after one gets all that, obtaining the absence of desire (*virakti*) from objects of worldly or sensual enjoyment, the (five) moral self-restraints or vows (of non-violence, etc.) (*yama*), calmness of mind due to subsidence of passions (*praśama*) is very difficult. *Kadācita* one gets all that due to the application of *puṇya*, to have the capability of deciding life principles (*tattva-nirṇaya*) is extremely difficult. —*Jñā* 6

Though people fortunately get the extremely difficult aforesaid things, they are (fallen, deviated or strayed from the virtuous, enlightened path) due to their subjection to negligence or laxity (*pramāda*) and very desirous/covetous of belonging or craving (*lālasā*) of desires, sexual desire, lust or passion (*kāma*) and wealth or worldly prosperity (*artha*) (*Jñā* 7) and engage themselves in worldly or sensual enjoyments (*viṣaya*) and passions (*kaṣāyas*) like anger.

Even after getting the enlightened (*samyak*) path of triple jewels (*ratnatraya*) (enlightened worldview or right belief, enlightened knowledge and enlightened conduct), some people give up the excellent path by being infatuated by severe delusion or deluded view (*mithyātva*) and worldly or sensual enjoyments (*viṣaya*). —*Jñā* 8

> Even after getting the jewel of *bodhi* (enlightenment of the nature of triple jewels (see *supra*), which is not easy, but extremely difficult, those who lose it, which is like dropping the jewel of great value from one's hand into the great ocean, to obtain it again is very difficult. — *Jñā* 12

Bhagavatī Ārādhanā describes the *bodhi-durlabha anuprekṣā* as follows:

> For the living being, wandering in the world, smeared, stained or sullied with *karmas*, to have *bodhi*, i.e. the triple jewels of enlightened worldview or right belief, enlightened knowledge and enlightened conduct, is very difficult. — *Bha* 1860

> It is difficult to get human birth in the infinite world. — *Bha* 1861

> This is because there is a great deal of inauspicious (*aśubha*) states-of-evolution (*pariṇāma*) (such as deluded-view (*mithyātva*) lack or absence of moral self-restraints (*asaṁyama*), passions (*kaṣāyas*) like anger and negligence or laxity (*pramāda*)). There being innumerable reincarnations (*yoni*) (including hellish, etc. conditions of existence), the human mode is very difficult.
> — *Bha* 1862

> Even after getting human condition or mode (*paryāya*), it is not easy to get or take birth in a good country, a good family or caste, good appearance, health, a long span of life, discerning or judicious intellect and grasping of the hearing of *dharma*.
> — *Bha* 1863

> Even after getting all the aforementioned things, it is not easy to have *bodhi* (the intellect) turned towards the discipline (*śāsana*) of the Omniscient Lord (Jina). This universe is full of perverse-minded and deluded persons imbued with powerful attachment (and aversion) faults. — *Bha* 1864

> Even after having the difficult to get *bodhi*, one engages in negligence or laxity (*pramāda*) (*Bha* 1865), with the result that it is difficult to get again the *bodhi* jewel fallen in the ocean.
> — *Bha* 1866

> Blessed are those who are enlightened in *dharma* (replete with instructions) of Lord Jina and adopt and follow that *dharma*.
>
> — *Bha* 1867

Human birth is a rare thing and enlightenment (*bodhi*) is rarer. The acquisition of enlightened worldview (*samyak darśana*) is the first step towards the accomplishment of enlightenment.

The following four things are increasingly difficult: (1) human birth; (2) listening to the scriptural texts; (3) to have faith in *dharma*; and (4) to undertake effort, or exertion needed for self-restraint, i.e. vigour and valour or valiance in *dharma* (*Uttarādhyayanasūtra* 3.1; *Samanasutta* 526-528).

In other words:

> After getting human birth, one who listens to *dharma* (righteousness and piety) and having faith in that makes efforts, i.e. behaves according to that, such *tapasvī* (one who undertakes austerities) while preventing future or fresh *karmas*, beats or destroys the kārmic dust of collected or accumulated (*sañcita*) *karma*.
>
> — *Uttarādhyayansūtra* 3.11

Understanding that it is difficult to get human birth, one should attain enlightenment (*bodhi*) (*Sūtrakr̥tāṅga* 1.7.11).

Conclusion

The twelve reflections are very useful in inculcating a realistic attitude in life. The first two reflections result in equanimity and a feeling of fearlessness. The next two (third and fourth) contemplations affirm the concept of *ekatva-vibhakta*. The fifth and sixth reflections remind one that the relentless cycle of births and deaths is full of sorrow and anxiety and that self-reliance is the only way out. The seventh to tenth contemplations speak of the influx of *karmas* (*āsrava*), etc. nine categories, including inanimate body, which are states-of-evolution of the Self. The pure nature of the Self is however quite distinct from them. The last two reflections of *dharma* and *bodhi-durlabha* emphasize that moral and spiritual discipline and discriminative insight alone lead to the path of liberation.

The above-mentioned twelve affirmations or reflections on different facets or angles of reality known as *bhāvanās* provide us valuable insights which help us stop clinging to a distorted or dogmatic view and correct our vision. These contemplations are, thus, inextricably linked with right perception/vision or enlightened worldview (*samyak darśana*). They enable us to view life and its problems in a realistic perspective and saves us from negative thoughts, which are indeed distortions or exaggeration of the truth.

A person who is equipped with *samyak darśana*, clarity of vision or a realistic perspective in life is better prepared to face its challenges and make mature and balanced decisions in difficult situations. As a result, a person confronts the situation in life with patience, courage, confidence, enthusiasm and energy. He neither reflects on the glories of the past nor indulges in wild expectations about the future. He remains a matter-of-fact person and does not live in a make-believe world.

It is wrong to think that these twelve affirmations or contemplations (*bhāvanās*) are designed or aimed at renunciation from the world and the worldly life (*vairāgya upavana*). These reflections are as much useful in this world as they are for moral and spiritual advancement. The five benefits of these affirmations or reflections may be summarized as follows. First, they enable a person to maintain one's cool in adverse situations and one is better prepared to face an untoward incident. Second, a person remains focused on the present and does not waste one's time and energy in reflecting about the past or the future. Third, one adopts a positive attitude in life. Fourth, they teach important lessons of self-reliance, detachment and equanimity. Fifth, they facilitate creativity, peace and happiness in life.

Jayasena's additional verses in *Samayasāra* (*SS* 10*1 and 10*2) (not found in Amrtachandra's recension) state:

> One should indeed contemplate on knowledge (*jñāna*), intuition or perception (*darśana*) and conduct (*caritra*), which are only Self alone. The saint, who contemplates on the Self attains liberation in a short time from all sufferings.

A person who has destroyed the blemishes of infatuation and being detached from sense objects, restrains his mind and unwaveringly situated (and engaged) the intrinsic (pure) nature of his own Self, becomes a contemplator of the Self (*PS* 196). In reply to the question as to what does such a person contemplate, Kundakunda provides the answer in *Pravacanasāra* 198 as follows:

> Set free from all afflictions and hindrances, rich with complete happiness and knowledge in all his faculties beyond or transcendental to (others) and sense organs, he without sense activities, contemplates supreme happiness.

The human body, mildness of passions like anger and also the company of good people are obtained by the devotion of the pure Self, i.e. attaining of enlightened worldview, enlightened knowledge and enlightened conduct is extremely difficult.

The twelve reflections, J.J. Jaini (1956: 150) states,

> must be meditated upon again and again. As to the first kind of meditation, viz. transitoriness, *anitya anuprekṣā*, it must be noted that as substance (*dravya*), everything is permanent. Only *paryāya* condition is transitory. Of the matter assimilated as *karma* and by the soul that which is accepted by the soul is called *upatta*. The rest is *anupatta* matter which is taken in by the soul.

Due to the availability or obtaining the proximity or presence (*sānnidhya*) of the twelve reflections like *anitya* and acquisition, maintenance and preservation of excellent (*uttama*) forgiveness (*kṣamā*), etc., there is great inhibition of *karmas* (*saṁvara*).

Anuprekṣā (contemplation) is the supportive factor (*nimitta*) [or the auxiliary cause (*nimitta kāraṇa*)] of both *kṣamā*, etc. *dharma* and *saṁvara*. That is why the term *anuprekṣā* is given in the middle of *dharma* and *pariṣaha-jaya* (see *Tattvārthasūtra* IX.2) which states:

> *Saṁvara* is produced by *guptī* (self-restraints of mind, speech and body), *samiti* (carefulness in walking, speaking, etc.), *dharma*, *anuprekṣā*, *pariṣaha-jaya* and *caritra* (conduct).

The Self by pondering over *anuprekṣās* cherishes and maintains a proper manner excellent *kṣamā*, etc. *dharma* and is enthusiastic, encouraged and inspired to conquer the hardships and sufferings (*pariṣaha*) (*SAS* 811).

For the sake of now-falling off from the path (*mārga*) of liberation and for the shedding off (*nirjarā*) (of kārmic matter, whatever sufferings are undergone (are called) the *pariṣaha* (sufferings (*TS* IX.8)), they are worth tolerance or forbearance (*Sarvārthasiddhi* 812).

Due to the exposition, treatment or topic of *saṁvara*, that is marking out or distinguishing (*viśāsana*) of the path (*mārga*) (of liberation). Therefore, the term coming in the aphorism (*TS* IX.8) one should grasp the path of *saṁvara*. For not falling therefrom and for *nirjarā* are *pariṣaha*, which are worth tolerance or forbearance.

Through tolerance or forbearance of hunger, thirst, etc. (twenty-two *pariṣaha* mentioned in *TS* IX.9), not falling from the *mārga* expounded by Lord Jina, through constant practice of the *mārga*, one obtains liberation by engaging in shedding off (*nirjarā*) or *karmas* in the sequence of doing *saṁvara* of the door of the inflow of *karmas* and experiencing of the fruition of *karmas* (*karmaphala*) successively (*aupakramika*) (*SAS* 813).

There are twenty-two *pariṣaha* (sufferings), which are mentioned in *Tattvārthasūtra* IX.9 (see *supra*).

Vilas Sangave (1990: iv) concluded his discussion on twelve *anuprekṣās* in these words:

> The twelve *anuprekṣās* (reflections) have been brought out in such an order that the aspirant may gradually go on diverting his thoughts from the outer world to his own pure nature of the Self. It is clear that these thoughts when reflected upon serve as a ladder for the soul of a man to rise up spiritually. It is also emphasized that these reflections are of great practical value because the practice of these contemplations makes the way clear for the attainment of *mokṣa*.

M.K. Dharma Raja, the translator and editor of *Bārasa Aṇuvekkhā* (1990: 5-6), concludes his description of twelve *anuprekṣās* as follows:

> An individual attached to worldly objects first perceives that they are but transitory. The gradual decay of one's own physical form — a predicament from which none can be saved – then becomes clear. Then follows the realization that one's present life cannot last indefinitely. This leads to the reflection that he is born all alone and that he alone endures all the troubles and tribulations in this life. He alone is responsible for all his miseries as well as

his good fortune. Similarly, he is left to face death all by himself marking his exit from this life.

The seeker proceeds to observe that all other things — animate and inanimate — are quite distinct from himself. Contemplating then on the continually revolving cycle of birth, death and rebirth that has been his lot, the seeker perceives that his immortal Self has been drifting, devoid of peace, all the time. The universe where the unending phenomena of births and deaths take place is eternal but, eternal peace, therefore, cannot be attained here. From this thought follows a progressive diminution of attachment to the impure body containing the pure Self. Attention then is focused on factors that determine the myriad varieties of existence. It is recognized that one's own acts cause the accumulation of kārmic dirt which holds him in bondage. Such activities then must be stopped and *karmas* previously accumulated, eliminated. This can be achieved by treading the path of the right faith, right knowledge and right conduct. The one and only rare opportunity to follow this path to salvation occurs in human life. It is, therefore, one's life as a human being that presents the most favourable conditions for the attainment of *mokṣa*.

Constant contemplations on these sublime aspirations enable the seeker to liberate himself from bondage. They are the stepping stones on the path to final salvation and supreme bliss.

Concluding his observations on the twelve *anuprekṣās*, A.N. Upadhye states:

> These bits of evidence, both positive and negative, culled together from the present-day canon leads us to the following conclusions: *Aṇṇuppehā* is recognized right from the beginning as a potent agency for the destruction of *karmas*; it accompanied *dhyāna* (meditation), both *dharma-dhyāna* and *śukla-dhyāna*; the four *anuprekṣās* of the latter did not get incorporated, like those of the former in the standardized list of the twelve *anuprekṣās*.
>
> The twelve *anuprekṣās* en bloc mentioned in the early canon (Schubring 1935: 119, 198, 199ff.; Atmaram 1936: 18ff.) which notes some other *anuprekṣās* than those included under the

> grouping of twelve. Later these *anuprekṣās*, when perhaps treatises were composed on them, came to be included under or associated with *svādhyāya* (study).
>
> The first four *anuprekṣās* stand as a group and very well represent the memorable themes of ascetic poetry: the next two also can go with them; then the seventh, eighth and ninth stand together as basic dogmas of Jainism, and the last three go together as a positive glorification of the doctrines preached by the Jina. Once the twelve *anuprekṣās* were enumerated, they served as a basis on which individual authors could compose comprehensive treatises which are not only valuable compendiums of Jaina doctrines but also repositories of great ethical sermons and of didactic poetry of abiding moral value and appeal. — Svami Kumar 1945: 8

Concluding his discussion on twelve *anuprekṣās*, Vaṭṭakera in *Mūlācāra* states:

> In brief, the twelve contemplations (*anuprekṣās*) are considered to give rise to detachment from the world (*vairāgya*) in Jaina scriptures. — *Mūlācāra* 765
>
> He who contemplates on the nature of the Self through these twelve *anuprekṣās* attains liberation (*mokṣa*) by being devoid of or free from all *karmas*. — *Mūlācāra* 766
>
> He who leads the destruction of *karmas* through meditation (*dhyāna*), he who opens the wooden bar or bolt (*argalia*) of *mokṣa*, he who is free from infatuation (*moha*) and he who delves deep into *tāmasika* and *rājasika* nature of things, that Lord Jina help us to cross over the world (of miseries) quickly or soon.
>
> — *Mūlācāra* 767

In this way, the eighth chapter of the narrative of the twelve *anuprekṣās* composed by Vaṭṭakera in *Mūlācāra* with the commentary thereon by Acharya Vasunandi ends.

In its concluding remarks on the twelve contemplations (*bhāvanās*), *Jñārnārṇava* describes the effect or reward and the grandeur or greatness of the contemplations of twelve *anuprekṣās* in the following words:

> By continuously contemplating the twelve reflections, the enlightened souls (*jñānī*) attain imperishable (*akṣaya*) happiness without any apprehension or fear. —*Jñā* 1
>
> By the continuous practice of the twelve contemplations, the fire of passions like anger is extinguished, the decaying of attachment towards other objects takes place and the lamp of enlightenment and understanding, intelligence or cognition (*bodha*) is illumined after the destruction of the darkness of ignorance or perverted knowledge (*ajñāna*). —*Jñā* 2
>
> The twelve contemplations are definitely the friend or confidante of the Goddess of fortune or prosperity (Lakṣmī) of the nature of liberation (*mukti*). —*Jñā* 3

Bhagavatī Ārādhanā concludes the discussion of the twelve *anuprekṣās* in the following words:

> The *anuprekṣās* are the support (*ālambana*) of righteous concentration (*dharma-dhyāna*). By taking refuge or shelter of these *ālambanas*, which are the supportive factors of *dhyāna*, one is not deviated or strayed from *dhyāna*. — *Bha* 1868
>
> Reading (*vācana*), questioning inquiry on a doubtful point (*pracchanna*), memorizing, using, application or reflection (*parivartana*) and all the contemplations (*anuprekṣā*) are favourable, comfortable or helpful support of righteous concentration (*dharma-dhyāna*). In other words, *dharma-dhayāna* is done with their help. — *Bha* 1869

Counterparts to Anuprekṣā in Buddhism

Buddhism, as stated earlier, lays a great deal of emphasis on the contemplation of *anitya* (called *anicchā* in Buddhism), the transitoriness of all worldly sufferings.

Jainism and Buddhism, according to A.N. Upadhye, have much in common in both ethical outlook and moral fervour. Both of them, in fact, belong to the same current of Indian thought, the Śramaṇic culture. It is natural therefore that ideas corresponding to *anuprekṣā*, individually and collectively, are found in Buddhism as well.

Upadhye goes on to list the following:

1. Objectively speaking, *anitya-a* has a better place in Buddhism than in Jainism, because, according to the latter, it is only the *paryāyas* (modes) that are *anitya*, the substance being *nitya* (*Dhammapada* 277).
2. Under *aśaraṇa-a*, it is stressed that death is certain and none can save one from its clutches (*Dhammapada* 128, 160 and 188-190; *Bodhicaryāvatāra* II.42, 46 — Śāntideva 1901).
3. As under *saṁsāra-a*, plenty of reflection on the nature of *saṁsāra* is found in Buddhist texts (*Bodhicaryāvatāra* II.28-29).
4. Corresponding to the *ekatva-a*, that the soul has to enjoy and suffer all alone is very similarly expressed in Buddhist texts (*Bodhicaryāvatāra* II.62, VIII.33).
5. Reminding one of *aśuci-a* and *anyatva-a*, that the body is separate from the soul and full of impurity is a favourite same in Buddhist texts (*Bodhicaryāvatāra* V.62-63, VIII.52).

Then for the *anuprekṣās*, as a whole, Upadhye adds, much similarity is found in what are known as ten *anussatis* (this list was first of six and later expanded to ten subjects) in Buddhism and elaborated in *Viśuddhi-Magga* (*VM*). They are enumerated thus: (1) *Buddha-anussati*; (2) *dhamma-a*; (3) *saṁgha-a*; (4) *śīla-a*; (5) *cāga-a*; (6) *devatā-a*; (7) *maraṇa-a*; (8) *kāyagata-a*; (9) *anapāna-a*; and (10) *upaśama-a*. The term *anussati* (*anu-smṛti*) closely resembles *anuprekṣā*. These are really topics for reflection and meditation.

The *dhamma-anussati*, according to Upadhye, basically corresponds to *dharma-a*. Though the details are differently elaborated, the term *svakhyāta* is common (VII.68ff.) and the way in which *dharma* is glorified has much similarity (88). In Buddhism, *śīla-a* (VII.101ff.) emphasizes topics (105) which correspond to those included under *saṁvara-a*. The *maraṇa-a* (VIII.1ff.) has some agreement in contents with *saṁsāra-a*.

Some of the expressions remind one of the topics coming under *anitya-a* and *aśaraṇa-a*. *Anussati* is a *bhāvanā*. The *kāyagata-a* deals with the impurity and the detestable constables of the body (VIII.45ff.) and thus corresponds to *aśucitva-a*. On the impurity of body, there is some discussion in the *aśubha-kammatthāna* (VI.89ff.). The *anapāna-a* contains some topics which remind one of *anitya-a* (VIII.234).

It is true, Upadhye concludes, that the details elaborated in the *Viśuddhi-Magga* are different from those found in Jaina works, but the basic community of ideas is strikingly similar. Some of these are included under *samādhi-bhāvanā*, and this *bhāvanā* leads to the stoppage of *karmas* as the commentary on *Catuḥśataka* (VII.14) puts it:

bhāvanāya kleśnirodhato niruddhatvāt ।

Thus, both in Jainism and Buddhism the object to be achieved through *bhāvanā* is the same (Svami Kumar 1945: 14-15).

PART TWO

Bārasa Aṇuvekkhā

Text, Transliteration, Translation and Commentary

Introduction

Acharya Kundakunda was an outstanding thinker, reformer, organizer, philosopher, teacher, poet, saint as well as a living legend. His importance within both Jainism and the Jaina philosophical tradition is incomparable. The Jainas always considered his name to be of great special significance. In fact, in the Digambara sect of Jains, he is revered next only to Lord Mahāvīra and his apostle Gautam Gaṇadhara. As the leader of Mūla Saṅgha (basic ascetics), he was indeed the most prominent. The origin of almost all the lineages of the Digambara monks is therefore traced to Kundakunda.

According to A.N. Upadhye, Kundakunda flourished in the beginning of the Christian era. Apart from *Bārasa Aṇuvekkhā*, his other prominent works are: *Samayasāra* (SS), *Pravacanāsara* (PS), *Pañcāstikāyasāra* (PKS) and *Niyamasāra* (NS).

Bārasa Aṇuvekkhā (*Twelve Reflections*) is the first-ever classic literature on the subject of the "Twelve Contemplations". According to Suresh Chand Jain (1990), Secretary, Kundakunda Bharati:

> Jain religion accords top priority to spirituality. The focus is on the soul in the realm of spirituality. Attention can be riveted on the soul (*ātmā*), only through proper understanding of the real nature of worldly distractions like relationship with one's kith and kin, the craving of the senses and the physical body. When this stark reality is grasped and is contemplated upon, a spirit of renunciation of these is bound to arise in the mind.
>
> The basic value of this classic lies in its stress on this truth from which emerges *dharma*. The very source of *dharma* and the sustaining stimulus for its blossoming in ultimate sublimation are derived from these twelve contemplations.

In his Foreword to M.K. Dharma Raja's book, Vilas Sangave (1990: iii) observes:

> *Bārasa Aṇuvekkhā* (i.e. Twelve Reflections or Contemplations) is of great significance both from the real and practical points of view.

> For cultivating the necessary religious attitude, it is enjoined on all to constantly reflect on twelve facts [or facets] of life. These reflections are known as *aṇuvekkhās* (*anuprekṣās*). It is laid down that these *anuprekṣās* should be thought upon . . . again and again. These twelve *anuprekṣās* have been discussed in minute detail by Acharya Kundakunda in his treatise *Bārasa Aṇuvekkhā*.

In his English translation, M.K. Dharma Raja has described and translated ninty-one verses, without mentioning that verse 91 is an interpolation. In his Hindi book on *Bārasa Aṇuvekkhā* edited by Devendra Kumar Shastri (1991), ninety-two verses are given and he has stated that verses 91 and 92 are interpolations.

The twelve contemplations (*anuprekṣās*), called *Bāraha Bhāvanā*, are extremely *pracalita* (in vogue), in force, or in use amongst Jains. All subsequent writers have followed Kundakunda in the description of these contemplations.

The distinguishing feature or characteristic of these contemplations is that at the end of each of the twelve contemplations (*bhāvanās*), there is a description of the internal, self-referential point of view/perspective (*niścaya naya* or *niścaya dṛṣṭi*). For instance, at the end of *ekatva bhāvanā*, it is stated:

> I am one, alone, solitary (*ekko-aham*), that nothing whatever or no other (living or non-living) is mine, that I am pure, characterized by knowledge and intuition and that identity or oneness (*ekatva*) with the pure nature of the Self is worth acquiring (*upādeya*) (or to be aspired for). The self-restrained person ought to contemplate in this manner.
>
> — *BA* 20

In the *saṁsāra bhāvanā*, Kundakunda mentioned the cycles of births and deaths or rounds of five kinds of transmigration. Other commentators including Pūjyapāda have adopted the very same without any changes. At the end of the treatise, he has written:

> I have described whatever contemplations in the form of *niścaya* (internal, self-referential) (or) *vyavahāra* (external, other of); one who contemplates on them with your mind, he attains supreme liberation.
>
> — *BA* 91

Bārasa Aṇuvekkhā is extremely splendid and unlike his other works, Kundakunda has also given his name at its end in verse 91.

Except contemplations on *saṁsāra*, *āsrava* and *dharma*, which have been described in fourteen, fourteen and fifteen verses respectively, the remaining nine verses have been described in not more than seven verses. *Nirjarā* has been described only in two verses and *anyatva* in three verses.

These contemplations have been the foundation on which Kundakunda has expounded splendid thoughts, which are the reflection or mirror of moral conduct and thoughts.

Invocation

1

णमिऊण सव्वसिद्धे झाणुत्तमखविददीहसंसारे।
दस दस दो दो व जिणे दस दो अणुपेहणं बोच्छे॥

ṇamiūṇa savvasiddhe jhāṇuttamakhavidadīhasaṁsāre ।
dasa dasa do do va jiṇe dasa do aṇupehaṇaṁ bocche ॥

Bowing to all Perfect Souls (*siddhas*), who through excellent meditation (*dhyāna*) had set at nought the protracted cycle of birth and death and, to the twenty-four Jinas, the Tīrthaṅkaras, I shall describe the twelve contemplations or reflections (*anuprekṣās*).

Commentary

The twenty-four Jinas or Tīrthaṅkaras are exalted, omniscient path-finders, those who have ascended the highest pinnacle of human existence through moral and spiritual attainment. They fulfil a mission of guiding all living beings towards emancipation from the miseries of modern existence. These supreme preceptors are worthy of the utmost veneration.

2

अद्ध्रुवमसरणमेगत्तमण्णसंसारलोगमसुचित्तं।
आसवसंवरणिज्जर धम्मं बोहिं च चिंतेज्जो॥

addhruvamasaraṇamegattamaṇṇasaṁsāralogamasucittaṁ ।
āsavasaṁvaraṇijjara dhammaṁ bohiṁ ca ciṁtejjo ॥

Verse 2 of *Bārasa Aṇuvekkhā* mentions only names of the twelve reflections or contemplations, which have been discussed in detail earlier (see *supra*).

Commentary

The sublime mental contemplations need to be meditated upon because action wilfully performed is enthusiastic and deliberate. Contemplation helps to guide the aspirant to realize enlightenment and salvation.

Shubhachandra, in his work *Jñānārṇava*, states:

> As a result of the constant practice of these twelve contemplations the fire of anger, etc. passions (*kaṣāyas*) are extinguished; attachment to other substances is checked and the dissolving of the darkness of ignorance or perverted knowledge (*ajñāna*) leads to the elimination of the lamp of knowledge.

According to Akalaṅka, when contemplation of *anitya* (transitoriness), etc. subjects becomes of the nature of knowledge and when one's mind is concentrated in those *anitya*, etc. subjects, then the same is called *dharma-dhyāna* (meditation of righteousness).

Adhruva (Impermanence) Anuprekṣā

Earlier we have seen what several commentators, including J.L. Jaini, Vilas Sangave, M.K. Dharma Raja and A.N. Upadhye and Chitrabhanu, have stated regarding *adhruva/anitya*, etc. twelve contemplations or reflections (*anuprekṣās* or *bhāvanās*) or what has been written in *Tattvārthasūtra*, *Sarvārthasiddhi* commentary on *Tattvārthasūtra*, *Maraṇa-Samādhi* and *Mūlācāra*. Now we have to see what Kundakunda has said in *Bārasa Aṇuvekkhā* and what is written in *Kārttikeyānuprekṣā* about each one of the *adhruva*, etc. *anuprekṣās*.

Chapter 1
Transitoriness

3

वरभवणजाणवाहणसयणासणदेवमणुवरायाणं।
मादुपिदुसजणभिच्चसंबंधिणो य पिदिवियाणिच्चा॥

varabhavaṇajāṇavāhaṇasayaṇāsaṇadevamaṇuvarā-
yāṇaṁ ।
mādupidusajaṇabhiccasaṁbaṁdhiṇo ya pidiviyāṇiccā ॥

All material possessions of celestials, human beings and kings — the magnificent mansions, vehicles and carriages, couches and seats as well as their attachment to their kith and kin, father, mother or uncle or to their attendants, etc. are ephemeral. None of these is permanent.

Commentary by M.K. Dharma Raja

The human body that receives so much care and attention is subject to the irrevocable process of decay and death. When life departs, it degenerates into a decaying corpse. The beauty and charm associated with the body is nothing but sheer fantasy. But the soul in the pure sense is real and indestructible or eternal. It is thus essential to free oneself from the worldly distractions of attachments and contemplate on the reality of the Self. The substance (*dravya*) is permanent, but its modes (*paryāya*) are transitory (1990: 8).

4

सामग्गिंदियरूवं आरोग्गं जोव्वणं बलं तेजं।
सोहग्गं लावण्णं सुरधणुमिव सस्सयं ण हवे॥

sāmaggiṁdiyarūvaṁ āroggaṁ jovvaṇaṁ balaṁ tejaṁ ।
sohaggaṁ lāvaṇṇaṁ suradhaṇumiva sassayaṁ ṇa have ॥

[The physical body with] all the sense organs, look or beauty, health and youth, strength, radiance, good fortune and charm – all resemble the rainbow which is ephemeral and vanishes within moments; they are impermanent.

Commentary by M.K. Dharma Raja

The human body, endowed with the faculty of deriving enjoyment and pleasure through its sense organs, is subject to decay. The charm and excellence of the human body are like the pleasant colours of the rainbow making its appearance in the monsoon sky only to recede out of sight, ever so quickly.

The different sense organs of the body yielding enjoyment and pleasure are subject to decadence. The transition from youth to advancing age is accompanied by a gradual weakening of the sense organs. With old age, a steep decline in their functioning sets in, through failing eyesight, weakened hearing, loss of teeth, graying hair and wrinkled skin. These serve as a forewarning of impending death. The charm and excellence associated with the most handsome and robust then are only eloquent reminders of the futility of being engrossed with these transient traits.

The wise would therefore rather contemplate on the unreality of worldly pleasures and the impermanence of the physical body. This introspection leads to a profound reflection on one's inner Self (1990: 9).

5

जलबुब्बुदसक्कधणुखणरुचिघणसोहमिव थिरं ण हवे।
अहमिंदट्ठाणाइं बलदेवप्पहुदिपज्जाया॥

jalabubbudasakkadhaṇukhaṇarucighaṇasohamiva thiraṁ ṇa have ।
ahamiṁdaṭṭhāṇāiṁ baladevappahudipajjāyā ॥

Neither the status of Ahamindras nor the modes (*paryāya*) of Baladevas and the like are everlasting. These are similar to the water bubble, the flash of the lightning and the splendour of the rainbow, which are ephemeral and unstable.

Commentary by M.K. Dharma Raja

The Ahamindras are the denizens of the super-paradise situated above the sixteen heavens and just below the *Siddhaloka* — the permanent abode of the liberated souls. All those who take their birth in these super-heavens and enjoy equal status; all are super-celestial Lords (*aham* (I am), *indira* (the celestial Lord)). They are endowed with the highest spiritual insight and are destined to attain salvation within a limited number of births (maximum of three) after being reborn in human existence.

The Baladevas — series of nine, in each half cycle of time are among the sixty-three most glorified humans (the *Triṣaṣṭi Śalākā Puruṣas*, among the Tīrthaṅkaras are the foremost), listed in canonical scriptures. The *baladeva* is the archetypal ideal of a princely hero, and endowed with all excellences and virtues and the one who attains salvation in that very life.

The Ahamindras and the Baladevas — occupants of the high status among the celestials and the humans — are cited here to underscore the theme of impermanence in mundane existence. Though superlatively endowed, neither an Ahamindra nor a Baladeva enjoys a permanent existence. It is bound to come to its end like the bubble on water, the attractive rainbow in the sky, the brilliant flash of lightning and the splendourous cloud — all fleeting phenomena. It is crystal clear that the status of the high celestial or the mightiest human is transient (1990: 10).

6

जीवणिबद्धं देहं खीरोदयमिव विणस्सदे सिग्घं।
भोगोपभोगकारणदव्वं णिच्चं कहं होदि॥

jīvaṇibaddhaṁ dehaṁ khīrodayamiva viṇassade sigghaṁ ।
bhogopabhogakāraṇadavvaṁ ṇiccaṁ kahaṁ hodi ॥

The body that is linked with the soul, like milk mixed with water, vanishes or disintegrates quite quickly. How can objects of physical consumption (*upabhoga*) and pleasure and enjoyment (*bhoga*) then remain permanent (*nitya*)?

Commentary by M.K. Dharma Raja

The soul leaves its physical body on death and transmigrates into a different body on its rebirths. It apparently remains indistinguishable from the body like milk mixed with water. But despite this close connection, the soul's exit from the body becomes inevitable when death intervenes. The everlasting soul enters into a different physical frame in its next birth. Death comes from the expiry of the age-*karma*. The new birth is determined by the totality of the *karma*-molecules clinging to the soul. While this apparently indissoluble link between the soul and the body is subject to separation, how can one's connection with the objects of worldly pleasure and enjoyment remain intact?

The clear fact of the transitoriness of attachment to worldly objects is here forcibly reinforced. So very slender in the connection between one's real Self and the worldly objects. It is utter folly, therefore, to long for and to remain attached to these transient mundane possessions.

Concentration on this reflection impels the aspirant to contemplate more intensively on the intrinsically detached attitude of the soul (1990: 11).

Commentary

None of the relations or connections is true and continuing, permanent, lasting or enduring (*sthāyī*). None of the objects goes with the soul into the other universe (*para-loka*).

7

परमट्ठेण दु आदा देवासुरमणुवरायविभवेहिं।
वदिरित्तो सो अप्पा सस्सदमिदि चिंतए णिच्चं॥

paramaṭṭheṇa du ādā devāsuramaṇuvarāyavibhavehiṁ ।
vadiritto so appā sassadamidi ciṅtae ṇiccaṁ ॥

From the transcendental (*paramārtha*) perspective, the soul is apart or distinct from the grandeur, majesty, power and wealth of the celestials, demons, humans and kings. The soul is (always) eternal, immortal (*śāśvata*).

Commentary

Having dealt with the impermanence of worldly objects and the sheer illusion of remaining attached to them, Kundakunda now emphasizes the distinguishing characteristic of the soul — its real, intrinsic attribute of being eternal.

People ordinarily are impressed by the magnificence of the celestials, the awesome powers of the superhuman demons and the majestic splendour of kings and rulers. But all this gloss and glitter, Kundakunda points out, are deceptive like the proverbial mirage. They all come to an end sooner or later. From the transcendental (*paramārtha*) perspective, the soul is distinct from these superficial and extraneous allurements.

The soul transcends superficial allurements, remaining all the while distinct from external encumbrances.

All life is like a stage where each plays his part as a celestial or a monarch, and departs when death intervenes. But the transcendental pure nature of the soul, uninvolved in material attachments, remains constant.

This reflection on the ephemeral nature of mundane life in all its permutations fortifies the aspirant's faith in the indestructible and eternal soul. Constant contemplation on the transience of mundane objects and attachments guides him forward on the path to liberation.

Kārttikeyānuprekṣā

Whatever originates is necessarily destroyed: there is nothing eternal insofar as its modifications are concerned. Birth, youth and wealth are accompanied respectively by death, old age and loss; thus everything is subject to decay. Acquaintances, relatives and possessions are all temporary like a newly-shaped mass of clouds. Sense-pleasures, attendants, domestic animals and conveyances are all temporary like the rainbow or flash of lightning. Meeting with kinsmen is temporary like that of travellers on the way. Howsoever nourished and decked, the body decays like an unbaked earthen pot which crumbles when filled with water.

The (Goddess of) Wealth is not steady even with merited monarchs, then what can one say about common men? She does not feel pleasure in the company of anybody; she stays for a couple of days and is fickle like ripples of water. Wealth, therefore, must be enjoyed and given to the worthy as kindly gifts; in this manner, human life is made more fruitful. Wealth that is hoarded is like a stone; it goes to others or serves the end of rulers and relatives. One, who earns wealth anxiously, greedily and sinfully, but never enjoys it, is verily its slave. By expending one's increasing wealth and religious duties and in giving gifts to the pious and poor, without expecting anything in return, one earns praise and makes one's wealth as well as life fruitful.

Wealth, youth and life are like a bubble of water; it is sheer delusion to understand that they are eternal. Knowing this, one should remove attachment from one's mind whereby the highest bliss is attained (*KA* 4-22).

Chapter 2
Aśaraṇa Anuprekṣā
(Helplessness)

8

मणिमंतोसहरक्खा हयगयरहओ य सयलविज्जाओ।
जीवाणं ण हि सरणं तिसु लोए मरणसमयम्हि॥

maṇimaṁtosaharakkhā hayagayarahao ya sayalavijjāo ।
jīvāṇaṁ ṇa hi saraṇaṁ tisu loe maraṇasamayamhi ।

Neither any immunity from an enchanted gem nor from incantations and medicine nor safety provided by such support like an elephant, a horse in the chariot or all the profundity of learning can afford real protection to anyone in the three worlds at the moment of death.

Commentary by M.K. Dharma Raja

In this verse, Acharya Kundakunda refers to the steps variously resorted to in the world in order to ward off ailments and to save the life of the afflicted.

Precious stones, believed to possess curative properties, were used in the past both to ward off evil and to heal those stricken by disease. Gems were also being used as talismans. The offering of prayers and the recitation of specially prescribed incantations were also in vogue as a device to facilitate recovery from ailments or to avert disasters.

The monarchs then, as now, had their lines of defence like horses, elephants and chariots comparable to armoured carriers, tanks or helicopters and the warplanes of today. But when death strikes, not all these aids and not even the most sophisticated and esoteric formula can rescue living beings anywhere in the three worlds from this irrevocable predicament.

The cosmos of the universe comprises of three layers or three worlds — the upper, the middle and the lower segments. All those living in these three worlds are, without exception, subject to the inexorable law of mortality. They are all bound to die at the expiry of their age-*karma*, when nothing anywhere can protect anyone from this inevitable end.

This sublime reflection generates in the seeker a sense of non-attachment to the physical body and the material possessions and objects of pleasure and enjoyment. He thus concentrates on the eternal soul that never dies (1990: 13-14).

9

सग्गो हवे हि दुग्गं भिच्चा देवा या पहरणं वज्जं ।
अइरावणो गइंदो इंदस्स ण विज्जदे सरणं ॥

saggo have hi duggaṁ bhiccā devā yā paharaṇaṁ vajjaṁ ।
airāvaṇo gaiṁdo iṁdassa ṇa vijjade saraṇaṁ ॥

No protection is available (at death) even to Indra (the celestial Lord), who has the heaven as his fortress, the celestials as his attendants, the *vajra* as his weapon and the Airāvata elephant (as his mount).

Commentary by M.K. Dharma Raja

Acharya Kundakunda, in this verse, elaborates on the theme that even the mightiest Indra is helpless in the face of death, which is inevitable.

The celestial Lord — the Indra — is looked upon as among the most formidable. The heaven — his domain — is an invulnerable fort. At his beck and call are celestial beings gifted with miraculous powers. His weapon is the *vajra* that can destroy any missile but is itself invincible. And for his mount, Indra has the wondrous

Airāvata elephant capable of getting him anywhere. Airāvata is, in fact, a celestial assuming the form of an elephant. He is endowed with the power of assuming any form, large and minute (macro and micro).

Despite all these resources, even this Lord of the celestials has nothing to save him when his ordained period of heavenly life comes to an end. Is it not utterly unwise, therefore, to harbour worldly attachments of any kind? (1990: 14-15).

10

णवणिहि चउदहरयणं हयमत्तगइंदचाउरंगबलं ।
चक्केसस्स ण सरणं पेच्छंतो कद्दये कालो ॥

ṇavaṇihi caudaharayaṇaṁ hayamattagaiṅdacāu-
raṅgabalaṁ ।
cakkesassa ṇa saraṇaṁ pecchaṅto kaddaye kālo ।।

When death comes even a *Cakravartī*, with his nine treasures, fourteen regal assets (described as gems), horses, the rampaging tusker (intoxicated elephant) and the four-tiered army — has none in sight to save him.

Commentary by M.K. Dharma Raja

The universal monarch, the *Cakravartī*, is the most opulent, the most resourceful, the mightiest and unrivalled on Earth — the ruler of all the six continents in Bhāratakṣetra. He has the most coveted assets on earth — the nine precious regalia, comprising the coffer of wealth, the lore of learning and the fine arts. He also owns the most desirable possessions, fourteen in number referred to as "gems". Among these is the all-conquering weapon — the radiant disc — the *Cakra Ratna*, which precedes his armed forces — setting out to quell any challenge. The universal monarch also has at his disposal a four-tiered fighting force [foot soldiers or infantrymen, those warriors riding on horses, elephants and on chariots], numerically, the largest.

But even this most resourceful and formidable universal monarch is powerless when death comes knocking at his door. How helpless then is the fate of ordinary mortals in such a predicament?

The inference here is that human life is brief. Since it is possible only for a human to attain the final liberation (*mokṣa*), every moment of the fleeting life on earth is to be devoted to achieve the supreme objective. Contemplation on this fact of absolute helplessness in facing death is yet another factor fortifying the aspirant in his self-purifying exercises. The Self alone is his own protector (1990: 15).

11

जाइजरामरणरोगभयदो रक्खेदि अप्पणो अप्पा।
तम्हा आदा सरणं बंधोदयसत्तकम्मवदिरित्तो॥

jāijarāmaraṇarogabhayado rakkhedi appaṇo appā ।
tamhā ādā saraṇaṁ baṁdhodayasattakammavadiritto ॥

The transcendental, pure nature of the Self, which is distinct or apart, is the only refuge, shelter or protection (*śaraṇa*) from birth, old age, death, disease and fear, devoid of the bondage of *karmas*, and their fruition as also their very existence or presence in the Self [i.e. the pure nature of the Self is distinct or apart from the defilement, impurity and limitations of *karmas*].

Commentary

The Self, which transcends the relative standpoint of the soul being bound by *karmas* and not bound with *karmas* (*SS* 142), is pure in the sense of being non-relational or independent of *karmas* (*karma-nirapekṣa*), *pāriṇāmika bhāva* (consciousness-as-such), not in the sense of being devoid of or free from *karmas* (*karma-rahita*), as in the liberated state. The transcendental pure Self has, however, the potential to be *karma-rahita* pure. Potential means that one has to make efforts to attain the objective of liberation.

Commentary by M.K. Dharma Raja

The mundane soul, on the other hand, is continually enmeshed in the cycle of birth, death and rebirth. Its continuous existence in varying conditions, high and low, with vulnerability to disease and fear, are determined by the accretion of *karmas* and by the coming into operation, rise (*udaya*) or fruition. There can be no immunity from the inexorable operation of *karmas* until the circumstances of the influx are stopped.

Arihanta, *siddha*, *ācārya* (head of saints), *upādhyāya* (teachers of saints) and *sādhu* are the five exalted, most favoured and adorable supreme spiritual dignitaries (*parameṣṭhi*) of Jainism, characterized by 46, 8, 36, 25 and 28 qualities respectively.

The five *Parameṣṭhi* are said to be the protection or shelter due to being immersed, engrossed or absorbed in their own pure nature of the Self; hence they are considered protection for me (*BA* 12). Moreover, they are described as protection from the external, other-referential point of view (*vyavahāra naya*). In reality, they are the particular condition or particular mode (*avasthā viśeṣa* or *paryāya viśeṣa*) of only the Self (*ātmā*) alone. Consequent upon the evolution of that condition, the said supreme, glorious, divine to be adored (*Bhāgavata* or *Bhagavān*) condition is on its own (*svayam*) illuminated; then the five *parameṣṭhi Bhagavān* are said to be the protection (Shastri 1991: 13).

Commentary

In view of the above, the enlightened or right worldview or belief (*samyaktva*), right knowledge, right conduct and right austerities (*sat tapa*) — these four are the features, qualities being the result of the soul's own efforts or attempts that inhere, exist or are comprised in the Self (*ādā* in Prākṛt and *ātmani* in Sanskrit) itself alone. Therefore, only the Self alone is my protection, shelter or refuge (*śaraṇa*) (*BA* 13) of Kundakunda from the internal, self-referential point of view (*niścaya naya*).

12

अरुहा सिद्धाइरिया उवझाया साहु पंचपरमेट्ठी।
ते वि हु चिट्ठदि आदे तम्हा आदा हु मे सरणं॥

aruhā siddhāiriyā uvajhāyā sāhu pañcaparameṭṭhī ।
te vi hu ciṭṭhadi āde tamhā ādā hu me saraṇaṁ ॥

All the adorable souls — the Arihantas, the *siddhas*, the *ācāryas*, the *upādhyāyas* and the *sādhus* — these exalted, most revered and adorable souls, known as *Pañca Parameṣṭhis* (the five most revered souls), themselves, in fact, remain absorbed in their own transcendental pure nature of the Self, which is my only refuge, shelter or protection.

Commentary

The Arihantas are the Omniscient Lords, the conquerors of their inner weaknesses or faults of attachment, aversion and infatuation, pride or ego, etc. The *siddhas* are the liberated pure souls, who have destroyed all *karmas*. The *ācāryas* are the heads of the saints, the noble souls. The *upādhyāyas* are the spiritual preceptors or teachers of the saints. The *sādhus* (saints) are the noble souls, who are continually engaged in the moral and spiritual advancement of their soul, so as to attain liberation, i.e. the state of *arihanta* and *siddha*.

The above-mentioned five dignitaries are the most revered souls. Since they are and have been engaged in self-absorption to reach or attain their present exalted and their revered status, we should also consider our own Self as the only protection or refuge (*śaraṇa*).

13

सम्मत्तं सण्णाणं सच्चारित्तं च सत्तवो चेव।
चउरो चिट्ठदि आदे तम्हा आदा हु मे सरणं॥

sammattaṁ saṇṇāṇaṁ saccārittaṁ ca sattavo ceva ।
cauro ciṭṭhadi āde tamhā ādā hu me saraṇaṁ ॥

Enlightened worldview (*samyaktva* or *samyak darśana*), enlightened knowledge, enlightened conduct (*samyak cāritra*) and enlightened penance or austerity (*samyak tapa*) — these four are the outcomes or results of one's endeavour or exertion for the purification of their own Self, in order to attain liberation, therefore my own Self alone is my refuge or protection (*śaraṇa*).

Commentary

The enlightened worldview or right belief, enlightened knowledge, enlightened conduct and enlightened austerities together constitute the path of liberation (*mokṣa*). The Self alone is capable of attaining these four characteristics which revel or inhere in the Self.

Kārttikayānuprekṣā

While Kundakunda expounds *aśaraṇa anuprekṣā* in six verses (*BA* 8-13), *Kārttikayānuprekṣā* describes this *anuprekṣā* in nine verses (*KA* 23-31) in these words:

> What protection is there in *saṁsāra*, when it is seen that Indra suffers ruin and Hari, Hara, *Brahman*, etc. are victims of time. There is no rescue from death as in the case of a deer which has come under the paw of a lion. No God, spell, ritual or *kṣetrapāla* can save a man from death. None, howsoever strong, fierce or well-guarded can escape death. It is only a pervert belief that makes one seek the shelter of planets, *bhūta*, *piśācī*, *yoginī* and *yakṣa*. Everyone has to die at the termination of his *āyuṣ*. The *ātman*, which is constituted of right faith, knowledge and conduct, is the only shelter; and it should be duly tempered with qualities like forbearance, etc.

Chapter 3
Ekatva Anupreksạ̄
(Being Alone/Solitary)

14

एक्को करेदि कम्मं एक्को हिंडदि य दीहसंसारे।
एक्को जायदि मरदि य तस्स फलं भुंजदे एक्को॥

ekko karedi kammaṁ ekko hiṅḍadi ya dīhasaṁsāre ।
ekko jāyadi maradi ya tassa phalaṁ bhuṅjade ekko ॥

Each (individual) Self alone performs its actions (*karmas*). Each one alone transmigrates in the long span of mundane existence. Each one is born alone; each one dies alone; and each one alone experiences the consequences of his/her actions (*karmas*).

Commentary

Every Self alone performs sinful or meritorious, good or bad actions (*karmas*) and, accordingly, attracts and binds *karma* molecules and suffers the consequences thereof. Each individual Self moves or transmigrates in the cycle of birth and death all alone.

Commentary by M.K. Dharma Raja

"Reap as you sow" is the inexhorable law governing the operation of bondage of *karmas*. Each individual is the architect of his/her own fate. The stark reality of the utter solitariness of the individual soul is the principle of mundane life enunciated in the verse. The logical corollary that follows is that each one alone has to strive for his/her salvation (1990: 20).

15

एक्को करेदि पावं विसयणिमित्तेण तिव्वलोहेण।
णिरयतिरियेसु जीवो तस्स फलं भुंजदे एक्को॥

ekko karedi pāvaṁ visayaṇimitteṇa tivvaloheṇa ।
ṇirayatiriyesu jīvo tassa phalaṁ bhuṁjade ekko ॥

The Self alone performs sinful action due to the objects of the sensual pleasures acting as a supportive factor (*nimitta*) and intense feeling of greed, and suffers the consequences thereof in hell or subhuman (animal and birds, etc.) existence all alone.

Commentary by M.K. Dharma Raja

The kārmic bondage that vitiates the soul is the direct outcome of its own actions. It is intense desire that impels an individual to commit sin. The desire arises in one's own mind. Individual volition is therefore the source of sensual desire — the great prompting sinful action.

The five senses of touch, taste, smell, sight and sound are the sources of one's desire. Those perversely inclined are driven to sinful action because of their undue attachment to sensual objects and their intense desire for sensual enjoyment. Perverse thoughts prompt individuals to do crimes like theft or deceit, the accumulation of wealth by wrong means or other sinful acts like debauchery and homicide.

The accretion of *karmas* tainting the individual Self due to such perversities and results in its rebirth in hell or in other subhuman conditions. Its next birth is conditioned by the degree and the kind of the sins committed. The nether-world of hell itself has seven categories marked by an increasing rigour or agony, downwards stage-by-stage in the scale. The miseries to be undergone are commensurate with the sin committed.

It is, therefore, essential to consider the mind from the distractions of sensual desires. A spiritually disciplined mind remains unsullied by the blemish of these temptations (1990: 21).

16

एक्को करेदि पुण्णं धम्मणिमित्तेण पत्तदाणेण।
मणुवदेवेसु जीवो तस्स फलं भुंजदे एक्को॥

ekko karedi puṇṇaṁ dhammaṇimitteṇa pattadāṇeṇa ।
maṇuvadevesu jīvo tassa phalaṁ bhuṅjade ekko ॥

The Self alone performs meritorious deeds by offering charity to the worthy, due to *dharma* (righteousness and piety) acting as a supportive factor (*nimitta*) in that regard and experiences the consequences thereof in human or celestial existence all alone.

Commentary by M.K. Dharma Raja

Righteous thoughts and deeds lead to the acquisition of virtue (*puṇya*). The impulse to do good and to tread the path of virtue is, in fact, an investment for the good of the soul. The virtuous perform meritorious acts not for personal benefit but as a matter of duty. The consequences are wholesome just as sinful thoughts and acts pave the way for misery in the future.

The pious perform a number of acts as daily duties. These are the worship of the adorable Perfected Souls — the *Arahanta* and *Siddha Parmeṣṭhis*, devotion to end the service of the worthy ascetics, study of scriptures, the practice of restraints, spiritual austerity and the offer of the right kind of charities.

The performance of righteous deeds imbues the soul with virtue (*puṇya*). Such acts arise from individual volition and the doer of the act himself is the beneficiary. The spiritual benefit is not something that can be bequeathed or gifted to others. The *puṇya* accrues to the doer and to none else. It can result in the transmigration of the individual to a higher status in the next birth of human or celestial existence.

Sublime reflection on these lines guides the seeker towards

further detachment and to a greater awareness of spiritual elevation of the Self.

The worthy recipient is one with right faith; those devoid of it are unworthy (1990: 22-23).

17

उत्तमपत्तं भणियं सम्मत्तगुणेण संजुदो साहू।
सम्मादिट्ठी सावय मज्झिमपत्तो हु विण्णेओ॥

uttamapattaṁ bhaṇiyaṁ sammattaguṇeṇa saṅjudo sāhū ।
sammādiṭṭhī sāvaya majjhimapatto hu viṇṇeo ॥

A saint endowed with the quality of enlightened worldview (*samyaktva*) is considered an excellent or most deserving recipient (of charity); while the noble householder having enlightened worldview and observing self-restraints and disciplines is said to be of middle-rung recipient.

Commentary by M.K. Dharma Raja

The dispensing of charity and providing help to the deserving are meritorious acts. Such acts inspire the giver to sublime thoughts. This leads to an accretion of *puṇya* to one's soul. However, this act of offering charity should itself be accomplished in the right manner. Thus, offering charity with devotion and reverence leads to happy consequences (1990: 24).

18

णिद्दिट्ठो जिणसमये अविरदसम्मो जहण्णपत्तो त्ति।
सम्मत्तरयणरहिओ अपत्तमिदि संपरिक्खेज्जो॥

ṇiddiṭṭho jiṇasamaye aviradasammo jahaṇṇapatto tti ।
sammattarayaṇarahio apattamidi saṁparikkhejjo ॥

In Jaina scriptures, a person endowed with enlightened worldview but devoid of self-restraints (*avirat samyak dṛṣṭi*) is said to be a lower-rung recipient (of charity); and he who is devoid of the jewel of enlightened worldview is considered an undeserving, unworthy and ineligible person for receiving charity. Therefore, one should properly examine the credentials of the recipients of charity.

Commentary

Charity (*dāna*) is of four kinds: offering of food (*āhāra dāna*), medicine and medical attention (*auṣadha dāna*), gifting of religious books or literature (*śāstra dāna*) and relieving one of fear (*abhaya dāna*). Of these, offering food is the first and primary. It serves the conditions of all other three *dānas*. It is the supportive factor (*nimitta*) in allaying hunger, thirst and disease. Due to the strength of food, a saint is able to devote himself to the study of scriptures and books. Because food protects the vitalities (*prāṇa*) of a person, it also relieves one of his fears.

There are two versions or descriptions of *Bārasa Aṇuvekkhā* 19: one given in the English translation of M.K. Dharma Raja and the other given by Devendra Kumar Shastri in his Hindi book on *Bārasa Aṇuvekkhā*. We give both of them.

19a

दंसणभट्ठा भट्ठा दंसणभट्ठस्स णत्थि णिव्वाणं।
सिज्झंति चरियभट्ठा दंसणभट्ठा ण सिज्झंति॥

daṁsaṇabhaṭṭā bhaṭṭā daṁsaṇabhaṭṭassa ṇatthi ṇivvāṇaṁ ।
sijjhaṁti cariyabhaṭṭā daṁsaṇabhaṭṭā ṇa sijjhaṁti ॥

Those, who are corrupted or debased of enlightened worldview or right faith, are indeed debased or perverted; they cannot attain salvation. Those who stray from right or enlightened conduct can be claimed and redeemed and, thus, can attain salvation, but those devoid of enlightened worldview or right belief (*samyak darśana*) cannot be reclaimed or redeemed.

Commentary

Those who are debased of the right worldview or faith, and whose belief is erroneous or perverted and who are seized or possessed of prejudice or bias, misguided zeal and stubbornness, it is not possible to set them right or improve them; their acquisition of enlightened or right conduct is difficult. Moreover, without internal *samyak darśana*, one cannot attain liberation by external conduct alone.

Samyak darśana is the source or the foundation of righteousness and piety (*dharma*). Without *samyak darśana*, neither knowledge can be of *samyak* (right or enlightened) nor conduct can be *samyak*, and all three together constitute the path of liberation. Thus, *samyak darśana* is the first step in liberation.

19b

In Devendra Kumar Shastri's *Bārasa Aṇuvekkhā*, this verse (19) is given as the last verse (verse 92) as interpolation. This verse is originally of *Darśana Pāhuḍa* (verse 3) and is coming in *Bhagavatī Ārādhanā* as verse 738.

The Self alone destroys difficult and burdensome (*viṣama*) *karmas* by striving towards the path expounded by the Omniscient Lord (Jina). In reality, the happiness of liberation is excellent (*utkṛṣṭa*); one who follows the path of true happiness experiences one's own pure Self all alone.

20

एक्कोहं णिम्ममो सुद्धो णाणदंसणलक्खणो ।
सुद्धेयत्तमुपादेयमेवं चिंतेइ संजदो ॥

ekkohaṁ ṇimmamo suddho ṇāṇadaṁsaṇalakkhaṇo ।
suddheyattamupādeyamevaṁ ciṅtei saṅjado ॥

I (*aham*) am *ekko* (*eka*, one, i.e. alone, solitary (*ekkoham*), that nothing whatever or no other living or non-living) is mine (*nirmama*), that I am pure (*śuddha*), characterized by intuition (*darśana*) and knowledge (*jñāna*) and that identity or oneness (*ekatva*) with the pure nature of the Self is worth-acquiring (*upādeya*) (or to be aspired for). The self-restrained (person) ought to contemplate in this way.

Commentary by M.K. Dharma Raja

An individual, disciplined in self-restraint, should contemplate on the reality that the Self in all respects is an independent entity – totally and absolutely unconnected with anything else. He should be well aware that neither his own body nor any other inanimate object has anything to do with his real Self. Individual salvation can be realized only through total detachment.

Such reflections on aloneness of the Self helps the process of progressive detachment. It leads to a state of mind free from both affection for the near and dear, and from animosity of the two adversaries.

Infinite comprehension and perception are the attributes of the soul in its pure state. A soul in mundane existence maintains its individuality. Striving for salvation is entirely an individual effort. The aspirant, therefore, is aware of this salient fact of his state of aloneness. This awareness of the implications of aloneness guides him steadfastly along the path towards liberation (1990: 25).

Krāttikeyānuprekṣā

Kundakunda has described *ekatva anuprekṣā* in seven verses (*BA* 14-20). *Kārttikayānuprekṣā* describes it in six verses (*KA* 74-79) as follows:

> One is all alone while being born, while growing, while suffering and while experiencing the fruits of one's *karmas*. No one else can share one's lot. Religion (consisting of *kṣamā*, etc.) is a good friend to save one from sorrow. When the *ātman* is realized as separate [it should be different or distinct] from the body, one knows what is worthy and what is fit to be relinquished.

Chapter 4
Anyatva Anupreksạ̄
(Otherness or Non-Identity)

21

मादापिदरसहोदरपुत्तकलत्तादिबंधुसंदोहो ।
जीवस्स ण संबंधो णियकज्जवसेण वट्टंति ॥

mādāpidarasahodaraputtakalattādibaṁdhusaṁdoho ।
jīvassa ṇa saṁbaṁdho ṇiyakajjavaseṇa vaṭṭaṁti ॥

The mother, father, brother, son, wife — this cluster of relations bears no relationship to the soul. They all exist, motivated for their own sake.

Commentary

In this verse, Kundakunda draws our attention to the distinctness, otherness or non-identity of the real nature of the Self from all the extraneous mundane affinities or relationships, which are due to attachment with the body. In fact, the motive of self-interest constitutes the basis of family bonds.

Acharya Amitgati remarks:

> That Self, which does not have identity with the body, how is it possible for that Self to have a relationship with the son, wife or friends.

Bhudhar Das, in his description of *anyatva*, states:

> Where the body is not mine, there can be no other relationship. The house, wealth are distinct or other (*para*) is quite obvious, the attendants, dependence and family (*parijana*) too are other (*para*) or distinct from the Self.

In this context, Gyalwang Drukpa (2016) observes:

We build a house and then say, "This is my house", and we are stuck with it. You become almost inseparable from the house, believing it to be part of you. We think of it as being forever, permanent, as if we can take it to the next life. We are too possessive. Of course, there is nothing wrong in having a house, nothing wrong in having wealth, but they are not a part of you. Your roots are not in your possessions, they are deep inside of you.

Pravacanasāra 160 states:

I am not the body, not mind, nor again voice, nor cause of these; neither the doer of action, nor getting it done by others, nor the approver of the same.

22

अण्णो अण्णं सोयदि मदो त्ति मम णाहगो त्ति मण्णंतो।
अप्पाणं ण हु सोयदि संसारमहण्णवे बुड्डं ॥

aṇṇo aṇṇaṁ soyadi mado tti mama ṇāhago tti maṇṇaṅto ।
appāṇaṁ ṇa hu soyadi saṁsāramahaṇṇave buḍḍaṁ ॥

(Under the spell of delusion), one grieves for the other thinking or being convinced that "He is mine; He is my lord (*nāyaka*)". But he does not grieve about himself while he is drowned, plunged or sinking into the ocean of mundane existence or the cycle of birth and death.

Commentary by M.K. Dharma Raja

People deceive themselves by harbouring feelings of attachment of their kith and kin. Such futile thoughts harm one's real Self. They only drown the soul deeper into the quagmire of worldly woes. Instead of grieving for others, one should really feel sorry that through such misplaced grieve his soul gets entangled in the coils of worldly existence. A wise person, therefore, should ponder over the fact that his physical body is distinct from his soul. There can thus be no real relationship with those whom he considers his kith and kin. Such unreal feelings arise from illusory sensual sentiments (1990: 28).

23

अण्णं इमं सरीरादिगं पि होज्ज बाहिरं दव्वं ।
णाणं दंसणमादा एवं चिंत्तेहि अण्णत्तं ॥

aṇṇaṁ imaṁ sarīrādigaṁ pi hojja bāhiraṁ davvaṁ ।
ṇāṇaṁ daṁsaṇamādā evaṁ ciṁttehi aṇṇattaṁ ॥

The body, etc. other extraneous substances/objects are other (*anya*) or distinct. I am of the nature of knowledge and intuition. One should contemplate of *anyatva* in this way.

Commentary

This verse makes it clear that the body and other objects (house, etc.) to which people are ordinarily attached are really other/distinct from the soul. These extraneous substances are inanimate and perishable.

But the true Self, though temporarily encased in the physical body, is eternal and not liable to decay or dissolution. Knowledge and perception are its attributes. These innate and inseparable attributes of the soul are not to be confused with the limbs of the physical body, its sensory feelings or with any other extraneous matter (1990: 28-29).

Kārttikeyānuprekṣā

Kundakunda has dealt with *anyatva anuprekṣā* in three verses (*BA* 21-23). *Kārttikeyānuprekṣā* also discusses it in three verses (*KA* 80-83) as follows:

> Relatives, etc. are different (other) and distinct from one's *ātman*. When the *ātman* is realized as distinct from the body, that is something fruitful.

Chapter 5
Saṁvara Anuprekṣā
(The Cycle of Birth and Death)

24

पंचविहे संसारे जाइजरामरणरोगभयपउरे।
जिणमग्गमपेच्छंतो जीवो परिभमदि चिरकालं॥

paṅcavihe saṁsāre jāijarāmaraṇarogabhayapaure ।
jiṇamaggamapecchaṅto jīvo paribhamadi cirakālaṁ ॥

The Self, which does not have faith in the path of liberation expounded by the Omniscient Lord (Jina), undergoes wanderings for a long time in the five kinds of cycle of birth and death or transmigratory existence (*saṁsāsra*) full of birth, old age or senility, death, disease and fear.

Commentary

The five kinds of *saṁsāra* transmigratory cycle refers to rounds (*parāvartana*) of transmigration undergone by the Self in matter (*pudgala* substance), place (*kṣetra*), time (*kāla*), birth in a particular condition of existence (*bhava*) and thought-activity (*bhāva*) *parāvartana*.

The seven kinds of fear are: (1) fear relating to this life; (2) fear relating to future life (*para-loka*); (3) fear of being without protection (*arakṣā*); (4) fear of the disclosure of what is kept in secret (*agupti*); (5) fear of pain (*vedanā*); (6) fear of accident (*asasmika*); and (7) fear of death.

An enlightened person is free from the seven kinds of fears (*SS* 228).

The next five verses (*BA* 25 to 29) describe five kinds of cycles of rounds undergone by the Self in *saṁsāra*.

25

सव्वे वि पोग्गला खलु एगे भुत्तुज्झिया हु जीवेण।
असयं अणंतखुत्तो पुग्गलपरियट्टसंसारे॥

savve vi poggalā khalu ege bhuttujjhiyā hu jīveṇa ।
asayaṁ aṇaṅtakhutto puggalapariyaṭṭasaṁsāre ॥

In the *saṁsāra* of the nature of *pudgala* (matter) round, the soul alone has enjoyed all the matter particles several times and given them up.

Commentary by M.K. Dharma Raja

Each mundane soul in the course of its transmigrations through the four conditions of existence wanders in this *saṁsāra* which abounds in an innumerable variety of material molecules and particles. The cycle of matter wandering is in relation to the outer gross physical body and the fine kārmic body of the mundane soul. It has therefore two kinds of wanderings; the cycle of physical (quasi-kārmic no-*karma dravya* (substance)/*parāvartana*) matter-wandering in the cycle of kārmic matter-wandering.

The quasi-kārmic cycle is the time which the soul takes in renewing exactly the same set of a particular number and quality of molecules as it took once. The object of taking into account each cycle of wandering is to underscore the fact that a mundane soul is bound to be weighed down for a long time in the cycle of transmigrations as a consequence of its own kārmic bondage.

A cycle of kārmic matter-wandering involves the time taken in renewing exactly the same set of a particular number and the quality of the knowledge-obscuring, etc. eight *karmas*, as the soul took in once. Each mundane soul absorbs new, mixed and old molecules innumerable number of times and also sheds them innumerable times.

Every mundane soul roams about in the cycles of matter wanderings for a long time until it finds a way to cross the ocean of recurring rebirths.

Kundakunda, thus, lays emphasis on the utter futility of chasing the chimera of happiness in worldly existence. The wise therefore set the mind on treading the path of liberation which takes the Self to the abode of eternal bliss (1990: 31-32).

26

सव्वम्हि लोयखेत्ते कमसो तं णत्थि जं ण उप्पण्णं ।
उग्गाहणेण बहुसो परिभमिदो खेत्तसंसारे ॥

savvamhi loyakhette kamaso taṁ ṇatthi jaṁ ṇa uppaṇṇaṁ ।
uggāhaṇeṇa bahuso paribhamido khettasaṁsāre ॥

Nowhere throughout space in the entire *saṁsāra* is there any place, where the (mundane) soul has not taken birth successively in many forms (big and small). The soul has thus traversed or wandered about in its cycle of transmigrations through places or space.

Commentary by M.K. Dharma Raja

There is no point in the entire space of the *saṁsāra* where each and every soul has not been born and reborn innumerable number of times. Each soul in the course of its transmigrations in every conceivable size from the minutest one-sensed (*nigoda*) being the largest in size like a whale, takes its birth innumerable times in each of its forms at each and every point in space throughout the *saṁsāra*.

The time taken in each of the successive births referred to as one cycle of space transmigrations.

The final release and redemption from this unending roaming about in space is secured only through liberation (1990: 32).

27

अवसप्पिणिउस्सप्पिणिसमयावलियासु णिरवसेसासु।
जादो मुदो य बहुसो परिभमिदो कालसंसारे॥

avasappiṇiussappiṇisamayāvaliyāsu ṇiravasesāsu ।
jādo mudo ya bahuso paribhamido kālasaṁsāre ॥

This mundane soul has been born and has died many a time through the entire progressive and regressive time-cycles. Thus, it has been revolving around the complete time-cycle.

Commentary by M.K. Dharma Raja

In this verse, Kundakunda speaks of the revolving cycle of rebirths with reference to the time factor. The transmigrations in time mentioned here referred to the Bhārata and the Airāvata parts of the Jambūdvīpa. The time-cycle in these regions consists of two equal halves — the progressive (*utsarpiṇī* (ascending)) and regressive (*avasarpiṇīs* (descending)) periods. The first is marked by a progressive increase in the happiness, strength, longevity, the power, the stature, etc. of living beings. Exactly the reverse process takes place in the second period marked by dimunition in the conditions.

The seeker on the path of spiritual advance is concerned with finding a way out of this continuing cycle of transmigrations. To liberate himself from this morass of rebirths, he has to follow the path expounded by the Omniscient Lord (the Jina) (1990: 33-34).

28

णिरयाउजहण्णादिसु जाव दु उवरिल्लया दु गेवेज्जा।
मिच्छत्तसंसिदेण दु बहुसो वि भवट्ठिदी भमिदो॥

ṇirayāujahaṇṇādisu jāva du uvarillayā du gevejjā ।
micchattasaṁsideṇa du bahuso vi bhavaṭṭhidī bhamido ॥

The mundane soul, deluded by delusion or wrong belief, has been roaming about many a time in varying durations in the various conditions of existence (*bhava*) *parāvartana* of life-span — from the briefest in hell (below) up to the highest heaven of *Graiveyakas*.

Commentary by M.K. Dharma Raja

The peregrination or wanderings in rebirths involves four conditions of existence — hellish, subhuman, human and celestial.

Life-duration in these conditions ranges between the minimum of one *antarmuhurtta* (within 48 minutes) in the subhuman existence and a minimum of 10,000 years and maximum of 33 *sāgaras* (multi-billion years) in infernal life in hells .... The minimum span of life in the celestial regions is 10,000 years and the maximum of 31 *sāgaras* up to the topmost heaven — the ninth *Graiveyaka* (1990: 34-35).

29

सव्वे पयडिट्ठिदिओ अणुभागपदेसबंधठाणाणि ।
जीवो मिच्छत्तवसा भमिदो पुण भावसंसारे ॥

savve payaḍiṭṭhidio aṇubhāgapadesabaṁdhaṭhāṇāṇi ।
jīvo micchattavasā bhamido puṇa bhāvasaṁsāre ॥

The Self has wandered in the cycle of rebirths of transmigrations in its thought-activity (*bhāva parāvartana*), repeatedly through all the four aspects of kinds of bondage, viz. *prakṛti* (nature, equality, class or type of *karma* that is bound); duration of bondage of *karmas* (*sthiti*), intensity of fruition of *karma* (*anubhoga*) and quantity or mass of material particles bound with space-points soul (*pradeśa bandha*), due to the subjection to deluded perception (*mithyātva*).

Commentary

At the very time when the soul assimilates kārmic material particles, the above-mentioned four aspects or kinds of bondage are generated. Of the four kinds or types of bondage, the *prakṛti* and *pradeśa* bondages are caused by the soul's vibratory activities of mind, speech and body (*yoga*). The duration (*sthiti*) of bondage and the intensity of the fruition (*anubhāga*) of the bondage of *karmas* caused passions (*kaṣāyas*) like anger. The quantity of kārmic material particles assimilated by the soul varies according to the intensity of passions.

Knowledge-obscuring (*jñānāvarṇīya*), deluding (*mohanīya*), etc. are eight kinds of *karmas*, with their 148 subdivisions, are bound with the soul.[1]

Commentary by M.K. Dharma Raja

Thus, the soul roams about in its thought-cycle for innumerable years in the various states of existence as a result of its deluded perception. Because of its deluded perception, the soul fails to gain insight into its transcendental, pure nature of the Self.

The ocean of transmigrations can be crossed only through an enlightened worldview of the reality of things as they are which illumine the path towards liberation. The souls released from the five cycles of transmigrations in matter, space, time, conditions of existence and thought activities are the liberated souls (*siddhas*) (1990: 36).

30

पुत्तकलत्तणिमित्तं अत्थं अज्जयदि पापबुद्धीए।
परिहरदि दयादाणं सो जीवो भमदि संसारे॥

puttakalattaṇimittaṁ atthaṁ ajjayadi pāpabuddhīe ।
pariharadi dayādāṇaṁ so jīvo bhamadi saṁsāre ॥

That Self which acquires and accumulates wealth for the reason of son and wife through sinful intellect, forsaking or avoiding compassion and charity, roams about or wanders in the cycle of birth and death (*saṁsāra*).

---

[1] The eight kinds of *karmas* are explained in Jain, J.P. 2005: 253-254.

Commentary by M.K. Dharma Raja

A person, blinded by deluded views and misplaced feelings of attachment only for his kith and kin, sets his sight on acquiring wealth only for the sake of his wife and children. He is unmindful of his duty to be compassionate and charitable to those around him. Such persons delude themselves and face harmful consequences. They continue to grope about in the ocean of birth and death (1990: 37).

31

मम पुत्तं ममभज्जा मम धणधण्णो त्ति तिव्वकंखाए।
चइऊण धम्मबुद्धिं पच्छा परिपडदि दीहसंसारे॥

mama puttaṁ mamabhajjā mama dhaṇadhaṇṇo tti tivvakaṅkhāe ।
caiūṇa dhammabuddhiṁ pacchā paripaḍadi dīhasaṁsāre ॥

"He is my son, she is my wife; that is my money and that is my grain." With such intense desire, one gives up or forsakes intellect of righteousness and piety (*dharma buddhi*) to be plunged into the prolonged cycle of worldly existence.

Commentary

The intellect of considering other substances/objects as one's own (*apanatva* or *aham buddhi*) is the deluded psychic state or disposition (*mithyā bhāva*). In *Samayasāra* 92, Kundakunda categorically states:

> Believing the non-Self to be the Self, and the Self to be the non-Self, the ignorant/deluded soul or the Self, imbued with perverted knowledge, becomes a causal agent of various *karmas*.

32

मिच्छोदयेण जीवो णिंदंतो जोण्हभासियं धम्मं।
कुधम्मकुलिंगकुतित्थं मण्णंतो भमदि संसारे॥

micchodayeṇa jīvo ṇiṁdaṁto joṇhabhāsiyaṁ dhammaṁ ।
kudhammakuliṅgakutitthaṁ maṇṇaṁto bhamadi saṁsāre ॥

The mundane soul, beset with delusions, perverted belief or conviction, i.e. not considering the reality of things as they are, blames/ridicules the tenets of righteousness and piety (*dharma*) spoken by the Omniscient Lord (Jina), follows perverse faiths, perverse cults and wrong places of pilgrimage, thereby wanders or roams about in the cycle of birth and death.

Commentary by M.K. Dharma Raja

Temptations abound in this materialistic world. Those who succumb to its temptations are liable to be misled by quacks and those who propagate superstitious myths and cults.

Those who are thus misled turn to denouncing the life of righteousness and piety reached by the Jinas. Such gullible individuals pin their faith in undesirable and distasteful cults and begin worshipping the unworthy.

The consequences of such sinful practices are disastrous. The passions aroused by the superstitious practices plunge the misguided being deeper into the labyrinths of the cycle of rebirths. Contemplation on these salutary ideas strengthens the aspirant's resolve to steadfastly follow the path of emancipation (1990: 38-39).

33

हंतूण जीवरासिं महुमंसं सेविऊण सुरयाणं ।
परदव्ववरकलत्तं गहिऊण य भमदि संसारे ॥

haṁtūṇa jīvarāsiṁ mahumaṁsaṁ seviūṇa surayāṇaṁ ।
paradavvavarakalattaṁ gahiūṇa ya bhamadi saṁsāre ॥

He, who kills a whole lot of creatures and consumes honey, meat and intoxicating liquor, takes or acquires other's wealth and cohabits with others' wives, continues to roam about in the cycle of worldly existence.

Commentary by M.K. Dharma Raja

The degraded individuals blindly indulge themselves in the gratification of their carnal desires. They resort to the senseless killing of innocent creatures as a way of life. They seek pleasures in consuming honey, eating meat and intoxicating themselves with liquor. It is a ruinous life that they lead in this manner.

It is sinful to consume honey since its extraction involves the killing of bees. Swarms of bees collected in cells are killed in the process of extraction. But people take to honey cultivation as an occupation unmindful of this cruelty.

Addiction to honey and meat entangles the mundane soul in ever greater bondage. This wretched condition becomes more vicious with the consumption of liquor which turns the addict senseless. The addict in his state of inebriation is rendered totally indiscreet and is driven to commit further sinful acts.

Those seized with greed and the desire to get richer are inclined to grab the property and wealth of others. Such sinful deeds drag the soul deeper into the pit of bondage.

Lust is yet another corrosive agent that drives people into the sinful act of adultery. Anti-social men who are not content with their own wedded wife covet other women and perpetrate a variety of crimes. All these demeritorious acts push the soul inextricably into the wheels of the remorseless cycle of innumerable wanderings (1990: 39-40).

34

जत्तेण कुणइ पावं विसयणिमित्तं च अहणिसं जीवो ।
मोहंधयारसहिओ तेण दु परिपडदि संसारे ॥

jatteṇa kuṇai pāvaṁ visayaṇimittaṁ ca ahaṇisaṁ jīvo ।
mohaṅdhayārasahio teṇa du paripaḍadi saṁsāre ॥

A soul shrouded in the darkness of delusion commits sin, through day and night, for the sake of sensual pleasures. He, therefore, wanders in the cycle of birth and death.

Commentary by M.K. Dharma Raja

A worldly soul blinded by delusion is lost in darkness, all around. Blinded by the stupor of delusion, such individuals are totally engrossed in sensual desires. Since their sole consuming passion is for the enjoyment of carnal pleasures, they are constantly preoccupied in perpetrating misdeeds. These unfortunate souls get irretrievably enmeshed in the cyclical effects of their sinful deeds. They are destined to grope about in the whirlpool of interminable existence[2] (1990: 40).

35

णिच्चिदरधादुसत्तय तरुदसवियलिंदिएसु छच्चेव।
सरणिरयतिरियचउरो चोद्दस मणुए सदसहस्सा॥

ṇiccidaradhādusattaya tarudasaviyalindiesu chacceva ।
saraṇirayatiriyacauro coddasa maṇue sadasahassā ॥

The birth categories of the permanent lowest forms of life (*nitya-nigoda*) and those which return to the lowest form (*itara-nigoda*), and of elements (earth, water, fire and air) are seven lakhs each, of plant-bodied ten lakhs, of the incomplete sensed (those with two, three and four senses) (ten lakhs of celestials), the hellish and animals (six lakhs each), and of human beings (fourteen lakhs). Thus, there are a total of 84 lakh categories of life-forms in which the worldly soul wanders or transmigrates.

---

[2] This verse is coming as verse 41 in *loka anuprekṣā* in Devendra Kumar Shastri's *Bārasa Aṇuvekkhā* (1991) in Hindi.

Commentary by M.K. Dharma Raja

The number of categories of life-forms based on the nucleus (*yoni*) of their birth totals 84 lakhs.

Life-forms range from the lowliest form of life to the most exalted. Most souls pass through them all before their final emancipation. A soul can be born into any of these categories. Most souls, indeed, go through innumerable repetition in the vicissitudes of almost every life-form.

At the very bottom of this classification are sub-microscopic creatures born in clusters inhabiting a single body. They are born together and die together. They are the permanently-placed *nigoda*—the lowest form of life pervading the earth and also inhabiting the tissues of plants, animals and human bodies. They have seven lakh birth-conditions.

There are seven lakhs of other birth conditions (*itara-nigoda*) of those which come out of the *nigoda* state and return to it. Then there are the single-sensed (sense of touch) organisms inside the subtlest units in the elements (earth, fire and air). They are referred to as earth-bodied (*pṛthvī-kāya*), water-bodied (*āpa-kāya*), fire-bodied (*tejo-kāya*) and air-bodied (*vāyu-kāya*). Their birth-conditions are also seven lakhs in each of the four elements.

There are also the plant bodies (*vanaspati-kāya*, in individual or collective life-forms) originating in ten lakh categories.

Life-forms with two, three and four senses are born in two lakhs each of different conditions.

The heavenly, hellish and subhuman beings (animals with five senses) take birth in four lakhs each of different conditions. And, finally, come the human beings with a total of fourteen lakhs of possible birth-conditions.

This vast amplitude in the range of the nucleus of births illustrates the staggering variety of conditions through which a soul in bondage travels about in the bottomless ocean of rebirths.

The mundane soul suffers this hapless fate due to the bondage of *karmas* of its own making.

It would be wise, therefore, to reflect that the only way out of this unfortunate predicament is the pursuit of the goal of everlasting bliss of liberation (1990: 41-42).

36

संजोगविप्पजोगं लाहालाहं सुहं च दुक्खं च।
संसारे भूदाणं होदि हु माणं तहावमाणं च॥

saṁjogavippajogaṁ lāhālāhaṁ suhaṁ ca dukkhaṁ ca ।
saṁsāre bhūdāṇaṁ hodi hu māṇaṁ tahāvamāṇaṁ ca ॥

The joining together or union and separation, gain and loss, pleasure and pain as well as honour and dishonour inevitably befall those born in this worldly existence (*saṁsāra*).

Commentary by M.K. Dharma Raja

The harsh realities of mundane existence are brought out in sharp relief in this verse.

Happiness and sorrow are but the two sides of the coin of life.

The joy in the coming together of the near and dear – of the husband and wife or the father and son – is only to be matched with the pangs of their separation on death. Gain and loss in the course of one's life, pleasure and misery or honour and dishonour follow each other as light and shade or like the night and day.

The wise, therefore, do not forget themselves in the pursuit of pleasure or plunge themselves in grief in the course of their life journey. On the other hand, they view life realistically and turn to meditation on the true nature of the Self as an independent entity. The discreet thus turns to thoughts of self-purification as the surest and the sole means of salvation from the miseries of worldly existence (1990: 42-43).

37

कम्मणिमित्तं जीवो हिंडदि संसारघोरकंतारे ।
जीवस्स ण संसारो णिच्चयणयकम्मविम्मुक्को ॥

kammaṇimittaṁ jīvo hiṅḍadi saṁsāraghorakaṅtāre ।
jīvassa ṇa saṁsāro ṇiccayaṇayakammavimmukko ॥

Weighed down by kārmic bondage, the Self wanders or roams about in the frightful, awesome or terrible forest of birth and death. [From the external, other-referential point of view (*vyavahāra naya*), the soul is associated with *karmas*, as a result of which it is impure and that body and the soul are united, combined or joined together as one or having oneness (*ekatva*) (i.e. released or granted amnesty by *karmas* (*SS* 27).] But from the [pure, transcendental] real point of view, [the Self is non-relational to or independent of *karmas* (*karma-anuprekṣā*) pure], i.e. *karma-nirmukta* (*BA* 37) in the sense of being not bound and unpatched (*abaddha aspr̥ṣṭa*) and not connected (*asaṁyukta*) with *karmas* (*SS* 14) and that the Self and body are never one, i.e. identical (having same nature or characteristics (*SS* 27)]. As a result thereof, it is the embodied soul, which wanders or transmigrates in the worldly existence, not the transcendental, pure Self.

Commentary

In this verse, *karma* is said to be only or merely the supportive factor (*nimitta*) in regard to the soul's wanderings in the terrible forest of life and death. But in reality, the transcendental, pure nature of the Self is *abaddha aspr̥ṣṭa* (not bound with *karma*s and untouched with *karmas*) in the sense described above. Even in the embodied existence, the transcendental, pure nature of the Self continues to remain ever-existing, eternal consciousness-as-such (*pāriṇāmika bhāva*) alone.

In *Samayasāra*, Acharya Kundakunda states:

> I (*aham*, the Self) is *ekko* [in *Bārasa Aṇuvekkhā*, it is said to be *ekkoham* (*BA* 14-16)] [the word *aham ekko* is also coming in *Samayasāra* 36-37 and 73], i.e. one, above, solitary, unique, indeed pure [in the sense described above], having intuition and knowledge, always non-corporeal or formless, and not even the minutest part of any other (*anya*) belongs to me or is mine (*SS* 38), i.e. *nirmama* (the word *nirmamatvas* is also coming in *SS* 36-37 and 73).

38

संसारमदिक्कंतो जीवोवादेयमिति विचिंतेज्जो ।
संसारदुहक्कंतो जीवो सो हेयमिति विचिंतेज्जो ॥

saṁsāramadikkaṅto jīvovādeyamiti viciṅtejjo ।
saṁsāraduhakkaṅto jīvo so heyamiti viciṅtejjo ॥

One should contemplate that the Self, which is transcendental from *saṁsāra* (cycle of birth and death), is worth acquiring (*upādeya*). And the Self which is assailed or overpowered (*akrānta*) by the miseries or sufferings in the worldly existence is worth discarding or not to be taken (*heya*); one should contemplate like this.

Commentary by M.K. Dharma Raja

The reflection on the bewildering variety of the soul's wanderings in the mundane circuit is aptly summed up in this verse.

It is clear beyond doubt that there is no happiness in any of the four conditions of existence, viz. the celestials, human beings, animals and those passing through their term in hell. All of them alike experience pain and misery of one kind or the other. Total bliss is obtained only on the final emancipation of the Self (soul) from all vestiges of kārmic bondage. This then is the worthy state of the soul which one should aspire to attain.

The soul in kārmic bondage in whatever state remains sullied and impure. This is a condition which ought to be discarded.

It is obvious that the attainment of perfection is the sole objective that the aspirant should set for himself. Constant contemplation on this theme rivets the mind securely on the supreme objective of the attainment of everlasting bliss. Acharya Kundakunda thus beckons the seeker to the path that takes him to the worthy state of absolute purity (1990: 44).

Chapter 6
Loka Anuprekṣā
(The Nature of the Universe)

39

जीवादिपयट्ठाणं समवाओ सो णिरुच्चए लोगो।
तिविहो हवेइ लोगो अहमज्झिमउड्ढभेएण॥

jīvādipayaṭṭhāṇaṁ samavāo so ṇiruccae logo ।
tiviho havei logo ahamajjhimauḍḍhabhe-eṇa ॥

The conglomeration of souls (living beings) and other substances is called the universe. It comprises of three different parts – the lower, the middle and the upper.

Commentary by M.K. Dharma Raja

The universe (*loka*) is situated in the midst of space (*ākāśa*). It contains souls (*jīva* – the living beings, sentient substance) and the other five substances, viz. matter, the time element, space, the medium of motion and the medium of rest.

The part of infinite space where the six substances exist is called the universe. The other part beyond this is void (without substances) (1990: 45).

40

णिरया हवंति हेट्ठा मज्झे दीवंबुरासयो संखा।
सग्गो तिसट्ठिभेओ एत्तो उड्ढं हवे मोक्खो॥

ṇirayā havaṁti heṭṭhā majjhe dīvaṁburāsayo saṅkhā ।
saggo tisaṭṭhibheo etto uḍḍhaṁ have mokkho ॥

In the lower part of the universe, the denizens of hell live, in the middle are innumerable continents and oceans; in the upper part are sixty-three layers of heavens. Above them is the abode of the Perfect Souls (*mokṣa*).

Commentary by M.K. Dharma Raja

The seven hells are located, one above the other, in the lower part of the universe. The nuances of the seven hells are: (1) *ratnaprabhā*; (2) *śarkarāprabhā*; (3) *bālukaprabhā*; (4) *paṅkaprabhā*; (5) *dhūmaprabhā*; (6) *tamaḥprabhā*; and (7) *mahātamaḥprabhā*. Those who inhabit them are condemned to the most disagreeable conditions of life.

Below them is the lowest part of the universe, the *nigoda*, where the lowest form of life exists. It is a region into which fall those who commit the worst kind of sins.

The middle world consists of innumerable continents and oceans. The continents and oceans lie in concentric circles, one beyond the other.

The Jambūdvīpa is the central element. The next two are the Dhātakī and Puṣkara *dvīpas*. Human beings inhabit only the first two-and-a-half continents, i.e. the Jambūdvīpa, the Dhātakīdvīpa and one half of the Puṣkaradvīpa which comprise the entire region illumined by the sun.

In the upper part of the universe is the celestial region comprising sixty-three layers of the heavens.

At the very top of the universe is *Siddhaloka* of the Pure and Liberated Souls (1990: 46-47).

41

इगतीस सत्त चत्तारि दोण्णि एक्केक्क छक्क चदुकप्पे।
तित्तिय एक्केक्केंदियणामा उड्डुआदि तेसट्ठी॥

igatīsa satta cattāri doṇṇi ekkekka chakka cadukappe ।
tittiya ekkekkendiyaṇāmā uḍḍa-ādi tesaṭṭhī ॥

Thirty-one layers (*pātāla*) in the first two heavens (*Saudharma* and *Īśāna*), seven layers (in the next two — *Sanatkumāra* and

Mahendra), four (in the next two — *Brahmā* and *Brahmottara*), two (in the next two — *Lantava* and *Kapiṣṭa*), one in *Śukra* and *Mahāśukra*), one in the next two — *Satārā* and *Sahasrāra*), six in four (i.e. three in *Aṇata* and *Praṇata,* and three in *Araṇa* and *Acyuta*). The nine super-heavens beyond the (*Graiveyakas*) have one each; the nine *Anudiśās* have only one and the last five (*Anuttaras*) have only one. Thus, there are sixty-three layers.

Commentary by M.K. Dharma Raja

This verse outlines the topography of the celestial region made up of sixty-three layers.

The first sixteen heavens are located on eight storeys. Above them are the super-heavens in an ascending order — the *Graiveyakas* (nine), the A*nudiśās* (nine) and the *Anuttaras* (five).

The celestial beings enjoy great felicity which increases progressively in an ascending order. Their longevity is very high. They never become old. They have a resplendent physical appearance and can, at will, assume any form. Celestials in the lower heavens have female companions. But the higher the heaven, the lesser is their essential desire. And the higher the heaven, the greater is also the spiritual disposition.

The denizens of the super-heavens have no sensual desires. They are all male; all enjoying the equal rank of Ahamindras.

Those born in the highest layers (*Anuttaras*) have the destiny of only one more life on earth from where they attain final emancipation.

In this verse, Kundakunda underscores the transience of all forms of existence from the lowliest inferno of hells to the most exalted tenure in the highest of the super-heavens. Birth and death, it is emphasized, are the inescapable destiny of all cast in the ocean of transmigrations.

The aspirant should therefore set his sight on attaining the loftiest status — of the liberated soul that abides eternally on the top of the universe — the *Siddhaloka* (1990: 47-48).

42

असुहेण णिरयतिरियं सुहउवजोगेण दिविजणरसोक्खं।
सुद्धेण लहइ सिद्धिं एवं लोयं विचिंतिज्जो॥

asuheṇa ṇirayatiriyaṁ suha-uvajogeṇa divijaṇarasokkhaṁ ।
suddheṇa lahai siddhiṁ evaṁ loyaṁ viciṅtijjo ॥

From evil or inauspicious (*aśubha*) thoughts, this mundane soul begets hellish subhuman destiny; from wholesome or auspicious (*śubha*) thoughts, the happiness of heavenly and human destiny and from pure thoughts, final emancipation. Thus, one should contemplate on the nature of the universe.

Commentary by M.K. Dharma Raja

The thought-activities of the mundane souls can be broadly classified as evil or inauspicious, unwholesome or inauspicious, wholesome or auspicious and pure.

The first category of the evil thought processes is caused by intense sensual passions like anger, pride, greed and deceit. These sensual passions, impelled by worldly desires, result in a vicious spiral of all kinds of sinful deeds and mean behaviour including killing, falsehood or theft, lechery and possessiveness and indulgence in seven calamatious addictions or habits (*vyasana*) of gambling, hunting, prostitution, stealing, adultery, drinking wine and meat-eating (one may add smoking and intoxicating drugs), which are harmful and reprehensible activities. They lead to the bondage of demeritorious *karmas*. The inevitable sequel is destiny in hell or in subhuman conditions.

The second category of wholesome, auspicious and desirable thoughts produce virtuous behaviour. They induce activities of piety and worship, study of the scriptures, charity, compassion or pity, righteousness, piety (*dharma*) and service and, generally, doing good to others. Acquisition of meritorious *karmas* from these virtuous deeds by the soul leads to a destiny of rebirth as humans or as celestial beings. But even life in the heavens like elsewhere on the mundane world is impermanent with the inevitable prospect thereafter of again being tossed about in the ocean of transmigrations.

Varying conditions of life prevail in the four different states or conditions of existence in the universe. But all these mundane destinies are fleeting and transient.

The true destiny of the Self lies in the realization of its innate purity. This is achieved through the pure thought-activity of absolute concentration on the Self, i.e. the contemplation of the *ātmā*. Thus, the third category of pure thought-activities are directed towards the ideal of the perfected Self.

The aspirant is, therefore, directed to shun the miseries of mundane existence and concentrate on the realization of the supreme destiny of the soul.

Contemplation of these aspects of the universe (*loka anuprekṣā*) leads to clarity of vision. It fosters distaste for worldly life and strengthens the resolve to realize the bliss that inherently resides in the pure Self (1990: 49).

Kārttikeyānuprekṣā

Kundakunda has described *loka anuprekṣā* in four verses (*BA* 39-42). *Kārttikeyānuprekṣā* describes it in 169 verses (*KA* 115-283) as follows:

> The *loka* (universe) which is constricted by the inner accommodation of various substances, situated right in the centre of infinite space; it is neither created by anybody nor supported by Hari, Hara, etc. It is eternal because the constituent substances are eternal; and it is subject to changes due to constant substances undergoing modifications at every moment.

The soul, though all-pervading in view of its knowability, gets the shape of its body by virtue of its nature of contraction–expansion. If it is not confined to its body, but if it were to be all-pervasive, pleasure and pain will fall to its lot ever and everywhere.

— *KA* 176-177

Knowledge is the very nature of the soul, as heat is of fire by nature; and both of them stand inseparable. Knowledge or *jīva* is not the product of elements. Knowledge, besides the *jīva,* is an impossibility; and this is patent to all those who are sensible. It is the *jīva* which experiences pleasures and pains, and comprehends the objects of senses. It is only in the company of body that the *jīva* experiences joy and sorrow, acts in various ways, is open to sense perception and has awareness of its position and ability; but it is wrong to take *jīva* to be the same as the body. *Jīva* (in the company of the body) becomes an agent. *Jīva* is a subject to *saṁsara* or attains liberation, according to *kāla-labdhi.* Likewise, *jīva* experiences the fruits of *karma* in this *saṁsāra.* Affected by acute passion, *jīva* is exposed to sin, but when the quiet psychic state is developed, *jīva* accumulates *puṇya. Jīva* crosses the ocean of *saṁsāra* in the boat of three jewels, viz. right faith, kowledge and conduct. — *KA* 178-191

Jīvas are classified into three types of *ātman*:

1. The *bahir-ātman* is one who is of perverted belief, a subject to acute passions and considers the *jīva* and body identical.
2. Those who are well-versed in the words of the Jina, discriminate between the soul and the body and are free from eightfold vanity stand for *antarātman.* They are the best when endowed with five *mahāvratas*, engrossed in *dharma* and *śukla-dhyāna* and free from all negligence and lapses. They are the mediocre who are devoted to the words of the Jina, follow the duties of a pious householder, and are magnanimous and quiet. They are the inferior who are devotees of the Jina, have faith but no conduct, realize their weakness and are yearning to follow the virtues of others.

3. The *Paramātman* is represented by *arhats* who still possess the body and knows everything through omniscience and by *siddhas* who possesses only knowledge of his body (i.e. who is an embodiment of knowledge) and has reached the highest happiness which arises out of the very nature of the soul consequent on the destruction of all the karmas and their influences. — *KA* 192-199

All the souls moving in *saṁsāra* are bound by *karmas* since beginningless time. That is how the pure nature is eclipsed by the interpretation of kārmic matter into space-points (*pradeśa*) of the soul. It is the situation that adds significance to the practice of religious life and penances which destroy *karmas* and the *jīva* becomes a *siddha*. *Jīva* is the best and the highest of the realities: it alone can discriminate between what is beneficial and what is harmful. — *KA* 200-205

The whole universe is replete with particles of matter, subtle and gross, and of manifold potencies. They are of the same variety of matter endowed with sense-qualities and capable of being perceived by the senses; in quantity, they are infinite times more than the multitudes of souls. Matter (*pudgala*) helps the spirit (*jīva*) in various ways by forming the body, sense organs, speech, breath and temperamental phases like delusion and ignorance till the end of *saṁsāra*. *Jīvas* too help each other. As a rule, *puṇya* and *pāpa* are the chief motive behind it. The matter has a remarkable potential power whereby it eclipses the omniscient character of the soul. — *KA* 206-212

The two substances of *dharma* and *adharma* are co-pervasive with the *lokākāśa* and serve as fulcrums of movement and rest (respectively) for all the substances, living and non-living. *Ākāśa* (space) gives accommodation to all the substances. It is of two kinds (*loka* and *aloka*); the latter standing for simple and pure space. The various substances are mutually accommodative; the space seven-points of *jīva* interpenetrate in *lokākāśa* like water in ashes; otherwise, how can all the substances be accommodated in one space-point of the *ākāśa*? Time which marks exchanges

in various substances is unitary in constitution, i.e. the points of time never mix with one another but always stand separate.
— *KA* 212-216

Every substance serves as the substantial cause of its modifications while other outside substances are only an instrumental cause. The mutual help of various substances is a cause of cooperative character. The various objects are potent with manifold power; and getting a suitable moment they undergo changes which none can stop. The subtle and gross modifications of *jīvas* and *pudgalas* spoken in terms of past, present and future, due to conventional or relative time. The past and future are infinite, while the present is confined to a single point of time. Every prior modification of a substance stands in causal relation with the posterior one which, as a rule, is an effect; and this relation persist through all the time. — *KA* 217-223

The various substances are infinite in character and extended over three tenses: this reality, as a whole, assumes an infinitely complex character. It is this manifold character of reality that is seen functioning in the universe: any isolated particular aspect of itself cannot explain the resultant effect. An eternal substance, if it is devoid of modification, neither originates nor is destroyed. Similarly, transitory modifications, if they do not have the substratum of the substance, cannot give rise to any effect of existential character. Attributes and modifications will have no basis, if they do not rest on something real. All along substances are subjected, in a single moment, to a series of new and newer effects which stand in a relation of priority and posteriority and of cause and effect. — *KA* 224-230

The *jīva* is eternal, without beginning and end. It is liable to various new forms according to the accessories available and shows resultant effects. It does not relinquish its real nature under any circumstances. If the souls were to give up their individuality, say being all-pervasive and of the nature of *Brahman*, there will result a chaos; and much less can all the effects be explained by presuming that the soul is atomic in size. — *KA* 231-235

All the substances form a type in view of their being a substance, but they vary from each other on account of their distinguishing qualities. The object which is characterized, at every moment, by origination, destruction and permanence, and is the substratum of qualities and modes, is said to be existent. Every moment the earlier form/mode is replaced by the succeeding one; this is what is called (in ordinary parlance) destruction and origination of a thing. As a substance, *jīva* neither dies alone nor is born; it is what it is eternally. In the constant process of development, *dravya* is marked by the persistence of its essential nature. But its modification is a specific phase: it is with reference to the specific phases that a substance is subject to origination and destruction. The inherent common property of a substance is its eternal attribute; it is inseparably associated with the substance. And what appears and disappears in a substance is a mode, a distinguishing and temporary property (according to the author, *guṇa* = *sāmānya-svarūpa*, but *paryāya* = *viśeṣa-rūpa*). The unitary collocation of substance, quality and mode is an object of factual experience. If the modes were not to change, disappearance/ destruction loses meaning; many modes which were absent earlier appear on the substratum of eternal substance. Substances get distinguished on account of specified modes; otherwise as substances they are not distinguishable. —*KA* 236-246

If knowledge alone is real and everything else unreal, then there remains no object of knowledge without which functioning of knowledge loses all meaning. The objects of knowledge are real and the *ātman* (which is an embodiment of knowledge) knows them as separate from itself. To deny the outside objective world, so patent to all, is a mockery of perverted understanding. What exists cannot be denied, and one does not exist cannot be grasped and described even as void. Names indicate objects which are facts of experience. — *KA* 247-252

That is knowledge which knows rightly the Self and other objectivity, endowed with manifold characteristics. The only signs (*kevala-jñāna*) and light of the physical world (*loka*) constituted of substances and modification and the pure space beyond (*alokākāśa*). The omniscient is called omnipresent by his all-pervasive functioning of knowledge, but the knowledge does not leave the soul and go beyond. The process of knowing functions without the knower and the object of knowledge leaving their respective places. As distinguished from the *Kevala* (which is *sakala-pratyakṣa*), *manaḥ-paryāya* and *avadhi* types of knowledge are *deśa-pratyakṣa*, i.e. of partial comprehension. Both *mati* and *śruta* types are indirect, the former being of more clarity and immediateness. *Mati-jñāna* (sensory knowledge) is possible through five sense organs and also the mind. It is the mind that comprehends the topics covered by senses and *śruta* (scriptural knowledge). Of the five sense-knowledge, only one functions at a time and the rest are latent. Every object has manifold aspects, and can be viewed only from a single aspect with the help of scriptural knowledge and of *nayas*. Any assertion about it is from some point of view or the other. The knowledge indirectly brings out the manifold aspects of objectivity, divested of flaws like doubt, etc. —*KA* 253-262

Naya is a variety of scriptural knowledge and originates from some characteristic of the other; it serves day-to-day worldly transactions with some aspect or object in view. The reality is a complexity, and when something is stated about it, it is with some aspect predominantly in view, and others being put in the background for the moment. *Naya* is threefold. That is a *sunaya* (a good point of view), which does not ignore or deny other points of view; but a bad point of view (*durnaya*) leaves no margin for other views. All worldly transactions are well explained by good points of view. — *KA* 263-266

Jīva is known from sense-functions and physical activities: that is *anumāna* (influence); it is also a *naya*, a point of view of which there are many a variety. Collectively speaking, *naya* is one; spoken from the points of view of the *dravya* and *paryāya*, it is twofold; and going into more particulars, it is other varieties like *naigama*, etc. The *dravyārthika naya* (substantial point of view), states reasonably the general (*sāmānya*), without

> denying the particular; while the *paryāya naya* states from various characteristics, etc. the particulars keeping in view the generality. —*KA* 267-270
>
> The *naigama naya* describes optionally the past and future in terms of the present. The *saṁgraha naya* states a class or group-point of view for a part or whole of a substance or modification, taking the common characteristic into consideration. The *vyavahāra naya* states a distributed view of the non-specified general by dividing or separating it into classes, etc. up to the minutest particle. The *ṛjusūtra naya* states the immediate condition of a thing as it is at present, at a particular moment. The *śabda naya* describes the difference between various objects with reference to their grammatical number, gender, etc. The *abhiryadha naya* specifies individual connotation of various objects with reference to the distinctions or the chief connotation (among them all). The *evambhūta naya* states the then aspect, situation or connotation of a thing. He also describes a thing in this world from these various points of view achieves faith, knowledge and conduct, and in due course, attains heaven and liberation. — *KA* 271-278
>
> The number of people who hear, understand, mediate and retain the principles (of religion) is always small: a firm grasp and steady reflection leads to a correct understanding of reality. Internal and external non-attachment brings therewith so many virtues. He who meditates quietly on the nature of the universe becomes a crest-jewel for the three worlds by destroying the stock of *karmas*. — *KA* 279-283

According to Jugal Kishore Mukhtar Yugantar (1956: 498-499), the instruction manner of verse *KA* 279 is not harmonious with the narration style of this chapter. Moreover, *KA* 281-282 are not consistent or in harmony with the subject of *loka-bhāva* and, in this treatise at no other place, the style of narration has been adopted. Hence, these two verses clearly seem to be an interpolation.

Chapter 7
Aśuci Anuprekṣā
(Impurity of the Body)

43

अट्ठीहिं पडिबद्धं मंसविलित्तं तएण ओच्छण्णं ।
किमिसंकुलेहिं भरियमचोक्खं देहं सयाकालं ॥

aṭṭhīhiṁ paḍibaddhaṁ maṁsavilittaṁ taeṇa occhaṇṇaṁ ।
kimisaṅkulehiṁ bhariyamacokkhaṁ dehaṁ sayākālaṁ ॥

This body is made of bones, composed with flesh, coated with skin and infested with swarms of insects. So it is ever dirty and *apraśasta*, i.e. not to be praised or commended.

Commentary by M.K. Dharma Raja

The human body is a compound of foul and filthy matter. The very source of its formation — the mother's womb itself is surrounded by filth. These dirty components constitute the basis of its growth. Its growth process is likewise nauseating; the body, in truth, is a pot of flesh covered with skin. Microbes and minute insects germinate and infest the putrid frame of bones covered by the skin-parchment.

This blatantly repulsive and dirty profile of the physical body becomes obvious on deeper reflection. It is, therefore, unwise to feel attached to this repository of foul and filthy matter (1990: 50).

44

दुग्गंधं बीभच्छं कलिमलभरिदं अचेयणं मुत्तं ।
सडणप्पडणसहावं देहं इदि चिंतए णिच्चं ॥

duggandhaṁ bībhacchaṁ kalimalabharidaṁ aceyaṇaṁ muttaṁ ।
saḍaṇappaḍaṇasahāvaṁ dehaṁ idi cintae ṇiccaṁ ॥

This body is foul-smelling, repugnant, filled with filth, inert or inanimate, corporeal and liable to rot and decay. One should always contemplate in this way.

Commentary by M.K. Dharma Raja

It is also obvious that the physical body is composed of stinking ingredients which are positively repugnant. It resembles a vessel overflowing with refuse like excreta. No amount of bathing or annointing with perfumes and scents can make it cleaner than what it is. In fact, beauty aids and cosmetics are apt to get polluted through contact with this repository of contaminating filth.

The physical body is nothing but an amalgam of inert, inanimate matter liable to decompose and wither away. It is, therefore, senseless to remain at the mercy of the mortal body which must really be looked upon as one's servant and not the master.

This should be the theme of constant contemplation of those seeking to cast away the shreds of attachment to the physical body (1990: 51).

45

रसरुहिरमंसमेदट्ठीमज्जसंकुलं पुत्तपूयकिमिबहुलं ।
दुग्गंधमसुचि चम्ममयमणिच्चमचेयणं पडणं ॥

rasaruhiramaṁsamedaṭṭhīmajjasaṅkulaṁ puttapūya-kimibahulaṁ ।
duggaṅdhamasuci cammamayamaṇiccamaceyaṇaṁ paḍaṇaṁ ॥

This body is filled with the bile, blood, flesh, fat, bones and marrow; it has a surfeit of urine and excreta; is foul-smelling, impure, skin-coated, impermanent, inert or inanimate and subject to disintegration.

Commentary by M.K. Dharma Raja

The utterly repugnant and despicable composition of the body is vividly brought out in this verse.

This body with its superficial gloss and an alluring, handsome exterior is really a perishable object. It is abominably filthy, containing foul-smelling matter like bile and phlegm, flesh, fat and bone marrow. It abounds with refuse and excreta.

The wise look upon the body realistically that it is inert, inanimate and utterly perishable (1990: 52).

46

देहादो वदिरित्तो कम्मविरहिओ अणंतसुहणिलयो ।
चोक्खो हवेइ अप्पा इदि णिच्चं भावणं कुज्जा ॥

dehādo vadiritto kammavirahio aṇaṁtasuhaṇilayo ।
cokkho havei appā idi ṇiccaṁ bhāvaṇaṁ kujjā ॥

The soul is distinct from the body. It is devoid of *karmas*; it is the abode of infinite bliss and is to be praised and commended (*praśasta*). Thus, one should contemplate all the while.

Commentary by M.K. Dharma Raja

A discerning and thoughtful aspirant on the path of spiritual advancement is aware of the soul being distinct from the physical body imprisoning it. He knows that this true Self (soul) is not tainted with the bondage of *karmas*. He is convinced that the soul freed from the shackles of mundane illusions attains its intrinsic state of infinite bliss.

The transcendental, pure nature of the Self is invisible or imperceptible, non-corporeal, formless, permanent, unborn, without support, intelligent, without defect or fault and indivisible. In *Pravacanasāra* 192, Kundakunda states:

> The Self is pure as it is only knowledge and intuition, a great thing, suprasensual, supreme reality, eternal, stable and without any proper support.

Constant contemplation on this weans the mind away from all afflictions of attachment of the allurements of the physical body. Continuous reflection on this theme is an effective aid to self-realization (1990: 52-53).

Kārttikeyānuprekṣā

Kundakunda has described the *aśuci anuprekṣā* in four verses (*BA* 39-42). *Kārttikeyānuprekṣā* describes it in five verses as follows:

> One's body is full of all that is impure, rotten and stinking: even the pure and fragrant stuff becomes detestable by its contact. Ordinarily people should be disgusted with it, but on the contrary, they are attached to it and want to derive pleasure from it. One should relinquish attachment for the body and engross oneself in one's own *ātman*. — *KA* 83-87

Chapter 8
Āsrava Anuprekṣā
(The Inflow of Karmas)

47

मिच्छतं अविरमणं कसायजोगा य आसवा होंति।
पण पण चउतियभेदा सम्मं परिकित्तिदा समए॥

micchataṁ aviramaṇaṁ kasāyajogā ya āsavā hoṁti ।
paṇa paṇa cautiyabhedā sammaṁ parikittidā samae ॥

Mithyātva (deluded view, delusion or perversity of vision), *avirati* (lack of moral self-restraints or non-abstinence), *kaṣāya* (passions) and *yoga* (the vibrating activities of mind, speech and body) are the four conditions or factors of the inflow of *karmas*. These have been properly enumerated in scriptures under five (deluded view), five (non-abstinence), four (passions) and three (*yoga*) categories. (These various kinds of deluded view, etc. are explained in subsequent verses.)

Commentary

In *Samayasāra* 109, the psychic states or modes of delusion or perverted worldview (*mithyātva*), the lack of moral discipline (*avirati*), anger, etc. passions (*kaṣāya*) and vibrations in the soul by the activity of body, speech and mind (called *yoga* in Jainism) (*TS* 6.1) are described as the four *pratyayas* (*SS* 109). These influence/condition kārmic matter to get transformed into knowledge-covering, etc. material or physical *karma* (*dravya-karma*). In this way, they act as the external condition or supportive factor (*nimitta*) of the influx and consequent bondage of physical *karmas*. Physical *karmas* are said to have the power (*śakti*) to act (as an external causal agent) to induce/produce changes (psychic impurity or distortion into anger, etc.) in the mental states of soul, called psychic *karma* (*bhāva-karma*) (*Gommaṭasāra Karmakāṇḍa* 6). Thus, psychic *karmas* are the defects (*doṣa*) of delusion and passions in the capacities of the soul. Physical *karma*, on the other hand, also called covers (*āvaraṇa*) consist of kārmic matter which brings about those defects, perversions and changes in the psychic states of the soul. In this way, the physical and the psychic *karmas*, corresponding to *dravya-karma* and *bhāva-karma* are said to be mutually related as cause and effect, each of the other.

Deluded or perverse views of the reality of things (*mithyātva*), non-abstinence (*avirati*), passions (*kaṣāyas*) and the vibratory activities of the mind, speech and body (*yoga*) are the causes of knowledge-covering or knowledge-obscuring, etc. eight kinds of material or physical *karmas* (*SS* 165), while the psychic states of infatuation, attachment and aversion are the conditions or the causes of deluded view, etc. psychic modes (*SS* 165). In reality, it is attachment that binds *karmas* (*SS* 150).

The psychic condition that makes possible the inflow of kārmic particles into the Self is known as *bhāvāsrava* (modifications, perversions or distortions of consciousness or the intrinsic nature and capacities of the Self), while the actual kārmic particles which enter into the Self constitute *dravyāsrava* (influx of material particles). The senses, passions and non-abstinence or non-observance of vows are the causes of the twenty-five kinds of activity, which are their effects (mentioned below).

Again, the inflow of *karmas* is of two kinds, viz. *samparāyika āsrava* and *īryāpatha āsrava* (*TS* IX.4). Souls affected with the passions have *samparāyika āsrava* (mundane inflow of kārmic matter which causes the cycle of births and rebirths). Those without the passions have *īryāpatha āsrava* (transient or fleeting inflow). Mundane inflow is the first ten and transient inflow in the eleventh, twelfth and thirteenth stages (*guṇa-sthāna*).

There are forty-two "doors" (causes) of kārmic inflow —

three instantaneous (the activities of body, speech and mind) and thirty-nine long-term, i.e. bondage proper. These thirty-nine causes are the five senses of touch, taste, smell, sight and hearing, four passions, five indulgences (*avrata*), i.e. non-observance of vows (these are causing injury, lying, stealing, incontinence and possessiveness) and twenty-five activities or urges (*kriyāḥ*).[1] These twenty-five urges are:

1. urges that lead to an enlightened worldview;
2. urges that lead to a deluded worldview;
3. evil urges of the body, speech and mind;
4. the inclination of the ascetic to abstain;
5. urges that produce instantaneous inflow;
6. physical enthusiasm;
7. using instruments of destruction;
8. malicious activity;
9. torturous activity;
10. murderous activity;
11. urges for visual gratification;
12. urges for tactile gratification;
13. inventing and manufacturing lethal weapons;
14. evacuating bowels or vomiting at gatherings of men and women;
15. occupying uninspected and unswept places and leaving things there;
16. undertaking others' duties out of anger or conceit;
17. approving of an evil act;
18. divulging the sins of others;

---

[1] *Tattvārthasūtra* VI.6 (*Svopajña Bhāṣya*), VI.5 (*Sarvārthasiddhi*); see Tatia 1998: 153.

19. arbitrary interpretation of scriptural teachings;
20. disrespect for the scriptural teachings;
21. damage to the environment such as digging the earth and shredding leaves;
22. possessive clinging;
23. deceitful actions;
24. promotion of deluded views; and
25. harbouring passions and possessiveness.

The senses, passions, indulgences (non-observances of vows) and urges to collaborate in the production of kārmic inflow. Any passionate act, whether good or evil, causes the inflow of long-term *karma*.[2]

The psychic condition that makes possible the inflow of kārmic particles into the Self is known as *bhāvāsrava* (the modifications, perversions or distortions of consciousness or the intrinsic nature and capacities of the Self), while the actual kārmic particles which enter into the Self constitute *dravyāsrava* (influx of material particles).

Unlike most Western philosophers, psychologists and neuroscientists, including Max Velmans and John Searle, who postulate only a single substrate (brain states) for mental states and lay emphasis on the neural correlates of consciousness, Jaina thought recognizes two substrates of psychic mind or mental states. The bible of the Jainas specifically states: *adhikaraṇam jiva ajiva* (*Tattvārthasūtra* VI.7).

When the mind has its substrate in *jīva*, it acts as a vehicle/instrument for giving vent to instinctive urges, primarily the survival instinct concerned with acquiring food, resorting to fight or flight syndrome, sexual activity and provision for future subsistence

[2] *Tattvārthasūtra* VI.6 (*Svopajña Bhāṣya*), VI.5 (*Sarvārthasiddhi*); see Tatia 1998: 153.

(possessiveness).[3] More than anything else, these subconscious motivations, having emotional preferences, determine the conduct of the individual and contribute to his worth.

These subconscious motivations may be considered as constituting derived intentionality, i.e. a mental wish to act which has its own unconscious antecedents or preceding unconscious processes, reflected in the onset of electrically observable cerebral processes, called readiness potential (RP), noticed in Libet's experiments, i.e. in *tejas śarīra* (electric body) of the Jainas. This wish to act is not to be confused with the true or real intentionality, the conscious will, representing conscious entity's "censor" potentiality which could block or "veto" the volitional processes initiated unconsciously by at least 350 msecs of RP, resulting in no motor act.

In this context, Benjamin Libet observes:

> The conscious veto is a control function, different from simply becoming aware of the wish to act. The conscious decision to veto could be made without direct specifications for that decision by the preceding unconscious processes (2003: 24-25).

Such a view, Libet states, "allows genuine conscious free will to be a controlling agent in the performance of a voluntary act" (2003: 25).

The "wish to act" is the psychic *karma* type of mental state which is the product or result of unconscious processes, i.e. physical *karma*, while the "conscious free will" is the decision of conscious entity or soul, which is not conditioned, affected or caused by physical *karma*, i.e. unconscious processes or brain states. The "wish to act" is the psychic disposition of the conditioned mind, while "conscious free will" is an act of conscious entity, unconditioned mind or consciousness-as-such. It is not without purpose that the phrase "conscious free will" is qualified by Libet with the adjective "genuine" so as to highlight the distinction between two kinds

3 For a detailed discussion on the Jaina concept of instincts and their comparison with William McDougall's enumeration, see Jain, J.P. 2005: 53-75.

of psychic states: conscious entity or Self and conditioned mind. However, no distinction is made in the West between consciousness and mind, so the words "mental", "psychic" and "conscious" have become synonyms in the English language and Western tradition and are used interchangeably without any thought of distinction between them.

The mental activities, that have their substrate in brain states, are "unconsciously planned and executed" and are primarily the result of neurophysiological processing of data in the brain, including past memory, by the so-called "interpreter", the special device (cortex) in our left brain, and hence are naturally full of "telling errors of perception, memory and judgement" (Gazzaniga 1998: xiii). These are obviously lacking in coherence, a balanced and detached view, discriminative insight and unity of conscious experience, which are the prerogatives of conscious entity and the domain of conscious attentiveness (*upayoga*).

Man, according to Jainism, recognizes that physical *karma* (the neurophysiological processes and brain states), has the power (*śakti*) to operate as *bhāva-karma* (psychic *karma*, i.e. mental states) (*Gommaṭasāra Karmakāṇḍa* 6). This may be said to be the nearest Jaina equivalent of neural correlates of "mental states". It should, however, not be forgotten that in Jainism these physical *karma* types of neural correlates are not deterministic in nature unless they are consented to and not vetoed by the conscious entity. They only act as an indirect, auxiliary cause of mental states. Likewise, mental states have the power to indirectly cause changes in neurophysiological processes or mental states.

48

एयंतविणयविवरियसंसयमण्णाणमिदि हवे पंच ।
अविरमणं हिंसादी पंचविहो सो हवइ णियमेण ॥

eyaṁtaviṇayavivariyasaṁsayamaṇṇāṇamidi have paṁca ।
aviramaṇaṁ hiṁsādī paṁcaviho so havai ṇiyameṇa ॥

Deluded belief or view (*mithyātva*) is of five kinds: (1) *ekānta* (one-sided view); (2) *vinaya* (indiscriminate veneration); (3) *viparīta* (perverse or contrary view); (4) *saṁśaya* (doubt or scepticism); and (5) *ajñāna* (ignorance or perverted knowledge).

And *avirati* (lack of moral self-restraints) is also of five kinds, violence or causing injury, etc.

Commentary

Deluded view is of five kinds:

1. One-sided view (*ekānta*), i.e. is taking only one aspect of a many-sided thing, e.g. man is mortal from the point of body and that man is immortal from the point of view of the soul or consciousness. It is erroneous to describe a man as only mortal or immortal.
2. Indiscriminate veneration (*vinaya*) or *vaināyika*, i.e. taking all goods, all scriptures or preceptors to be equally worthy of veneration).
3. Perverse (*viparīta*) belief, e.g. animal sacrifices lead to heaven, etc.
4. Doubt, scepticism (*saṁśaya*), i.e. doubt as to path of liberation.
5. Ignorance (*ajñāna*) or deluded view or wrong belief caused by perverted knowledge, e.g. lack of awareness in choosing between right and wrong, good and bad.

Ekānta, etc. five kinds of delusion (*mithyātva*) are the kinds of *grāhatā* (acquired) *mithyātva* which is grasping or taking of contrary view (*anyathā*) than what it really is, of the six principles:

1. Worthy Lord (*deva*).
2. Preceptor (*guru*).
3. Righteousness or piety (*dharma*).
4. *Āpta*, i.e. Omniscient Lord, Jaina Tīrthaṅkaras or true Gods (*āpta*) who are free from faults and weaknesses of the lower nature. They are also free from eighteen kinds of blemishes

like hunger, thirst, senility, disease, birth, death, fear, pride, attachment, aversion, infatuation, worry, conceit, hatred, uneasiness, sweat, etc. (*RKS* 6). Pride is the intoxication of the Self in respect of eight particulars: (i) learning, (ii) worship, (iii) family; (iv) tribe; (v) power; (vi) influence on accomplishment; (vii) religious austerities; and (viii) person (*RKS* 25).

5. *Āgama*, i.e. true scripture which is the word of a Tīrthaṅkara[4]; cannot be overridden in disputation, nor falsified by a perception, reason or testimony, which reveals the nature of things as they exist, which is helpful to men into other beings and which are potent enough to destroy all forms of falsehood (*RKS* 9).
6. The nature of objects of things (*padārtha*) (Sastri 1991: 48).

Those who suffer from any of the above-mentioned kinds of deluded view are subject to the constant inflow of kārmic molecules.

Lack of moral self-restraints or vowlessness (*avirati*) is also of five kinds: (1) violence and causing injury to living being; (2) falsehood; (3) theft; (4) unchastity; and (5) possessiveness (*parigraha*).

The seven kinds of fear are: (1) fear relating to this life; (2) fear relating to future life; (3) fear of being without protection; (4) fear of the disclosure of what is kept in secret; (5) fear of pain; (6) fear of accident; and (7) fear of death.

Avirati (abstinence or vowlessness) is also of five kinds: (1) violence (*hiṁsā*); (2)falsehood (*anṛta* or *jhūṭha*); (3) theft (*steya* or *corī*); (4) unchastity (*abrahma* or *kśīla*); and (5) possessiveness (*parigraha*) (*TS* VII.1).

These five kinds of vows (*vrata*) are of two kinds for householders and for houseless ascetics (*TS* VII.19) are classified as:

---

[4] For details, see commentary on *BA* 55.

1. *aṇuvrata*, i.e. partial vow (that is limited abstention from the five or sources mentioned above) is practised by laymen or householders according to their capacity; and
2. *mahāvrata*, i.e. total or complete six abstentions of the five sins, is adopted by ascetics.

Thus, those who practise the five vows or abstentions are of two kinds: (1) *āgārī*, i.e. householders and laymen; and (2) *anāgāra*, i.e. houseless ascetics (*TS* VII.19).

Defining violence, Umāsvāmi or Umāsvāti states: *pramatta yogāt prāṇa vyāpāropaṇam hiṁsā*, i.e. violence means the destruction of vitalities or life processes (*prāṇa*) on account of *pramāda* (carelessness, negligence, passions, thoughtless activity, etc.) (*TS* VII.13).

Commenting on this aphorism, Acharya Pūjyapāda (1992: 196-197) observes:

> The qualifying phrase "arising from passionate activity" is intended to indicate that mere severance of the vitalities is not wicked. "Even with the severance of life one is not stained with the sin of injury." Again it has been said thus in the scriptures: "When a monk goes on foot with carefulness, sometimes small insects get crushed under his feet and die. Still there is not the slightest bondage of sin in his case. From the spiritual standpoint, infatuation is called attachment." Now, has it not been admitted that mere passionate attitude even without the severance of vitalities constitutes violence? "He who acts with negligence commits injury whether death is caused to organisms or not."

In this regard, Kundakunda points out:

> Let the creature die or live, on the part of the careless one the act of hurting is certain: by the mere fact of hurt he who is careful in his observances incurs no bondage. — *PS* 217

Commenting on *Pravacanasāra* 217, Amrtachandra states:

> Impure psychic attention is negligence; the taking of another's life is external. Whether the taking of another being's life occurs or does not occur, to the actual impure psychic attention, proved by the careless conduct, which does not occur without it, the nature of hurting certainly belongs: and to the non-existence of impure psychic attention, proved by the careful conduct, which occurs without it, the nature of hurting certainly does not belong, as is shown by the fact that the taking of another's life does not involve bondage: therefore, internal negligence is the more serious, and not the external. Even so, the external should be recognized, simply as being an occasion for the internal negligence.
>
> —Jain, J.P. 2014: 355-356

Amrtachandra further states that the "material vitalities (*dravya prāṇa*) of "the other" are sometimes injured and sometimes not, but (always) the soul binds (itself with) *karmas*, through being impassioned, causing injury to the subjective *prāṇas* (*bhava-prāṇa*) to itself, the soul binds (itself with the *karmas*) (*PS* 149 AC).

In his work *Puruṣārthasiddhyupāya*, Amrtachandra clearly points out that irrespective of whether there is an injury or not, the absence of care and caution under the influence of passion, *hiṁsā* (violence) is certainly committed (*PSU* 46).

Jaina thinkers have classified violence into 108 varieties so that the aspirant can detect even the minutest form of violence. The violence is threefold inasmuch as it can be

1. committed by the person himself (*kṛta*), or
2. got committed by other (*kārita*), or
3. consent (*anumodana*) is given to the violence committed by others.

This threefold violence becomes ninefold as it can be committed by either of the three agencies of the mind, speech and body. This ninefold violence becomes twenty-sevenfold as it has three stages:

1. thinking of violent action (*samārambha*),

2. making preparation for violence (*samārambha*), and
3. actual committal (*ārambha*).

This twenty-sevenfold violence becomes one-hundred-and-eightfold as it could be inspired by either of the four passions (*kaṣāyas*), viz. anger, pride, deceit and greed (Amitgati 1968: 109, vv. 6.12-13).

The *kaṣāyas* are the four evil motives for *hiṁsā*. These 108 types of *hiṁsā* can become 432 types of *hiṁsā* if each of the four passions is further subdivided by four degrees of intensity.[5]

There are four kinds of violence (*hiṁsā*):

1. *ārambhī* (injury involved in activities like cooking and washing);
2. *udyoginī* (occupational);
3. *virodhinī* (that involved in the protection of one's life and honour); and
4. *saṅkalpī* (intentional).

The householder is required to abstain only from intentional violence (*hiṁsā*).

Falsehood (*anṛta*) is speaking of hurtful words out of passions (*TS* VII.14). Taking anything which is not given by the owner on (*adattadāna*) out of passion is stealing (*steya*) (*TS* VII.15). Unchastity (*abrahma* or *kuśīla*) is sexual or lustful activity out of passion (*TS* VII.16).

Parigraha (possessiveness), the fifth non-abstinence is defined in Pāṇini's *Aṣṭādhyāyī* as *parigrahaṇam parigraha*, i.e. that which entangles, binds, entraps or enslaves one from all sides. The term *aparigraha* (non-possession, non-grasping) has its root in the term *parigraha* which means to amass, to grasp, to accumulate, to compile, to seize, to hold, to fence in and to receive or accept

[5] For the degrees of intensity of passions, see commentary on the next verse.

possessions or property. Etymologically, it consists of two terms: *pari* and *graha*. *Graha* is rooted in *grahaṇa* meaning to take hold of, to accept, to receive or to possess something, while *pari* means round, round about, abundant, rich or fullness (Jain, K. 1998: 61).

Thus, *parigraha* means the entrapping or clutching of the soul from all sides. Under its effect, the soul comes to be possessed by the acquisitions and possessions and comes under the influence of alien, non-soul or foreign matter and thus loses its purity, calm, equanimity and freedom. It becomes subject to the enslavement of material goods or objects. Umāsvāmi defines *parigraha* by the term *mūrcchā* (*TS* VII.17), thereby meaning that attachment or mental clinging to worldly belongings or objects is responsible for generating a sort of hallucination, senselessness, forgetfulness or delusion on account of which it is bound to go astray.

According to Acharya Pūjyapāda, *mūrcchā* (infatuation) is an activity relating to the acquisition and safeguarding of external possessions and also inward thoughts like desire. The word *mūrcchā* denotes fainting or swooning and is used in the sense of insensibility (Pūjyapāda 1992: 199).

One becomes helpless and bewildered under the grip of enslaving desires and passions. Attachment is born out of "mineness" which ultimately binds the soul. All miseries suffered by the Self are the result of attachment towards alien objects. Amrtachandra defines *mūrcchā* as the development of acquisitive egotism, attachment, affectionate regard or belongingness (*mamatva pariṇāma*) to worldly possessions arising from the operation of the delusion (*moha*) (Jain, J.P. 2007: 130, v. 111).

Parigraha is of two kinds: internal or psychic (*ābhyantara* or *antaraṅga*) and external (*bāhya* or *bahiraṅga*). Mental attachment, passions and infatuation or delusion in regard to worldly belongings is internal *parigraha*. Actual possession of property, wealth, servants, farms and houses (*kṣetra-vastu*), gold and silver (*hiraṇya-suvarṇa*), bipeds and quadripeds (*dvipada* and *catuṣpada*), diverse commodities, grains, furniture, etc. is external *parigraha*. The possession of external things is not possible without internal attachment, desire or craving.

49

कोहो माणो माया लोहो वि य चउव्विहं कसायं खु।
मण वचिकाएण पुणो जोगो तिवियप्पमिदि जाणे॥

koho māṇo māyā loho vi ya cauvvihaṁ kasāyaṁ khu ।
maṇa vacikāeṇa puṇo jogo tiviyappamidi jāṇe ॥

Anger, pride, greed and deceit are the four kinds of passions (*kaṣāya*). And the vibratory activity of mind, speech and body are the three kinds of *yoga*. Thus, one should know that.

Commentary

Kaṣāya (passions) is one of the most fundamental concepts of Jainism and is, indeed, central to the understanding of Jaina psychology, philosophy, ethics and spirituality. The control of passions plays a significant role in spiritual awakening as well as in moral and spiritual advancement. *Kaṣāya* is the main cause of kārmic bondage (*TS* VIII.2) and in the absence of passions, which provides the glue, the activities of mind, body and speech cannot cause any kārmic bondage. According to Haribhadra, liberation from passions is the real liberation (*kaṣāyamukti kila muktivaha*). The Jaina concept of passions is not purely psychological, but psycho-ethical in character.

According to Kundakunda, however, passions (*kaṣāyas*), along with the delusion (*mithyātva*), lack of moral self-restraints (*avirati*), and the vibrations of mind, speech and body (*yoga*) are considered as four *pratyayas* (*SS* 109), which are the influencing factors, which act as the conditions (*hetu*), the supportive factor (*nimitta*) or the auxiliary cause (*nimitta-kāraṇa*) for the inflow of and the consequent bondage of knowledge-covering, etc. eight kinds of physical or material *karmas*.

The psychic states of attachment, diverse and infatuation of the real causes of delusion (*mithyātva*), etc. psychic modes and the influx and bondage of *karmas*. In *Samayasāra* 150, Kundakunda has categorically stated that attachment binds *karmas* (*ratto bandhādi kammas*).

The root cause of all our sufferings and mental tensions is our attachment to the objects of worldly enjoyment. But when there is any hindrance, obstruction or opposition in this regard we react by expression of our dislike or aversion. Thus, our attachment (*rāga*) and aversion (*dveṣa*), or likes and dislikes, are the sources of all our problems and miseries. The four passions, viz. *krodha* (anger), *māna* (pride or ego), *māyā* (deceit) and *lobha* (greed), are considered to be the offshoots or manifestations of *rāga* and *dveṣa*. *Krodha* and *māna* come within the fold of *dveṣa*, while *māyā* and *lobha* belong to the category of *rāga*. The four passions give rise to negativities, impurities and distortions in the Self and are the cause of all our sufferings. That is why it is said: *moha rāga ruṣ* (*dveṣa*) infatuation or delusion, attachment and aversion (*duḥkha kī khāna*)[6] are the cause of our sufferings.

Desires and passions are closely related. According to Champat Rai Jain, "desires develop into passions", as passions are but violent forms of desire, which means mental agitation. He observes:

> An active longing for a thing is termed greed. The state of the fury which blazes up when one is thwarted in the obtainment or enjoyment of an object of desire is anger. The cunning that is resorted to secure an object of desire is deceit. The state of intense self-glorification which results by the possession of the desired object or state is pride. —Jain, C.R. 1929: 13

Passions stand in the way of our moral and spiritual advancement. It is because of these passions that man cannot attain enlightened vision, enlightened knowledge and enlightened conduct, which together lead to liberation (*mokṣa*). Again, it is due

---

6 *Ātma Kīrtana* by Manoharlal (Sahjanand) Varni.

to these passions that one can neither practise the five rules or vows (*vratas*) of moral conduct nor follow the ten virtues. Intense passions manifest themselves or give rise to all the five vices or sins, viz. violence, falsehood, stealing, unchastity, and unlimited wants and possessions. One cannot commit violence unless one is nursing anger inside. Violence is an effect, an outward manifestation of anger. One resorts to falsehood or lying because of deceit or greed or both. And because of greed, intense attachment to objects and persons, one indulges in acquiring material possessions without any limits, hoarding, adulteration, stealing and unchastity. Unbridled desires for possessions compel a person to resort to falsehood, stealing and exploitation of others. It is for these reasons that greed is said to be the source of all the sins (*lobha pāpa kā bāpa bakhānā—Daśalakṣaṇa Dharma Pūjā*).

Each of the four passions are further subdivided into four subcategories, depending upon their degrees of strength or intensity. These imply the proportional density of fusions of kārmic particles, i.e. the higher the degree, the larger is the fusion, longer is its time to decay and stronger is the kārmic force (Mardia 1990: 43). These are:

1. *Anantānubandhī* (tenacious, irresistible, uncontrollable, extremely severe or most intense): When the four passions of anger, pride, deceit and greed are of great intensity, they keep the soul immersed in the darkness of delusion leading to deluded conduct and unending worldly wanderings. They are called tenacious (Tatia 1998: 194). This group of passions is the worst. It completely hinders enlightened vision (*samyak darśana*), lasts a very long time and is the cause of indefinite transmigration in worldly existence.
2. *Apratyākhyāna* (non-abstinent, overwhelming or severe): This group prevents the soul from observing the vows, i.e. the twelve *vratas* (vows) of the householder. A person is, thus, not able to practise even partial self-restraint. This

group, however, does not prevent a person from attaining discriminating insight or enlightened vision.

3. *Pratyākhyāna* (partially abstinent or moderate): In this group of passions, the passions are further weakened. They allow the soul to undertake the vows, i.e. partial self-restraint. But they cover the capacity for complete abstinence.
4. *Sañjvalana* (flickering or mild): When the passions get rid of their gross nature and become subtle forces, they are called flickering passions which disturb the soul's higher states of spiritual development. They are detrimental to the practice of perfect conduct which requires complete absence of passion, i.e. complete non-attachment (*vītarāgatā*). It is said that intense passion is vice or sinful, while mild passion is *śubha* (auspicious or wholesome) and virtuous (*KA* 90).

Of the four types of bondage of *karmas*, viz. nature or class (*prakṛti*), duration (*sthiti*), the intensity of fruition (*anubhāga*) and quantity or mass of material particles assimilated by the soul (*pradeśa bandha*), nature and quantity of assimilated kārmic particles depend on the vibratory activities of mind, speech and body (*yoga*), while the duration and intensity are determined by the passions.

50

असुहेदरभेदेण दु एक्केकं वण्णिदं हवे दुविहं ।
आहारादी सण्णा असुहमणं इदि विजाणेहि ॥

asuhedarabhedeṇa du ekkekaṁ vaṇṇidaṁ have duvihaṁ ।
āhārādī saṇṇā asuhamaṇaṁ idi vijāṇehi ॥

Each of the three vibratory activities of mind, speech and body is of two kinds: (1) good, wholesome or auspicious (*śubha*); and (2) bad, unwholesome and inauspicious (*aśubha*). Food, etc. instincts (*saṁjñā*) from inauspicious motivations in thought activities are to be known as inauspicious mind (*aśubha mana*).

Commentary

The soul (*jīva*), which is endowed with consciousness, and the inert, inanimate matter (*pudgala*) undergo states-of-evolution (*pariṇāma*), which is of two kinds: (1) *bhava pariṇāma*, i.e. evolution into being; and (2) *parispanda* or *kriyā pariṇāma*, i.e. evolution and characterized by vibrations and action (*PS* 129; *PS* 129 AC). (The other substances, including space and time, however, undergo only *bhava pariṇāma.*)

The vibration (*parispandana*) that takes place in the space-points (*pradeśa*) of the soul due to the vibratory activities either of mind only, speech only or body alone (separately) is called *yoga*, not the combination of all three.

The inflow (*āsrava*) of auspicious *karmas* (*śubha karma*) takes place through auspicious vibratory activities (*śubha yoga*) and the inflow of inauspicious *karmas* (*aśubha karmas*) takes place through inauspicious vibratory activities (*aśubha yoga*) and the inflow of inauspicious *karmas* (*aśubha karmas*) takes place through inauspicious vibratory activities (*aśubha yoga*). The tendencies, inclinations or dispositions of mind, speech and body, obtained by desire, craving of passion through auspicious or inauspicious conscious attentiveness (*upayoga*) are the conditions (*hetu*) of the inflow (*āsrava*) of *śubha* or *aśubha karmas* (*Yogasāra* 3.1; Shastri 1991: 50).

51

किण्हादि तिण्णि लेस्सा करणजसोक्खेसु गिद्धिपरिणामो।
ईसा विसादभावो असुहमणं त्ति य जिणा वेंति॥

kiṇhādi tiṇṇi lessā karaṇajasokkhesu giddhipariṇāmo ।
īsā visādabhāvo asuhamaṇaṁ tti ya jiṇā veṁti ॥

The three thought-paints (*leśyās*) of black, etc. arise from intense lustful craving or desire for sensual pleasures, thought of envy and jealousy and grief and are described by the Omniscient Lord as inauspicious mind (*aśubha mana*).

Commentary

The tendency, inflation or disposition of the activities of mind, speech and body (*yoga*), tainted, conciliated, attached to or imbued with (*anurañjita*) due to the coming into operation or rise of passions.

The three thought-paints, colouration or soil-soiling tints (*leśyā*) referred to in this verse are: (1) black (*kṛṣṇa*); (2) blue (*nīla*); and (3) grey (*kapota*). The black thought-paint is wrathful, wicked, having intense craving for sense objects and are imbued with the extremely severe or most intense degree of passions (*anantānubandhī kaṣāya*). The blue thought-paint is deceitful, having intense desire for worldly objects and severe degree of passions. The grey thought-paint is imbued with sorrow, fear, envy or jealousy.

These three thought-paints are unwholesome or inauspicious (*aśubha*), which affect the soul with the inflow of sinful (*pāpa*) *karmas*.

Thought-paint (*bhāva-leśyā*) is distinguished from material or physical *leśyā* (*dravya-leśyā*), i.e. matter paint or colour of the matter.

There are other three thought-paints, viz. (1) pale or yellow (*pīlā*); (2) pink (*padma*); and (3) white (*śukla*). These three are wholesome or auspicious thought-paints, which lead to the inflow of wholesome or auspicious (*śubha*) *karmas*. The first of these two have mild and milder degree of passions. In the third, i.e. *śukla-leśyā*, there is total absence of anger, etc. passions.

The six thought-paints are best illustrated by the example of six travellers who have lost their way in a forest and become very hungry but fortunately see a large *jambu* tree laden with fruits. The first person with black *leśyā* thought of uprooting the tree. The second person with blue *leśyā* thought of cutting the large branches. The third one with grey *leśyā* thought of cutting small branches. The fourth one with yellow *leśyā* thought to bring down the bunches of fruits. The fifth with pink *leśyā* thought of plucking ripe fruits from the branches. The sixth one with white (*śukla*) *leśyā* picked up and ate the ripe fruits that had fallen on the ground.

52

रागो दोसो मोहो हास्सादिणोकसायपरिणामो ।
थूलो वा सुहुमो वा असुहमणे त्ति य जिणा वेंति ॥

rāgo doso moho hāssādiṇokasāyapariṇāmo ।
thūlo vā suhumo vā asuhamaṇe tti ya jiṇā veṅti ॥

Attachment, aversion, infatuation and laughter, etc. quasi-passions (no-*kaṣāya*) are the states-of-evolution of the soul, whether gross, cruel or intense (*sthūla*) or subtle, slender, mild or minute (*sūkṣma*); they are said to be of inauspicious mind (*aśubha mana*) by the Omniscient Lord (Jina).

Commentary

Attachment and aversion are the causes of bondage of *karmas*. Infatuation (*moha*) relates or pertains to deluding (*mohanīya*) *karmas*. It is of two kinds: view-deluding (*darśana-mohanīya*) and conduct-deluding (*caritra-mohanīya*). View-deluding *karmas* distort enlightened vision, while conduct-deluding *karmas* cause delusion in the form of attachment, aversion and passions and, thus, obstruct enlightened conduct. These *karmas* are considered to be the greatest obstacle in the path of liberation and needs to the attenuated, eradicated and overcome in order to attain equanimity, peace, happiness and social well-being. Of the eight types of *karmas*, only deluding *karmas* can be suppressed.

Jaina texts describe nine no-*kaṣāyas* (quasi-passions or minor passions). They are called quasi-passions because they are incapable of harming the soul in the absence of the primary passions of anger, pride, deceit and greed (Tatia 1998: 195). They inspire, trigger or give rise to the main passions and coexist with them. The quasi-passions go out of existence as soon as the twelve passions, i.e. the four main passions in their extremely severe, severe, moderate and mild forms are conquered or annihilated. The nine quasi-passions are: (1) *hāsya* (scornful laughter); (2) *rati* (love or relish); (3) *arati* (dislike, hatred or ennui); (4) *śoka* (grief or sorrow); (5) *bhaya* (fear); (6) *jugupsā* (disgust or abhorrence); (7) *puruṣaveda* (feminine-sexuality or cause of sexual desire for women); (8) *strīveda* (masculine sexuality or cause of sexual desire for men); and (9) *napuṁsakaveda* (hermaphroditic sexuality or cause of sexual desire for both men and women).

The ninth quasi-passion should not be understood in the sense of impotency or frigidity, inasmuch as both impotency or frigidity are of the nature of negation of the sex-drive and, hence, not positively real which is an essential condition of emotion (e-motion) or passion. It is to be taken in the sense of a twofold desire directed towards the male and the female. The sexual desires should not be mistaken for the sexual organs. The desires relating to sex are mental dispositions, whereas the organs corresponding to these desires are physical (Mehta 1957: 133).

Jayasena includes anger, pride and four quasi-passions, viz. *arati* (hatred), grief, fear and disgust in aversion (*dveṣa*) and deceit, greed and the rest of the quasi-passions in attachment (*rāga*). The sixteen kinds of passions (the four primary passions, each subdivided into four degrees of intensity) and the nine quasi-passions are synonymous with conduct-deluding (*caritra mohanīya*) *karmas*, which is the deadliest of enemy of moral and spiritual discipline.[7]

53

भत्तित्थिरायचोरकहाओ वयणं वियाण असुहमिदि ।
बंधणछेदणमारणकिरिया सा असुहकायेत्ति ॥

---

[7] Commentary on *Samayasāra*, *gāthā* 282.

bhattitthirāyacorakahāo vayaṇaṁ viyāṇa asuhamidi ।
baṅdhaṇachedaṇamāraṇakiriyā sā asuhakāyetti ॥

Talk about food, women, politics and thefts are to be known as inauspicious speech (*aśubha vacana*). Acts of binding (restraining) piercing or severing (cutting) and beating or killing are inauspicious acts of the body (*aśubha kāya*).

Commentary

The talk or indulgence in conversations concerning inauspicious speech is considered *vikatha*, i.e. frivolous, useless, idle gossip or reprehensible talk. *Vikatha* is of four kinds: those concerning food (*bhojana katha*), women (*strī katha*), affairs of state politics (*rāja katha*) and thefts (*cora katha*). Praising, smelling, etc. in regard to various kinds of dishes is *bhojana katha*. Talk about the beauty, appearance, etc. of women inducing lustful thoughts is *strī katha*, which abets inauspicious thoughts of attachment. Indulgence in conversation pertaining to kings, their grandeur, wealth, etc. and the affairs of state or politics is *rāja katha*. And talk about the wealth, ornaments, etc. stolen by thieves and the punishment suffered gives rise to inauspicious thoughts. In the same way, the bodily activities of binding, cutting and killing are the inauspicious activities of the body.

54

मोत्तूण असुहभावं पुव्वुत्तं णिरवसेसदो दव्वं ।
वद समिदिसीलसंजमपरिणामं सुहमणं जाणे ॥

mottūṇa asuhabhāvaṁ puvvuttaṁ ṇiravasesado davvaṁ ।
vada samidisīlasaṁjamapariṇāmaṁ suhamaṇaṁ jāṇe ॥

Giving up the aforesaid inauspicious thoughts and acts, one should engage in thoughts of moral self-restraints or non-violence, etc. five vows (*vratas*), five self-regulations or carefulness (*samiti*), other rules of moral conduct (*śīla*) and self-discipline (*saṁyama*), which are known as auspicious mind (*śubha mana*).

Commentary

The five vows (*vratas*), as stated earlier, are: (1) non-violence (*ahiṁsā*); (2) truthfulness (*satya*); (3) non-stealing (*asteya*); (4) chastity or sex-fidelity (*brahmacarya*); and (5) non-possessiveness (*aparigraha*). The five self-regulations or carefulness (*samitis*) are:

1. *īryā-samiti*, i.e. carefulness in walking, so that no living being is injured and even harm to oneself is avoided;
2. *bhāṣā-samiti*, i.e. speaking what is beneficial to oneself and to others, and using blameless and concise speech, devoid of passions and avoiding backbiting, ridiculing other and self-condemnation. It also involves speaking wholesome words that are measured, indubitable, harmless and meaningful (Tatia 1998: 220);
3. *eṣaṇā-samiti*, i.e. carefulness in taking food. One should take wholesome, pure and balanced food observing regularity in eating, avoiding overeating or eating for the sake of taste;
4. *ādāna-nikṣepaṇa-samiti*, i.e. carefulness in receiving, lifting, putting and handling things in order to avoid injury to small beings such as flies and insects; and
5. *pratiṣṭhāpana-samiti*, i.e. carefulness in disposing excrements, stools, urine, phlegm, spit, mucus, uncleanness of the body, dead body, waste products, etc. in a proper place and in such a manner as would cause no harm or inconvenience to others.

Bacteriology informs us that excreta and urine remaining undisposed for long generate poisonous germs which spread diseases. This *samiti*, thus, helps maintain cleanliness which is beneficial to health and conducive to mental delight and prevent infectious and other diseases.

For maintaining one's health, proper and moderate food,

pure water, fresh unpolluted air, sunlight, cleanliness, sufficient manual labour, sufficient rest and sufficient sleep are essential. Neglecting all or any one of them invites bodily disorders, ailments and diseases, which, in turn, lead to mental unease and tension. It is, thus, evident that all these rules of carefulness are aimed at preserving the health of people, inculcating good social habits, avoiding injury to living beings and promoting social well-being.

In addition to the five vows observed as limited abstention (*aṇuvrata*), the householders are also required to observe three *guṇa-vratas* (augmenting or supporting vows) and four *śikṣā-vratas* (self-disciplinary vows or practices), collectively known as *śīla-vratas* (supplementary vows) (*TS* VII.21). They are said to serve the useful purpose of guarding the basic five vows and effecting a positive improvement in their observance.

GUṆA-VRATAS: SUPPORTING VOWS

Guṇa-vratas are so called because they help, support, strengthen or enhance the value, quality and practice of the five basic vows. They increase the capacity of observing the five vows with greater determination and purity (*RKS* 67) and are accepted for permanent life-long observance.

DIG-VRATA: REFRAINING FROM MOVEMENT BEYOND A LIMITED AREA

This vow, which is taken for life, enjoins on a person to limit the area of his physical and mental activity or the range of movement in all the ten directions, with the result that one cannot be present in the areas beyond the bounds one has drawn for himself. Accordingly, one automatically renounces committing any sin, whether gross or subtle, or unvirtuous activity beyond or outside that limit. The passions of greed and *hiṁsā* are controlled at least in the fixed limits. By the avoidance of even the subtle sins beyond the determined limits, the *aṇuvratī* (householder) becomes like *mahāvratī* (ascetic) in respect of the regions lying beyond those limits (*RKS* 70).

ANARTHADAṆḌA-VRATA: ABSTAINING FROM PURPOSELESS HARMFUL ACTIVITIES

In Sanskrit, this vow is called *anarthadaṇḍa-vrata*. The term *anartha* means purposeless, aimless, unnecessary, etc. And the term *daṇḍa* means harmful, bad, evil activities. Thus, the term *anarthadaṇḍa* means unnecessary and purposeless harmful activities. And refraining from such activities is *anarthadaṇḍavratī*. Since it is not possible to pinpoint exactly what unvirtuous activities could be regarded as unnecessary and purposeless harmful activities, the Jaina thinkers have attempted to give some idea of these activities by laying down broad guidelines which are as follows:

1. *Pāpopadeśa*: Malicious sermons, harmful advice or preaching of sin. It covers selfish propaganda, stories of violence, garrulity or use of vulgar, prolix [tediously lengthy], nonsensical and impertinent speech, cruelty to living beings, swindling and advice in regard to indulgence in corrupt, passionate and life-injuring ways, including indulgence in harmful activities and vices (*vyasanas*) like drinking wine, taking intoxicating drugs, smoking and gambling.
2. *Hiṁsādāna*: Giving objects of offence or supplying means of violence. It implies the giving of the instruments of *hiṁsā* such as knife, poison, fire, sword, weapons, bow, chain, whip, stick, etc. (*RKS* 77) (Sogani 1967: 98). However, this does not prevent a person from giving weapons to an innocent man for defence of one's life, property, etc. against the violent attacker. The main criterion is the motive or the intention to save the life of an innocent man (Nyayavijaya 2000: 57-58).
3. *Apa-dhyāna*: Harmful contemplation, evil thought or thinking ill of others. This involves peeping into another man's faults and infirmities, coveting others' wealth, seeing wives of others with a lusty eye, taking interest in others' disputes (Svami Kumar 1945: v. 344), evil thoughts of conquest, subjugation, mutilating, imprisoning, hurting and killing

other living beings (*RKS* 78), and taking interest in hurting, victory, defeat, war, adultery, theft, gambling, etc. (*PSU* 141 and 146). One should refrain from evil thoughts in the form of wishing defeat, punishment, mutilation, confiscation of possessions, etc. of others. Hemachandra (2002: 185, v. 57) and Asadhara (*SDGA* v. 9, tr. Sogani 1967: 98) include *ārta-dhyāna* (concentration of mind on pain, misery or sorrow) and *raudra-dhyāna* (concentration on cruelty, harmful ideas or callousness) in *apa-dhyāna*.

4. *Pramādacaryā*: Negligent acts, thoughtless behaviour. It consists in doing such actions purposelessly as digging or flooding fields, recklessly cutting, chopping and damaging plants and trees, igniting fire, trampling lawns, plucking leaves, fruits and flowers, thereby aimlessly committing violence and harm to plant life and environment. One should also refrain from such purposeless harmful activities as striking a standing or moving animal with a stick while walking, joking which hurts others, backbiting, talking ill of others and indulgence in four *vikathas* (unnecessary, unprofitable, useless, time-wasting gossiping) pertaining to women, food, theft, affairs of politics and state, etc.

5. *Duḥśruti*: Listening to and teaching such stories which excite passion (*TS* VII.21; Jain, J.P. 2007: 138, v. 145). It consists in refraining from faulty reading and writing material, hearing, distributing and propagating exciting literature and works, including propagandist material dealing with violence, crimes, hatred, false doctrines, irrationalism, delusion, attachment, aversion, pride, lust, obscene words and gestures arousing sex-passion, which disturb, defile and pollute the mind with evil or impure thoughts of attachment, vanity and passions (*RKS* 79). This abstention is indeed of extreme relevance and importance in modern times.

BHOGOPABHOGAPARIMĀṆA-VRATA: LIMITING USE AND ENJOYMENT OF CONSUMABLE AND NON-CONSUMABLE GOODS

There are two types of things, viz. *bhoga* and *upabhoga*. *Bhoga* things are those that can be used only once, viz. eatables, water, etc. *Upabhoga* things are those that can be used repeatedly, viz. clothes, etc. The vow implies limitation in the use of objects of sense enjoyment, as food, drink, cosmetics, perfumes, rich clothes and jewellery, beds, chairs, vehicles, houses, etc. as well as refraining from wasteful expenditure, and excessive and even perverse enjoyment of sensual pleasures in order to reduce attachment to the objects. It is not only a positive process of limitation but also the negative process of renunciation.

By insisting on moderation in eating, clothing, etc. this vow seeks to inculcate the virtue of moderation, simple and frugal living which is not only good for one's physical health but also relieves one's mind from unnecessary worries and tension, thereby ensuring mental peace and happiness.

Unrestrained consumerism and excessive indulgence in *bhoga* and sensual pleasures are now playing havoc with people's health and happiness. Hunger is not the only reason people eat. Stress, boredom and pleasure all come into play. Excessive indulgence and obsession with *bhoga* leads to *roga* — physical and mental maladies. Medical science now proves that over-indulgence in *bhoga* or sensual pleasures affects our digestive, respiratory and nervous systems resulting in a wide range of ailments. Moral and spiritual degradation is also the natural outcome of overindulgence in sensual pleasures.

ŚIKṢĀ-VRATAS: DISCIPLINARY VOWS

The *śikṣā-vratas* aim at raising the householder to such a standard of purity of character that he is well-equipped to undertake a higher level of moral and spiritual discipline.

DEŚA-VRATA: LIMITING THE SPHERE OR FIELD OF ONE'S ACTIVITY STILL FURTHER AND FOR FIXED PERIODS

The idea behind both *dig-vrata* and *deśa-vrata* is to restrict one's egoistic activities and movements to certain spheres and directions. An attempt is, thus, made (on the part of the individual, family, a tribe, a social group or a community or even a country or nation) to progressively check and control intentions and tendencies for boundless expansion, thereby avoiding violence and minimizing greed as regards the prescribed limits. In *deśa-vrata* the sphere of one's activity is still further limited from day-to-day and for fixed periods within the larger field fixed in the *dig-vrata* (*RKS* 79). It sets narrower limits of the area and for shorter time than *dig-vrata.* The curtailment, thus, takes place in terms of shortening of both area and time.

SĀMAYIKA: EQUANIMOUS STATE OF MIND FOR A FIXED PERIOD

Sāmayika is observed by sitting in a suitable place (free from disturbance of noise, insects, etc. in a convenient posture, sitting or standing and without indolence or laziness for a set period, usually 48 minutes. It is to be performed once, twice or three times in a day depending on one's convenience, capacity and state of purity. During that time, one tries to keep himself aloof from all sinful and injurious activities by controlling one's mind, body and speech, and cultivates an equanimous state of mind by renouncing attachment and aversion to the objects of the world.

The purpose of *sāmayika* is the cultivation of

1. equal goodwill (sympathy) (*samabhāva)* towards all religions, towards all races and castes, and towards man and woman;
2. equality and evenness (*samatā*), i.e. to regard all living beings equal with one's own Self and to maintain evenness (equanimity) of mind on all occasions, favourable and adverse; and
3. tranquillity (*sama*) to suppress and weaken passions (Nyayavijaya 2000: 121).

Thus, by the practice of *sāmayika* one seeks to attain gradually "inward balance" or mental equanimity or tranquillity. It is an exercise in *samaya,* etymologized as the attainment (*aya*) of equanimity or tranquillity of mind (*sama*) (*TS* VII.16, p. 91, quoted in Williams 1991: 131).

PROṢADHOPAVĀSA: OBSERVING FAST

It means observing fast by abstaining from all kinds of food, and being in close proximity of one's soul (*up* means near and *vāsa* means to be, exist or sitting or remaining) by utilizing the time in the study and discussions of spiritual literature, thereby nourishing, fostering, supporting, elevating and ennobling (*poṣadha* means that which nourishes, fosters, supports or causes to grow and develop) the soul. This vow enjoins a person to undertake occasional fasting, usually on the eighth and the fourteenth day of the fortnight, for the purification of one's body and soul. Fasting can be observed for 48 hours, 24 hours or a lesser period, one can take only one meal a day (*ekasan*) or even eat less amount of food than what one normally eats (*avamaudārya*).

During the fast period, one abstains from physical adornments such as use of cosmetics, perfumes and ornaments, indulgence in the pleasures of the senses, refrains from all kinds of sinful activities in all respects, including *hiṁsā*, falsehood, stealing, feelings of attachment and acquisition, sexual intercourse or unchastity, renounces all worldly attachment, observes the restraint of body, speech and mind, and spends his time by keeping himself engaged in the study of the scriptures, contemplation of pure thoughts and meditation.

ATITHISAṀVIBHĀGA-VRATA: OFFERING ALMS TO WANDERING ASCETICS OR SHARING WITH DESERVING GUESTS

Saṁvibhāga means sharing together, participation. The use of the word "sharing" is much nobler than helping others, which gives you the idea of being a saviour, of being superior and as a result of which the ego enters from the back door again. You become important, the centre of the group, everybody is looking to you. The participant, on the other hand, is not someone who is inferior to you. *Atithi* is made up of *a* (not) and *tithi* (date), i.e. the homeless or wandering saints who come without any regularity, definiteness or prior appointment. They should be offered necessities of life, such as suitable food, drink, religious equipment, books, wholesome and proper medicine and shelter with devotion, humility, respect (*satkāra*) and purity of mind. The alms offered must be righteously acquired (*nyāyagata*) by oneself. Samantabhadra denominates this vow as *vaiyyāvṛttya* probably to extend the scope of vow, so as to include removal of ailments of those pursuing the path of righteousness as well as serving them in various other ways (*RKS* 112).

In observing this vow, one has to take into consideration four things:

1. the recipient (*pātra*) should be a deserving person (a saint, a person endowed with *samyak darśana* or one observing self-restraint);
2. the giver (*dātā*) must give with a feeling of joy, humility and enthusiasm;
3. the alms (*dravya*) must be worthy of gifts, i.e. food, medicine, etc.; and
4. the manner of giving (*vidhi*) should be such that it is indicative of due respect.

In *Śīla Pāhuḍa*, *śīla* is considered one's nature (*svabhāva*), so the transcendental, pure nature of the Self is of the nature of inclusion and knowledge. The family of *śīla* consists of compassion towards living beings (*jīva dayā*), subduing or disciplining (*damana*) of the senses, truthfulness, non-stealing unchastity or sex-fidelity (*brahmacarya*) and contentment (*santoṣa*), enlightened worldview or right belief (*samyak darśana*) and the austerity of knowledge (*jñāna tapa*) (*Śīla Pāhuḍa* 19). Being inclined towards liberation is *suśīla* (desirable or good *śīla*). Without *śīla*, one does not attain liberation by knowledge alone (*Śīla Pāhuḍa* 30).

According to the commentator of *Śīla Pāhuḍa*, joining of *karmas* since beginningless time, the Self evolves in unnatural and perverse ways.

As a result of delusion (*mithyātva*), attachment, aversion and infatuation are numerous, which are divided into 84 lakhs, known as *kuśīla*. Their absence is called *śīla*. From the external, other-referential aspect of association or connection with women, there are 18,000 divisions, the absence thereof, *śīla* is said to be of 18,000 kinds.

Self-discipline (*saṁyama*) consists of *pratikramaṇa* (repentence) of past misdeeds and negative thoughts; *pratyākhyāna*, i.e. resolve not to repeat the sinful and unrighteous conduct in future; *ālocanā* (confession), i.e. voluntary acknowledgement of one's own faults existing at present; and *prāyaścitta* (expiation or atonement).

Prāyaścitta accounts for conquering passions: anger by forgiveness, pride by humility, deceit by straightforwardness and greed by contentment (*NS* 115). About contentment, Robert Greene says in his poem:

Such sweet content such minds, such sleep, such bliss,
Beggary enjoy, when princes oft do miss.

Thought processes and psychic dispositions involved in observing the rules of moral conduct (five vows in five carefulnesses), *śīla* (wholesome character), *saṁyama* (self-restrained) and control of senses help in inculcating forgiveness, etc. virtues and, thus, facilitate expiation. Hence, they should be constantly practised (*NS* 113). Moreover, observance of austerities (*tapa*) (*NS* 117-118) and concentration or meditation (*dhyāna*) on the intrinsic nature and real attributes of the Self (*NS* 119-120), which is facilitated by the subduing of passions, necessarily constitute true expiation.

55

संसारछेदकारणवयणं सुहवयणमिदि जिणुद्दिट्ठं ।
जिणदेवादिसु पूजा सुहकायं त्ति य हवे चेट्ठा ॥

saṁsārachedakāraṇavayaṇaṁ suhavayaṇamidi
jiṇuddiṭṭhaṁ ।
jiṇadevādisu pūjā suhakāyaṁ tti ya have ceṭṭhā ॥

The speech, which is the cause of bringing to an end the wanderings in the cycle of birth and death, is auspicious speech (*śubha vacana*). Worship or reverence of the Omniscient Lord (Jinadeva), etc. (i.e. true scripture/Jina-*vāṇī*) and true preceptors (*sadguru*) is the activity of the wholesome or auspicious body (*śubha kāya*).

Commentary

The characteristics of the Omniscient Lord (Jinadeva) or true God (*āpta*), true scripture (*āgama*) and true preceptors (*guru*) are described in *Ratnakaraṇḍa Śrāvakacāra* of Samantabhadra. The true God (*āpta*) is free from faults and weaknesses of the lower nature or the internal enemies of attachment, etc. He is also free from eighteen kinds of blemishes. These are: hunger, thirst, senility, disease, birth, death, fear, pride, attachment, aversion, infatuation, worry, conceit, hatred, sweat, sleep, comments and surprise (*RKS* 6). Pride is the intoxication of the Self in respect of eight particulars:

1. learning,
2. tribe, caste, genus or race;
3. family;
4. greatness
5. power;
6. affluence, wealth or accomplishments;
7. religious
8. body or personality (*RKS* 25). austerities; and

The seven kinds of fear are: (1) fear relating to this life; (2) fear relating to future life; (3) fear of being without protection; (4) fear of the disclosure of what is kept in secret; (5) fear of pain; (6) fear of accident; and (7) fear of death (Chakravarti 1971: 146-147, v. 228).

The Jaina texts speak of seven kinds of fear, viz. fear of (1) death; (2) ailment, pain or suffering; (3) loss of reputation, i.e. dishonour and shame; (4) injury to wife and children; (5) loss of wealth; (6) helplessness or accidental fear; and (7) anxiety about the other world.

Fear can also be of failure in examination, fear of the unfamiliar or unknown, a ghost, loss in trade or business, etc.; it could be of any other thing. Fear begets anxiety and leads to doubt and indecisiveness.

The true scripture (*āgama*) is the word of a Tīrthaṅkara, which cannot be overridden in disputation nor falsified by prescription, reason or testimony, which reveals the nature of things as they exist, which is helpful to men and other beings and which are potent enough to destroy all forms of falsehood (*RKS* 9).

According to *Ratnakaraṇḍa Śrāvakācāra* 10, the preceptor (*guru*) is

> praiseworthy who has no desires for sensual pleasures, who has renounced all worldly preoccupations and possessions, and who is always absorbing study, meditation and contemplation about the Self.

56

जम्मसमुद्दे बहुदोस बीचिये दुक्खजलचराकिण्णे।
जीवस्स परिब्भमणं कम्मासवकारणं होदि ॥

jammasamudde bahudosa bīciye dukkhajalacarākiṇṇe ।
jīvassa paribbhamaṇaṁ kammāsavakāraṇaṁ hodi ॥

Where there are waves of many faults and weaknesses (attachment, passions, etc.) and which is replete with aquatic creatures of the nature of or in the form of miseries, that transmigration or wanderings of the soul in the ocean of birth (and death) is the cause of the inflow of *karmas.*

Commentary by M.K. Dharma Raja

Worldly existence in its myriad permutations is like a dreadful ocean interspersed with a host of frailties in the form of temptations as well as a bewildering assortment of treacherous circumstances.

The waves buffeting the hapless soul in the ocean of life are passions like greed, anger, deceit which result in miseries of existence because of the influx of *karmas*. It is, therefore, imperative to plug the very sources of the inflow of *karmas*. This is best accomplished through disciplined efforts to overcome and surmount the deceptive frailties of worldly life (1990: 65).

57

कम्मासवेण जीवो बूडदि संसारसागरे घोरे।
जं णाणवसं किरिया मोक्खणिमित्तं परंपराया॥

kammāsaveṇa jīvo būḍadi saṁsārasāgare ghore ।
jaṁ ṇāṇavasaṁ kiriyā mokkhaṇimittaṁ paraṁparāyā ॥

The soul is plunged or immersed in the fearful, awesome and terrible ocean of life and death, the mundane worldly existence due to the inflow of *karmas*. Conduct or action based on knowledge is the supportive factor (*nimitta*) or the auxiliary cause (*nimitta kāraṇa*) of liberation.

Commentary

Samayasāra 167 observes:

> The psychic states imbued with attachment, etc. of the Self bind the soul. The Self, which is free from attachment, etc. does not bind the soul; the Self is of the nature of knowledge consciousness (*jñāyaka*).

Samayasāra 150 categorically states *ratto bandhādi kammam* (it is attachment that binds).

Commentary by M.K. Dharma Raja

As already elaborated, it is the phenomenon of the inflow of *karmas* that plunges the soul into the terrible ocean of mundane existence. The constant surge of *karmas* keeps the soul submerged in this ocean. The mosaic of *karmas* in all its manifestations rockets the soul into the world of the four states or conditions (*gati*) of transmigrations. The substantive factor that determines the bondage of *karmas* is the soul itself.

The kārmic molecules, as stated earlier, staining the soul are attracted to the Self by its own vibrations set off by the activities of the mind, speech or body in their movements.

Kundakunda points out in this verse that conduct or action based on right perception and knowledge also plugs the inflow of *karmas* which tarnish the soul and thus keep it immersed in the ocean of life and death. Perseverance in this liberating action progressively eliminates the kārmic molecules from the Self until it ultimately regains the state of liberation.

The Self enlightened by enlightened knowledge is thus guided to the path that leads to perfection. Enlightened knowledge is a prime factor in this evolution of the Self to final emancipation (1990: 65-66).

58

आसवहेदू जीवो जम्मसमुद्दे णिमज्जदे खिप्पं।
आसवकिरिया तम्हा मोक्खणिमित्तं ण चिंतेज्जो॥

āsavahedū jīvo jammasamudde ṇimajjade khippaṁ ।
āsavakiriyā tamhā mokkhaṇimittaṁ ṇa ciṁtejjo ॥

Due to the condition (*hetu*) of the inflow of *karmas*, the soul is immersed or plunged in the ocean of births. Therefore, the activity, which is the condition of kārmic inflow, is not the supportive factor (*nimitta*) [or auxiliary cause (*nimitta-kāraṇa*) of liberation — one should contemplate in this manner.

Commentary by M.K. Dharma Raja

This verse clarifies that any action causing the inflow of *karmas* has the effect of keeping the soul submerged in the ocean of mundane existence. And the process of calming the influx takes place in respect of the nature of *karmas*, whether it is auspicious (*śubha*) or inauspicious (*aśubha*). A meritorious deed generates auspicious *karmas* though the result is the influx of *karmas* (*āsrava*). The difference between the effect of a virtuous deed and a sinful deed can be likened to that between a golden chain and an iron chain. In fact, both are chains, which prolong the soul's bondage. Thus, nothing that fosters the inflow of *karmas*, whether auspicious or inauspicious, can be construed as a cause of liberation from bondage.

The state of final emancipation from the vicious circle of life and death cannot be attained until the soul sheds its last vestige of *karma* molecules. This sublime status is attained in the fourteenth *guṇa-sthāna* (stage) of moral and spiritual advancement (1990: 66-67).

59

पारंपज्जाएण दु आसवकिरियाए णत्थि णिव्वाणं।
संसारगमणकारणमिदि णिंदं आसवो जाण ॥

pāraṁpajjāeṇa du āsavakiriyāe ṇatthi ṇivvāṇaṁ ।
saṁsāragamaṇakāraṇamidi ṇiṅdaṁ āsavo jāṇa ॥

There is no liberation even customarily through the action of the nature of the inflow of *karmas* (*āsrava*), which is the cause of wandering in the mundane worldly existence. Therefore, that *āsrava* is to be known as blameworthy or reprehensible.

Commentary by M.K. Dharma Raja

Any auspicious or inauspicious activity of the mind, body and speech that induces the influx of *karmas* (*āsrava*) has the effect of subjecting the soul to the cycle of birth and death. The total cessation of activities and vibrations is essential for the soul to attain the goal of liberation. The aspirant is thus admonished to steer clear of any action that may tarnish the soul with *karmas* even in the remotest way (1990: 67).

60

पुव्वुत्तासवभेदा णिच्छयणयएण णत्थि जीवस्स।
उहयासवणिम्मुक्कं अप्पाणं चिंतए णिच्चं॥

puvvuttāsavabhedā ṇicchayaṇayaeṇa ṇatthi jīvassa ।
uhayāsavaṇimmukkaṁ appāṇaṁ ciṁtae ṇiccaṁ ॥

From the pure, transcendental point of view, the aforesaid kinds of inflow of *karmas* are not connected (*asaṁyukta*) with *karmas* (*SS* 14) of the Self (*jīva*), who is non-relational to or independent of *karmas* (*karma-nirapekṣa*, pure), i.e. released from *karmas* (*karma-nirmukta*) in the sense that the soul is not bound and untouched (*abaddha, aspṛṣṭa*) and not connected (*asaṁyukta*) with both kinds of *dravyāsrava* (the influx of material particles) and *bhāvāsrava* (the inflow of *karmas* due to the psychic states of attachment, etc.). One should always contemplate in this manner.

Commentary by M.K. Dharma Raja

Kundakunda now points out that both kinds of the inflow of *karmas* (auspicious and inauspicious) from the real standpoint of the various categories of the inflow of *karmas* enumerated in this chapter are characteristics of the soul.

In the mundane world, as viewed from the *vyavahāra naya* point of view, the soul is held in bondage. It is this bondage of *karmas* that submerges the captive soul in the ocean of repetitive births.

Both auspicious and inauspicious *karmas* constitute the factors that subject the soul to continued suffering in worldly existence. The inflow of inauspicious *karmas* brings in its wake a welter of unhappiness and miseries. The inflow of inauspicious *karmas* brings the glitter of worldly pleasures. But the end result of both categories of the influx of *karmas* is identical, viz. the continued subjection of the soul to mundane existence.

The ultimate destiny of the soul is perfection — a state free from all *karmas*. The aspirant who aspires for perfection is, therefore, enjoined by Kundakunda to constantly remind himself of the transcendental pure nature of the Self.

Such reflection on the causes and conditions of the inflow of *karmas* has the effect of elevating the seeker to give up passions, etc. and to make efforts for the liberation of the soul (1990: 68).

Kārttikeyānuprekṣā

Kundakunda has described *āsrava anuprekṣā* in fourteen verses (*BA* 47-60). *Kārttikeyānuprekṣā* describes it in seven verses (*KA* 88-94) as follows:

> The activities of the mind, speech and body, causing a stir in the space-points of the soul, with or without *moha*, lead to kārmic influx, developing into *mithyātva*, etc. Lower degree of passion (to be illustrated by appreciation of virtuous, sweet words and forgiveness even in the face of provocation) leads to merit; while acute passion (illustrated by egotism, fault-finding and sustained hatred) leads to demerit. By avoiding infatuatory and deluding *bhāvas* (moods or temperaments), and by using engrossed in *upaśama*, one grasps the causes of kārmic influx.

Chapter 9
Saṁvara Anuprekṣā
(Stoppage of the Inflow of Karmas)

61

चलमलिनमगाढं च वज्जिय, सम्मत्तदिढकवाडेण।
मिच्छत्तासवदारणिरोहो होदित्ति जिणेहि णिद्दिट्ठं॥

calamalinamagāḍhaṁ ca vajjiya, sammattadiḍhakavāḍeṇa ।
micchattāsavadāraṇiroho hoditti jiṇehi ṇiddiṭṭhaṁ ॥

Though forbidding or abandoning of fickle, impure and intense defects or faults and from the firm door of enlightened worldview, enlightened perception or right belief, the stopping, prohibition or preventing (*nirodha*) of the door of the inflow of delusion (*mithyātva*) *karmas* takes place; this is directed as advised by the Omniscient Lord (Jina).

Commentary by M.K. Dharma Raja

Right perception is to be acquired by getting rid of the infirmities or defects of perception. These defects arise from the fickleness or the lack of steadfastness in belief, vitiated or impure belief and the high intensity of false beliefs.

One should therefore acquire enlightened right belief and be vigilant against the influx of *karmas*.

The aspirant on the path of spiritual progress is advised to fortify himself with an immaculate right perception as a safeguard against any further inflow of *karmas* (1990: 69).

62

पंचमहव्वयमणसा अविरमणणिरोहणं हवे णियमा।
कोहादि आसवाणं दाराणि कसायरहियपल्लगेहि॥

pañcamahavvayamaṇasā aviramaṇaṇirohaṇaṁ have ṇiyamā ।
kohādi āsavāṇaṁ dārāṇi kasāyarahiyapallagehi ॥

Through rigorous, stringent and complete observance of five great- or major-scale vows (*mahāvratas*) (see *supra*) and the moral self-restraints or non-abstinence (of violence, etc. five sins), the stopping, prohibition or preventing (*nirodha*) of the incoming *karmas* take place, as a rule. The door of the inflow of *karmas* of the nature of passions like anger are plugged or stopped by the doors of being dispassionate, i.e. by being completely devoid of or free from the passions (*kaṣāyas*).

Commentary by M.K. Dharma Raja

While an individual with the right insight takes up the five vows of the mendicants, he advances from the fourth to the fifth stage of spiritual progress (*guṇa-sthāna*). The five are the vows of non-injury (*āhiṁsā*), truthfulness, non-stealing, celibacy and non-attachment.

The observance of these vows stems the inflow of *karmas* which would have sullied the soul had they not been observed. Likewise, the *karmas* are accruing through passions of anger, greed, etc. are stopped by complete abstinence from passions. The influx of *karmas* is thus stopped at the very source.

The total elimination of passions elevates the aspirant to the eleventh stage of spiritual progress (1990: 70).

Commentary

According to *Tattvārthasūtra* IX.2, the stopping (*saṁvara*) takes place through

1. the three self-restraints or controls of the mind, speech and body (*guptī*) (*TS* IX.4);
2. five self-regulations or carefulness (*samiti*) (*TS* IX.5) are in walking, speaking, eating, lifting and putting things or objects, and cleanliness;

3. observance of forgiveness, etc. ten types of righteousness and piety (*dharma*) (*TS* IX.6);
4. twelve contemplations (*anuprekṣā*) (*TS* IX.7);
5. conquering of twenty-two hardships (*pariṣaha jaya*) (*TS* IX.9) of hunger, thirst, etc. (see *supra*); and
6. five kinds of conduct (*caritra*) (*TS* IX.18).

By [external and internal] austerities (*tapa*) (*TS* IX.19 and IX.20) the shedding of *karmas* (*nirjarā*) is also stoppage of inflow of *karmas* (*saṁvara*) takes place (*TS* IX.3).

The ten kinds of *dharma* are:

1. Forgiveness (*kṣamā*): It implies control of anger.
2. Humility (*mārdava*): It signifies absence of pride.
3. Straightforwardness (*ārjava*): It is freedom from deceit or crookedness.
4. Purity (*śauca*): It is contentment or freedom from greed.
5. Truth (*satya*): It is the absence of falsehood, to which one resorts because of deceit or greed.
6. Self-control (*saṁyama*): It means desisting from injury to *prāṇas* (life forces or vitalities), which is caused because of anger or greed, etc.
7. Austerities (*tapa*): As already stated, one cannot practise austerities because of passions.
8. Renunciation (*tyāga*): A greedy person who indulges in falsehood, stealing, deceit, etc. cannot observe renunciation, bestowing of knowledge, etc.
9. Non-attachment or non-acquisitiveness (*akiñcanya*): A greedy man cannot give up "mineness" or acquisitiveness.
10. Chastity or sex-fidelity (*brahmacarya*): A greedy and lustful person will not hesitate to indulge in unchastity.

The word "excellent" (*uttama*) is added before each of the ten *dharmas*.

The five kinds of moral conduct is also said to consist of the following practices, viz. equanimity towards all friends and foes alike (*sāmayika caritra*), suitable amendments with a view to regaining equanimity after accidental transgression (*chedopasthāpanā caritra*), purification of heart through inoffensive conduct (*parihāraviśuddhi caritra*), control of passions in subtle forms (*sūkṣmasamprāya caritra*) and the sublime conduct characterized by the utter cessation of passions (*yathākhyāta caritra*) (cited in Shiv Kumar 2000: 101).

63

सुहजोगस्स पवित्ती संवरणं कुणदि असुहजोगस्स ।
सुहजोगस्स णिरोहो सुद्धुवजोगेण संभवदि ॥

suhajogassa pavittī saṁvaraṇaṁ kuṇadi asuhajogassa ।
suhajogassa ṇiroho suddhuvajogeṇa saṁbhavadi ॥

The tendency, application of auspicious thought-activities of mind, speech and body (*yoga*), the checking or stopping (*saṁvaraṇa*) of inauspicious (*aśubha*) thought-activities of *yoga* takes place; the stopping, prohibition or preventing (*nirodha*) of auspicious (*śubha*) *yoga* is possible through pure conscious attentiveness (*śuddha upayoga*).

Commentary by M.K. Dharma Raja

Auspicious (*śubha*) thoughts motivate good deeds like the worship of *Pañca-Parameṣṭhi*s, offering charities or rendering service to the deserving ascetics. These good thoughts prevent the bad or unwholesome vibrations of the mind rising from passions. Auspicious thoughts thus have the prophylactic effect of integrating the Self from the contamination of bad thought-activities.

The objective of the aspirant, however, is the highest spiritual status of the total cessation of the process of the influx of *karmas*. That becomes possible only by eliminating all desires; the wholesome or the unwholesome. This implies the cessation of all activities of the body, mind and speech.

The elimination of the influx of auspicious *karmas* is brought about by pure thought-activity or the self-absorption. Pure thought-activity is attained in the fourteenth stage of spiritual ascent in which the soul is in total self-absorption.

The total absence of any relation or vibration is the hallmark of this status within the minutest activity — the last remaining cause of the bondage of the Self — comes to an end (1990: 71).

64

सुद्धुबजोगेण पुणो धम्मं सुक्कं च होदि जीवस्स।
तम्हा संवरहेदू झाणो त्ति विचिंतए णिच्चं॥

suddhubajogeṇa puṇo dhammaṁ sukkaṁ ca hodi jīvassa ।
tamhā saṁvarahedū jhāṇo tti viciṅtae ṇiccaṁ ॥

Through the pure conscious attentiveness, the righteous (*dharma*) and pure (*śukla*) concentrations or meditations (*dhyāna*) takes place. Therefore, one should always contemplate that the checking or stopping (*saṁvara*) is a condition (*hetu*) of *dhyāna*.

Commentary by M.K. Dharma Raja

Pure thought-activity, which is continuous self-absorption, is the exercise of the mind's concentration. This state of intense absorption in the Self generates the quality of the most sublime spiritual concentration. All loopholes of the influx of *karmas* are plugged in this process.

Kundakunda thus directs the aspirant to be continuously meditating on the thought that concentration is the way to stop the influx of *karmas*.

65

जीवस्स ण संवरणं परमट्ठणएण सुद्धभावादो।
संवरभावविमुक्कं अप्पाणं चिंतए णिच्चं॥

jīvassa ṇa saṁvaraṇaṁ paramaṭṭhaṇaeṇa suddhabhāvādo ।
saṁvarabhāvavimukkaṁ appāṇaṁ ciṅtae ṇiccaṁ ॥

From the transcendental, pure perspective (*paramārtha*), the pure psychic disposition of the Self needs no checking or stopping of the inflow of *karmas* (*saṁvara*). Therefore, the Self is released, set free or exempt (*vimukta*) from [the thought-constructions (*vikalpa*) of] *saṁvara*. Thus, one should always contemplate in this manner.

Commentary by M.K. Dharma Raja

The aspirant's attention is once again drawn here to the innate purity of the soul. Viewed from the real or absolute standpoint, the soul is pure. Hence, it does not need the devices of stopping the influx of *karmas* into itself. The conventional view that the soul should be selected from the process of the influx of *karmas* is reported in this verse.

The emphasis in this verse is on the discipline of pure concentration in the Self which is immaculate (1990: 72).

Kārttikeyānuprekṣā

Kundakunda has described *saṁvara anuprekṣā* in five verses (*BA* 61-65). *Kārttikeyānuprekṣā* describes it in seven verses (*KA* 95-101) as follows:

> Right faith, partial or total observance of vows, subjugation of passions and absence of activities of mind, speech and body: these are the synonyms of *saṁvara* (stoppage of kārmic influx). The causes of *saṁvara* are *guptī*, *samiti*, *dharma*, *anuprekṣā*, *pariṣaha-jaya* and excellent *caritra*. *Guptī* means control of mind, speech and body; *samiti* is carefulness, and absence of negligence; *dharma* is characterized by compassion; *anuprekṣā* consists in reflecting on the principles; *pariṣaha-jaya* means ungrudgingly putting up with various troubles like hunger; and the best conduct to discipline one's self-meditation, free from all attachment and aversion. One who abstains from pleasures of senses and guards oneself fully against all temptations stops the kārmic influx and curtails the journey in this miserable *saṁsāra*.

Chapter 10
Nirjarā Anupreksā
(Shedding of Karmas)

66

बंधपदेसग्गलणं णिज्जरणं इदि जिणेहि पण्णत्तं ।
जेण हवे संवरणं तेण दु णिज्जरणमिदि जाण ॥

bandhapadesaggalaṇaṁ ṇijjaraṇaṁ idi jiṇehi paṇṇattaṁ ।
jeṇa have saṁvaraṇaṁ teṇa du ṇijjaraṇamidi jāṇa ॥

The dissolving or decaying of the material particles bound with the Self is shedding of *karmas* (*nirjarā*) is declared by the Omniscient Lord (Jina). *Nirjarā* takes place from the same conditions from which the stoppage of the inflow of *karmas* (*saṁvara*) takes place — this is to be known.

Commentary by M.K. Dharma Raja

The elimination or destruction of *karmas* is the culmination of the process of stopping the inflow. This involves the cleansing of the soul by eliminating the residue of molecules still left in it.

Concentration on the Self is the commended formula both to check the inflow of *karmas* and for the process of self-purification, totally eliminating the *karma* molecules from the soul (1990: 73).

67

सा पुण दुविहा णेया सकालपक्का तवेण कयमाणा ।
चदुगदियाणं पढमा वयजुत्ताणं हवे विदिया ॥

sā puṇa duvihā ṇeyā sakālapakkā taveṇa kayamāṇā ।
cadugadiyāṇaṁ paḍhamā vayajuttāṇaṁ have vidiyā ॥

Nirjarā is of two kinds: the first one is that in which *karmas* fall off after being ripe or mature in their normal course or in their own time; the second kind of *nirjarā* (shedding of *karmas*) is that in which the *karmas* are made to fall off prematurely, i.e. even before their fruition (through the practice of austerities). The first kind of *nirjarā* takes place when the soul is in the four conditions (*gatis*) of mundane existence, while the latter, i.e. the second kind of *nirjarā* takes place in respect to those who observe moral self-restraints or vows.

Commentary

The word *nirjarā* is derived from the Sanskrit verbal root *jṛ* which means to wear down, to rub to pieces, to crush, etc. Thus, falling away of all *karmas* attached to the Self is called *nirjarā*, which is of two types: the first is due to ripening (*vipākaja*) and the second is due to process other than ripening (*avipākaja*) (Shiv Kumar 2000: 101). If the *karma* ripens by itself, i.e. wears down on its own in due course of time, it is called *vipāka nirjarā*; but if it is plucked unripe and then ripened by an artificial device, it is known as *avipāka nirjarā* (*TS* VII.2-4, cited in ibid.). The process and activities of the Self whereby the effect of kārmic coating on the texture of the Self is neutralized resulting in their falling away from the Self are called *nirjarā* (ibid.).

Nirjarā consists of the observance of austerities (*tapas*), both external and internal, which are an effective means of inhibiting (*saṁvara*) as well as wearing off (*nirjarā*) of *karma* (*TS* IX.3).

The *avipāka* (voluntary shedding of *karmas*) in the highest degree of each condition occurs to an innumerable-fold extent in each of the following stages, compared with the one immediately preceding it.

The first mention is of the condition of right belief, i.e. the fourth stage (*guṇa-sthāna*) in spiritual development. In this the shedding is of innumerable-fold, compared with a condition of the soul just before it acquired right belief. The stages as mentioned are:

1. *Samyak-dṛṣṭi*: one who has right belief, the fourth *guṇa-sthāna*. This stage is reached by *upaśama* (subsidence, cessation). The subsidence or by *kṣayopaśama*. Partial destruction subsidence and operation of the passions which feed wrong belief (*anantabandhī*) and of three kinds of *darśana mohanīya*, right belief deluding *karmas*.
2. *Śrāvaka*: One who takes the layman's vows (partial vows), the fifth stage. By *kṣayopaśama* of four passions which obscure renunciation.
3. *Vrata*: A saint with full vows in the sixth and seventh stages. By *kṣayopaśama* of the four passions (*pratyākhyāna*) which obscure total renunciation.
4. *Anantaviyojaka*: The same, when it transforms the kārmic matter of passions, which feed wrong belief, into a less injurious kind of kārmic matter of passions.
5. *Darśanamohakṣapaka*: The same when it destroys the three kinds of right belief-deluding *karmas*.
6. *Upaśamaka*: A saint in the eighth, ninth and tenth *guṇa-sthāna*, when his *caritra mohanīya* right conduct-deluding *karmas* are subsiding.
7. *Upaśāntamoha*: In the eleventh *guṇa-sthāna* (stage) when his right conduct-deluding *karmas* have totally subsided.
8. *Kṣapaka*: A saint in the eighth, ninth and tenth stages when he is destroying the right conduct-deluding *karmas*.
9. *Kṣīṇamoha*: In the twelfth stage, when he has destroyed totally the right conduct-deluding *karmas*.
10. *Jina*: In the thirteen states, when he becomes Omniscient (Kevalī) after having destroyed all the four *ghātīya* (destructive) *karmas*, i.e. knowledge (*jñānāvarṇīya*), conation

(*darśanīya*), right belief and right conduct-deluding (*mohanīya*) *karmas* and obstructive (*antarāya*) *karmas*.

In the fourteenth stage (*guṇa-sthāna*), the four non-destructive *karmas* are also totally destroyed (Jaini 1956: 162-163).

Commentary by M.K. Dharma Raja

The twin-process of the inflow of kārmic matter and of its evaporation is common to all the four kinds of mundane existence. Each of the kārmic molecules bound with the soul has its own duration. This period varies with the degree of passion that vitiates the mundane Self.

The kārmic molecule drops off from the soul after fully working itself out – having stretched itself to all its consequences. Its falling off is like a ripe fruit dropping from the tree.

This mechanical process of "evaporation" of *karmas* is common to all souls found in captivity in all the forced states of mundane existence. It is known as *savipāka nirjarā*. This implies the elimination of matter particle from the *kārmaṇa śarīra* (the transmigrate body) in its normal course.

The other kind of *karma* elimination is *avipāka nirjarā*. This is the process of the removal of matter and the consequent disassociation of the forces vitiating the soul through one's exertion. It is accompanied by observing the vows, i.e. by practising restraints through austerities. Elimination of *karmas* as a result of this discipline of self-effort is achieved by the laity (humans) and ascetics.

The shedding of *karma* molecules by self-volition (*avipāka nirjarā*) starts when the mundane soul acquires right faith. Right faith takes the seeker to the fourth round of spiritual advancement. Progress on the path is achieved by means of stepping up the discipline of restraints and austerities. This step-by-step ascent in spiritual progress reaches its culmination of the fourteenth stage which is attained on the destruction of *karma* molecules.

Avipāka nirjarā is achieved by *dhyāna* (concentration) of the mind. This concentration is the direct means of attaining *mokṣa*.

A spiritual aspirant should, therefore, set his thoughts on this sublime course of wilful elimination of *karma* residue (1990: 74-75).

Kārttikeyānuprekṣā

Kundakunda has described *nirjarā anuprekṣā* in two verses (*BA* 66-67). *Kārttikeyānuprekṣā* describes it in thirteen verses as given below:

> Eradication of *karmas* is possible through the practice of twelvefold penance without any remunerative hankering (*nidāna*) for one who is not vain, who is detached and who is endowed with knowledge. The various *karmas* come into operation, give their i.e. fruit and the drop out, i.e. *nirjarā* shedding of the *karmas*. It is of two kinds: *karmas* fall off after being ripe or mature, according to the schedule; and they can be made to fall off prematurely by the practice of penances. The former is normal in all the grades of life, while the latter belongs to those who undertake religious practices. In the case of monks, this *nirjarā* increases more and more along the steps of the ladder of *guṇa-sthānas*, as one progresses in spiritual quiet and penances, especially by twofold meditation, *dharma* and *śukla-dhyāna*. Plenty of *karmas* are eradicated by putting up with abuses, ill treatment and various troubles, by subjugating the senses and passions, by realizing one's defects and appreciating the virtues of others, and by repeatedly concentrating oneself on one's *ātman* which is pure in eternal embodiment of faith, knowledge and conduct. Thus, alone life becomes fruitful, merits increase the highest happiness is attained.
>
> — *KA* 102-114

Chapter 11
Dharma Anupreksā
(Righteousness and Piety)

68

एयारसदसभेयं धम्मं सम्मत्तपुव्वयं भणियं ।
सागारणगाराणं उत्तमसुहसंपजुत्तेहिं ॥

eyārasadasabheyaṁ dhammaṁ sammattapuvvayaṁ bhaṇiyaṁ ।
sāgāraṇagārāṇaṁ uttamasuhasaṁpajuttehiṁ ॥

The Omniscient Lord (Jina) has ordered/spoken of the elevenfold code of conduct of righteousness (*dharma*) for the householders (*sāgāra*) and tenfold conduct of righteousness (*dharma*) for the saints. This *dharma* is endowed with enlightened worldview or right belief (*samyaktva*).

Commentary by M.K. Dharma Raja

The scripture is based on the teachings of the Tīrthaṅkaras (Lord Jinendra). It lays down the codes of conduct both for householders (the laity) and ascetics.

These codes are based on the primacy of right perception. It is right perception that sets the soul on the Right Path. Hence, it is to be regarded as the cardinal requisite for those in quest of spiritual progress culminating in final liberation.

The code of conduct for laymen is based on the principle of partial renunciation and total renunciation is the basis of the ascetics' code (1990: 69).

69

दंसणवयसामाइयपोसहसच्चित्तरायभत्ते य ।
बम्हारंभपरिग्गह अणुमणमुद्दिट्ठ देसविरदेदे ॥

daṁsaṇavayasāmāiyaposahasaccittarāyabhatte ya ।
bamhāraṁbhapariggaha aṇumaṇamuddiṭṭha desaviradede ॥

The elevenfold stages of a householder's *dharma* are: *darśana, vrata, sāmayika, proṣadha, sacitta tyāga, rātri-bhojana tyāga, brahmacarya, ārambha tyāga, parigraha tyāga, anumati tyāga* and *uddiṣṭa tyāga.*

Commentary

While the *vratas* are said to be "horizontally conceived", the eleven stages of moral and spiritual progress (*pratimās*) are considered to be their "vertical projection" (Schubring 1935 cited in Williams 1991: 172). The eleven *pratimās* are:

1. *darśana*, the basic purpose of this is the attainment of *samyak darśana.* In some Jaina texts, the observance of *mūla-guṇas* and eschewing of seven *durvyasanas* are also insisted;
2. *vrata* (the observance of 12 *vratas*);
3. *sāmayika* (the practice of equanimity);
4. *proṣadha* (fasting on particular days);
5. *sacitta-tyāga* (giving up the use of animate food, i.e. having life or in contact with animate food, uncooked or insufficiently cooked);
6. *rātri-bhukti-tyāga* (giving up having meals at night);
7. *brahmacarya* (control of sex-feeling and avoidance of physical contact with women);
8. *ārambha-tyāga* (renunciation of worldly occupations such as service, cultivation and business);

9. *parigraha-tyāga* (abandonment of external possessions, except clothes, books and bare necessities of life as well as inner faults, perverted attitude, infatuation, desire for sex, scornful humour, passions, attachment and aversion);
10. *anumati-tyāga* (abandonment of giving or offering advice or suggestion regarding worldly affairs); and
11. *uddiṣṭa-tyāga*, i.e. not taking food specially prepared for oneself, renouncing home, living like a quasi-ascetic on food obtained by begging, wearing a piece of loincloth and drinking only water that has been rendered sterile by boiling (*prasūka*). A comparison of the *pratimās* and the *śīla-vratas* reveals many similarities.

Commentary by M.K. Dharma Raja

The elevenfold code of conduct prescribed for the householder represents a graph of progressive spiritual ascent – each successive rung moving up higher and higher on the ladder. The renunciation involved at each higher step signifies increasing austerity in his mode of life.

The aspiring householder progressively enlarges the scope of his detachment, finally withdrawing from all activities of his mundane occupation. In the final stage (designated as *aillaka*), he retains only a single piece of cloth, gives up the food cooked for him and renounces his own Self. At this stage, he is ready to take up an ascetic's life (1990: 77).

70

उत्तमखममद्दवज्जवसच्चसउच्चं च संजमं चेव।
तवचागमकिंचण्हं बम्हा इदि दसविहं होदि॥

uttamakhamamaddavajjavasaccasauccaṁ ca sañjamaṁ ceva ।
tavacāgamakiñcaṇhaṁ bamhā idi dasavihaṁ hodi ॥

The tenfold *dharmas* of the saints are:

1. excellent (*uttama*) forgiveness (*kṣamā*);
2. humility (*mārdava*);
3. straightforwardness (*ārjava*);
4. truth (*satya*);
5. purity (*śauca*);
6. restraint (*saṁyam*);
7. austerity (*tapa*);
8. renunciation (*tyaga*);
9. non-attachment or non-inquisitiveness (*akiñcanya*); and
10. chastity or sex-fidelity (*brahmacarya*).

The word "excellent" (*uttama*) is put before each of the ten *dharmas*.[1]

Commentary

The first three and the fifth of the above-mentioned tenfold *dharmas* are the result of the subsidence of four passions of anger, pride, deceit and greed respectively. The fourth, sixth and eighth to tenth of the tenfold *dharmas* mentioned above represent the five moral self-restraints or five vows of restraining oneself from untruthfulness, causing injury to others, non-stealing, *aparigraha* and *brahmacarya* respectively. In addition to these, there are austerities and penance (*tapa*), which are a condition for both stoppage (*saṁvara*) of the inflow of *karmas* and shedding of (*nirjarā*) of *karmas*.

Commentary by M.K. Dharma Raja

In advancing on the path of self-realization, an ascetic strengthens his practice of restraints and self-regulation by observing the ten forms of righteousness.

---

[1] For explanation of these, see *supra* and subsequent verses.

Each of these ten supreme virtues forms an integral part of one or the other of the highest vows (*mahāvratas*) of the ascetic. He goes through a life of the utmost simplicity, having reduced his needs to the barest minimum and suffering hardship with equanimity.

Absolute excellence in self-realization is attained through strict adherence to the tenfold righteous path (1990: 78).

71

कोहुप्पत्तिस्स पुणो बहिरंगं जदि हवेदि सक्खादं।
ण कुणदि किंचि वि कोहो सस्स खमा होदि धम्मो त्ति॥

kohuppattissa puṇo bahiraṅgaṁ jadi havedi sakkhādaṁ ।
ṇa kuṇadi kiñci vi koho sassa khamā hodi dhammo tti ॥

One who does not indulge in anger remains unruffled and cool in the least, even though externally the provocations are present as a supportive factor (*nimitta*) [or auxiliary cause (*nimitta-kāraṇa*)] to anger. Such a person is considered to be adorned with forgiveness (*kṣamā*) *dharma.*

Commentary

All the major religions of the world lay great emphasis on forgiveness, which is considered a cardinal virtue of immense importance. In Islam, the *Koran* (51:1) enjoins on the believers: "Be foremost in seeking forgivenees". In Christianity, Jesus spoke from the Cross: "Father forgive them (executioners), for they know not what they do" (Luke 23:34). In the *Manusmṛti* too, forgiveness is included among the ten virtues. Kindness (*karuṇā*) of Buddhism obviously includes forgiveness.

The Jainas have been observing a Day of Forgiveness (Kṣamāvāṇī Divasa) every year at the end of their religious festival (Paryuṣaṇa Parva) for the last 2,000 years. Forgiveness also figures as the foremost virtue in the list of ten moral and spiritual virtues. These ten virtues or characteristics of *dharma* (called *dasa dharma*) are: forgiveness (control of anger and practice of tolerance in adverse situations), humility (absence of pride, vanity and overbearing attitude), straightforwardness, purity of both body and mind (*śauca*), i.e. contentment or freedom from greed, self-restraint, truthfulness, renunciation/non-attachment, non-acquisitiveness, continence or chastity and austerities.

The first four of these moral and spiritual virtues are the result of subsidence of four passions of anger, pride, deceit and greed (the internal enemies of the purity of the soul) and the next five represent five basic moral values, while the last one pertains to austerities. These qualities or virtues are also highly valued by other religions of the world in some form or other.

The Jainas are advised to recite a verse which means:

> I forgive all living beings, let all living beings forgive me; let there be friendliness, or loving kindness (*maitrī*, *mitti*, in Prākr̥t or *metta* in Buddhism) towards all living beings, including ourselves and our enemies, and enmity or hatred with none.

The four parts of this verse signify: It is only when one gives up anger, he will be inclined to forgive others; and unless one gives up pride he will not seek forgiveness from others; one cannot desire friendship with others unless he abandons deceit, jealousy and envy within himself; and only when there is limitation or renunciation of greed, i.e. of wants and possessions or contentment one cannot give up exploitation or enmity with others.

Forgiveness can ostensibly help to heal relationships by overcoming resentment, soothe painful emotions and serve as an example of the religious life. It means forbearance. It implies control of anger and practice of tolerance in adverse situations. It is a positive emotion and a conscious act of will. It decreases the feeling of hurt and insult; it also enables human beings to forget the weaknesses, shortcomings and faults of others. It not only enhances interpersonal relationships but also leads to improved understanding of both the Self and others.

Forgiveness is an attribute of a calm and peaceful mind, and heralds the beginning of enlightenment, peace and happiness. There is no rest for a person who constantly broods over slights and injuries and wrongs, who feels that one has been unjustly treated and who conspires how best to act for the discomfiture of one's enemy.

Hatred and violence multiplied in retaliation creates a spiral of destruction. An eye for an eye leaves the world blind, as Mahatma Gandhi stated. Revenge, which is the antonym of forgiveness, is a virus that eats into the very vitals of the mind and poisons the entire spiritual being. Resentment is a mental fever which burns up the wholesome energies of the mind and "taking offence" is a form of moral sickness which saps the healthy flow of kindliness and goodwill. Forgiveness is, thus, beneficial at both personal and social levels.

Some researchers have identified five key components of an apology: (1) a statement of apology (I am sorry); (2) remorse (I feel bad); (3) an offer of restitution; (4) self-castigation (I was an idiot); and (5) a request for forgiveness.

Goodwill and trust, which are fragile, easily broken and hard to repair, are essential to day-to-day business. And "when it comes to trust, actions matter, but they do not always speak louder than words". In other words, in addition to the expression of regret, an apology and a specific request for forgiveness, it is also necessary to dispel the misgivings and lurking doubts in the minds of person(s), hurt by your harsh words or misdeeds, besides appropriate actions to restore trust and rebuild goodwill.[2]

On the Day of Forgiveness, observed by the Jainas every year at the end of their religious festival (Paryuṣaṇa Parva), they have the practice of writing in e-mails, postcards, letters, etc. *micchāmi*

---

2 "Knowledge@Wharton", University of Pennsylvania, reproduced in *Economic Times*, 11 August 2006.

dukkaḍam (I seek apology or forgiveness). These days, it seems to have become a mere formality.

While the importance of practising forgiveness has been extolled for centuries, it is only recently that research studies have demonstrated its important health benefits. The practice of forgiveness, therefore, is being increasingly used as a stress management tool for reducing anger and depression as well as for enhancing hopefulness and self-efficacy. For instance, the Stanford Complementary Medicine Clinic runs a regular workshop series of six 90-minutes sessions on forgiveness throughout the year and charges about Rs 10,000 for the course, which is said to provide, among others, medical, clinical and psychological benefits to the trainees.

People with a forgiving nature are said to have lower blood pressure than less-forgiving ones. That hostility and anger, or resentment and bitterness, have been linked with poor health, hypertension and heart problems, is proved in the largest ever study conducted by the Stanford Forgiveness Project. The forgiveness training, the study revealed, resulted in a 70 per cent decrease in feeling of hurt, a 13 per cent reduction in long-term experience of anger, a 27 per cent reduction in physical symptoms of stress (back ache, dizziness, headache, etc.) and a 15 per cent decrease in the emotional experience of stress.

The chief beneficiary of forgiveness is the one who forgives. It is in our own interest to forgive those with whom we are even justifiably angry. Those who try to get even with their enemies discover to their dismay that they hurt themselves more in the process. We forgive for our own sake, not for others. Of course, one has to suffer the consequences of one's actions. There are no such things as sins being forgiven; the evil will have to be paid for. Yet forgiveness is sound ethics that safeguards our mental and physical health and spiritual well-being.

HOW TO CONTROL ANGER

Anger is considered to be a strong negative emotion (e-motion, i.e. energy in motion). It is an adventitious mental state, not the intrinsic nature of the Self, and lasts only for a short while. But in that short period, it can do tremendous harm both to oneself as well as to others. In a fit of anger, one can commit the most sinful act, even killing one's elders. It signifies the loss of self-control and spoils relationships. It is also injurious to our health since it leads to the contraction of arteries and muscles, increases blood pressure, affects our digestion and causes fatigue. If it is directed inward, it creates corrosive energy, which can be extremely self-destructive. It is the cause of agony, distress and enmity, and may take the form of revenge; often there is a feeling of repentance and guilt after anger. It mars one's peace of mind and happiness. Anger, it is said, is only one letter short of danger. It kills you by-and-by, it is a poison.

Anger is inherently a reaction, not action. One becomes angry either in response to frustration, or to an action by other person, that is considered harmful, insulting and abusive, or when someone acts against our wishes or obstructs the fulfilment of our desires. Thus, it is not a well-thought out, deliberate act of will of a conscious being, but the outcome or reaction of the conditioned, unconscious or subconscious mind, which bursts forth in an instantaneous reaction.

Anger makes people insensible, be it a good friend or sibling. Psychologist Charles Spielberg says:

> Anger is an emotional state that varies in intensity from mild irritation to intense fury and rage.

Forgiveness could be the most powerful thing we will ever do. Forgiveness does not mean giving in. It means letting go. Once we forgive, we are no longer emotionally handcuffed to the person who hurt us. When we forgive, we reclaim our power to choose.

Commentary by M.K. Dharma Raja

An ascetic remains unruffled even in the face of the gravest provocation to anger. Howsoever serious the provocative circumstances, his response is not only cool but positively forgiving.

An ascetic, indeed, regards someone who tries to drive him to anger as a friend who does a good turn. For, such an apparently malicious act enables the saint to practise the virtue of forgiveness. He regards such provocative acts as only the operation of the *karma* factor. The forgiving ascetic actually sympathizes with the wrong-doer since according to him, the person concerned was not that he does anything wrong. He is therefore to be forgiven (1990: 78-79).

72

कुलरूवजादिबुद्धिसु तपसुदसीलेसु गारवं किंचि।
जो ण वि कुव्वदि समणो मद्दवधम्मं हवे तस्स॥

kularūvajādibuddhisu tapasudasīlesu gāravaṁ kiñci ।
jo ṇa vi kuvvadi samaṇo maddavadhammaṁ have tassa ॥

The saint who does not in the least feel proud about his ancestry or lineage, appearance, birth, wisdom, austerity, scriptural learning and conduct (*śīla*), observes the virtue (*dharma*) of humility.

Commentary by M.K. Dharma Raja

An ascetic has no conceit of any kind; nor does he feel proud for any extraneous reason.

In the work-a-day world, people usually feel elated but consider themselves superior to others on the ground of one or the other of their attributes. Their parentage, physical excellence, intellectual attainment and the like are among the factors that make people feel superior to others. But an ascetic ought to be free from any trace of conceit. Supreme humility is the hallmark of an ascetic (1990: 80).

73

मोत्तूण कुडिलभावं णिम्मलहिदएण चरदि जो समणो।
अज्जवधम्मं तइयो तस्स दु संभवदि णियमेण॥

mottūṇa kuḍilabhāvaṁ ṇimmalahidaeṇa caradi jo samaṇo ।
ajjavadhammaṁ taiyo tassa du saṁbhavadi ṇiyameṇa ॥

Giving up crooked, guileful or wicked (*kuṭila*) thought-activity, the saint practises conduct with a pure heart; in that case, the *dharma* of straightforwardness (*ārjava*) is possible.

Commentary by M.K. Dharma Raja

An ascetic is scrupulously straightforward and utterly honest in his conduct. He has no desire of deceiving anyone. Always impelled by the purist of motives, he does not swerve from the right conduct. Such an ascetic is truly endowed with a virtue of lofty uprightness (1990: 80).

74

परसंतावयकारणवयणं मोत्तूण सपरहिदवयणं।
जो वददि भिक्खु तुरियो तस्स दु धम्मो हवे सच्चं॥

parasaṅtāvayakāraṇavayaṇaṁ mottūṇa saparahida-vayaṇaṁ ।
jo vadadi bhikkhu turiyo tassa du dhammo have saccaṁ ॥

The holy man (*bhikṣu*) living by begging alms, who giving up the words which cause anguish, grief or remorse (*santāpa*) to others, speaks what does good or is beneficial, affectionate and serves the well-being of one's own Self as also of others (*sva-parahita*); in that case, it is the fourth truthfulness *dharma.*

Commentary by M.K. Dharma Raja

Abstention from causing injury is the very essence of righteousness. An ascetic dedicated to the highest principle of truthfulness takes the utmost care to ensure that his words will not cause injury to anyone.

An ascetic's vow of truthfulness has a positive dimension. His utterances do good both to himself and to those to whom he speaks. They ennoble both himself and those whom he addresses. This is the excellence of the loftiest truthfulness, the characteristic of an ascetic (1990: 80-81).

75

कंखाभावणिवित्तिं, किच्चा वेरग्ग भावणा जुत्तो।
जो वट्टदि परममुणी, तस्स दु धम्मो हवे सोच्चं॥

kaṅkhābhāvaṇivittiṁ, kiccā vēragga bhāvaṇā juttō ।
jo vattadi paramamuni, tass du dhammo have sochcham ॥

He who abstains from desire or longing (*kāṅkṣā*) and is free from worldly desires and concerns, that saint of the highest stage is said to be endowed with the immaculate purity (*śauca*) *dharma*.

Commentary by M.K. Dharma Raja

Total purity of the mind is attained by stamping out the impulse of desires. Having subjugated all desires, the ascetic is totally averse to mundane interests. His conduct, therefore, is exemplary. Such a venerable saint observes the immaculate vow of purity of mind, speech and action (1990: 81).

76

वदसमिदिपालणाए दंडच्चाएण इंदियजएण।
परिणममाणस्स पुणो संजमधम्मो हवे णियमा॥

vadasamidipālaṇāe daṇḍaccāeṇa iṅdiyajaeṇa ।
pariṇamamāṇassa puṇo sañjamadhammo have ṇiyamā ॥

The saint, who observes non-violence (*ahiṁsā*), etc. vows (*vrata*) and self-regulations or carefulness (*samiti*) in walking, speaking, etc. (see *supra*), restrains the afflictions of mind, speech and body, and overcomes all sensual desires is considered to observe a practice of self-discipline (*saṁyama*) *dharma* as a rule.

Commentary by M.K. Dharma Raja

A saint conducts himself with supreme restraint, strictly abstaining from all mental, physical and vocal afflictions. He observes the entire range of vows and regulations, and joins in the mendicant order. By subjugating and overcoming the sensual impulses, he attunes himself to concentrate his mind on the real nature of the Self. The discipline of the highest form of self-restraint enables a saint to feel completely detached from the mundane world (1990: 82).

77

विसयकसायविणिग्गहभावं काऊण झाणसज्झाए।
जो भावइ अप्पाणं तस्स तवं होदि णियमेण॥

visayakasāyaviṇiggahabhāvaṁ kāūṇa jhāṇasajjhāe ।
jo bhāvai appāṇaṁ tassa tavaṁ hodi ṇiyameṇa ॥

He, who restrains sensual desires (*vyasana*) and passions like anger, and through meditation (*dhyāna*) and study (*svādhyāya*) contemplates on the Self, practises the austerities of penance (*tapa*) *dharma*.

Commentary

There are six kinds of external austerities (*TS* IX.19) and six kinds of internal austerities (*TS* IX.20) (see *supra*).

Commentary by M.K. Dharma Raja

Austerity involves the most exacting discipline of the complete insulation of one's mind from the pollution of desires and passions. An ascetic achieves this sublime mental poise of a total absence of carnal cravings by means of the rigorous discipline of meditation and through absorption in scriptural studies. This is the exercise that enables ascetics to burn up kārmic impurities through penance. Total absorption in the contemplation of the Self becomes possible through observing austerities like fasting and living in isolation and mindful of sufferings (1990: 82).

78

णिव्वेगतियं भावइ मोहं चइऊण सव्वदव्वेसु ।
जो तस्स हवे चागो इदि भणिदं जिणवरिंदेहिं ॥

ṇivvegatiyaṁ bhāvai mohaṁ caiūṇa savvadavvesu ।
jo tassa have cāgo idi bhaṇidaṁ jiṇavariṅdehiṁ ॥

He, who giving up attachment to and infatuation for all objects, takes a dispassionate and detached view of things (*nirveda*) or is imbued with detachment (from the mundane world and disinterest in his own body and sensual pleasures), is considered to practise renunciation (*tyāga*) *dharma*; so the Omniscient Lord (Jina) has uttered.

Commentary by M.K. Dharma Raja

Renunciation involves giving up the desire for all objects; total lack of concern with all things extraneous to one's own Self.

The saint who practises this virtue remains free from the feelings of attachment either for the outside world, or his own body or for external comforts. He practises the strict discipline of severing all ties with the extraneous objects. The renunciation is deliberate and all hardships which come his way are borne cheerfully.

Constant contemplation on this supreme virtue of total renunciation of all worldly attachment further strengthens the aspirant's resolve to tread the path towards perfection (1990: 83).

79

होऊण य णिस्संगो णियभावं णिग्गहित्तु सुदुहदं।
णिद्दंदेण दु वट्टदि अणयारो तस्स किंचण्हं॥

hoūṇa ya ṇissaṅgo ṇiyabhāvaṁ ṇiggahittu suduhadaṁ ।
ṇiddaṅdeṇa du vaṭṭadi aṇayāro tassa kiñcaṇhaṁ ॥

The homeless (*anāgāra*) saint, who gives up and forsakes possessiveness and restrains his own thoughts, is indifferent to pleasure and pain, is endowed with the non-attachment and non-inquisitiveness (*akiñcana*) *dharma.*

Commentary by M.K. Dharma Raja

The acquisitive instinct of claiming objects as one's own does not assail an ascetic. Nor is he motivated by thoughts which induce either pleasure or anguish.

Having given up his home as well as all kinship, an exemplary saint radiates an equal disposition which is reflected in his actions.

The saintly virtue of supreme selflessness is a worthy theme of contemplation (1990: 83-84).

80

सव्वंगं पेच्छंतो इत्थीणं तासु मुयदि दुव्भावं।
सो बम्हचेरभावं सक्कदि खलु दुद्धरं धरिदुं॥

savvaṅgaṁ pecchaṅto itthīṇaṁ tāsu muyadi duvbhāvaṁ ।
so bamhacerabhāvaṁ sakkadi khalu duddharaṁ dhariduṁ ॥

He, who, seeing all the parts of a woman's body, refrains from the thought of relish, love or attachment (*rati*) to her, that noble saint is able to practise the mighty (*durdhara*) *brahmacarya dharma.*

Commentary by M.K. Dharma Raja

A saint, who attains the high standard of spiritual excellence of having subdued all sex impulses, is capable of observing supreme celibacy.

The vow of celibacy signifies absolute purity in sex-passion both in conduct and intention. Those taking this vow remain totally impervious to the sex inclination even when seeing the naked bodies of women.

A saint sees and feels no difference between the body of either sex. Sex, in fact, has no meaning to a saint who views the physical body as inert and extraneous matter (1990: 84).

81

सावयधम्मं चत्ता जदिधम्मे जो हु वट्टए जीवो।
सो णय वज्जदि मोक्खं धम्मं इदि चिंतए णिच्चं॥

sāvayadhammaṁ cattā jadidhamme jo hu vaṭṭae jīvo ।
so ṇaya vajjadi mokkhaṁ dhammaṁ idi ciṅtae ṇiccaṁ ॥

That soul, which gives up or abandons the noble householder's vows and virtues (*śrāvaka dharma*), practises a saint's righteousness and piety (*dharma*), necessarily, without fail attains liberation. One should always contemplate in this manner.

Commentary by M.K. Dharma Raja

The ascetic's path is commended here as the surest stepping stone to final liberation. The attainment of perfection is the culmination of a graduated spiritual advance. It has been explained in the preceding verses that a layman qualifies himself to follow the ascetic's way of life after passing through the initial eleven stages of spiritual evolution.

The most exacting regimen of the ascetic's path culminates

with a thirteenth stage at which the Self realizes its potential of omniscience. This marks the threshold to final liberation.

Thus, focusing the mind on this lofty radius path is the ideal subject for constant contemplation (1990: 85).

82

णिच्छयणएण जीवो सागारणगारधम्मदो भिण्णो ।
मज्झत्थभावणाए सुद्धप्पं चिंतए णिच्चं ॥

ṇicchayaṇaeṇa jīvo sāgāraṇagāradhammado bhiṇṇo ।
majjhatthabhāvaṇāe suddhappaṁ ciṅtae ṇiccaṁ ॥

From the internal, self-referential point of view (*niścaya naya*) the householder's (*sāgāra*) *dharma* and the term of homeless (*anāgāra*) are distinct. Therefore, by practising indifferent or equanimous thoughts (*madhyastha bhāvas*) one should always contemplate on the (*transcendental*) pure nature of the Self (*BA* 82). The Self or the path of liberation is not to be identified with either *sāgāra* or *anāgāra dharma*.

Commentary by M.K. Dharma Raja

In this verse, the aspirant is once again directed to grasp the essence of the purity of the soul. This theme ought to be the central point of constant contemplation.

With due consideration to practical norms, different codes of conduct have been prescribed for the pious householder and the ascetic. But this distinction is purely conventional.

From the strictly real standpoint, it is the pristine purity of the soul that is to be contemplated upon. Self-realization is the ultimate goal of the householder and the ascetic alike. The layman in his spiritual quest adopts the ascetic's vows as he advances spiritually. His aim is to liberate himself from the kārmic bondage.

The worthy seer, therefore, elucidates the cardinal point that differences between the two ways in pursuit of the ultimate goal should be viewed equitably in their real perspective (1990: 86).

Commentary

The concept of being indifferent (*madhyastha*) is explained by Antaratma Swamiji in the following words:

> Understand that no negative thought has any effect if you do not own it and act upon it. You are not responsible for the arising of any thought. Your responsibility commences from the time you act upon it. The difference is crucial. If negative thoughts come, and you are not prepared to act upon them, they will simply disappear, leaving it to yourself, as before. If their incidence has no effect or purpose, automatically they will stop coming again. If at all once in a while, they happen to intrude, or simply be indifferent.[3]

Joseph Goldstein (2002: 140-141) points out:

> Thoughts are tremendously seductive. When they go unnoticed, they have compelling power; they become the dictators of the mind. Yet when they are noticed, we realize the only power thoughts have is the power we give to them.

In *Samayasāra* 408-409, Kundakunda states:

> The ignorant/deluded persons (*mūḍha*) put on various types of external insignia or marks of pseudo-ascetics or laymen (householders) and (mistakenly/erroneously) maintain that these (external) paraphernalia or outer marks constitute the path of liberation.
>
> Bodily marks on external insignia are certainly not the path of liberation. [This is evident from the fact that] the Omniscient Lords (Arhat or Arihanta) do not have any attachment (*nirmama*) to the body and give up/abandon these bodily marks and devote their attention to enlighten worldview or right belief, knowledge and conducts.

---

3 *Vicharasetu: The Path of Introspection* (monthly), Thrissur, Kerala: Narayanashrama Tapovanam, January 2005, p. 25.

Kundakunda further states:

> The external insignia or marks of the householders in the pseudo-ascetics never constitute the path of liberation (*mokṣa mārga*). The Omniscient Lords (Jina) declare that enlightened worldview, knowledge and conduct together constitute the path of liberation. — *SS* 410
>
> Therefore, giving up (attachment to) the external insignia and bodily marks adopted by the householders of the homeless ascetics, one should join with and devote oneself (*juñja* in Prākr̥t) to the task of concentrating fully upon the path of liberation comprising of the enlightened worldview/right belief, knowledge and conduct. — *SS* 411

Kundakunda observes:

> Those (ignorant, deluded) persons who have attachment to various kinds of ascetic symbols or householders' marks [consider these to be essential for liberation and mistakenly imagine themselves to be real ascetics] do not know the real transcendental pure nature or the essence of the Self. — *SS* 413
>
> From the external, other-referential point of view (*vyavahāra naya*), the two (*dve*), i.e. both types of external insignia and marks [i.e. of the ascetics and householders) are also (*api*) considered to be useful and relevant in the path of liberation. However, from the internal, self-referential point of view (*niścaya naya*), all kinds of external insignia and marks are not desired for the path of liberation. — *SS* 414

In view of what is stated above, Kundakunda emphasizes:

> Keeping the Self firmly established (*sthāpya*) on the path of liberation, contemplate, meditate upon [and be absorbed only in the Self] and become aware of it, experience only (the Self), and always moving in, wander or roam about (*vihāra*) in the Self; do not move in, wander or roam about in other (*anya*) substances (*dravyeṣu*). — *SS* 412

Kārttikeyānuprekṣā

Kundakunda describes *dharma anuprekṣā* in fifteen verses (*BA* 68-82). *Kārttikeyānuprekṣā* describes it in 187 verses (*KA* 302-488) as given below.

The omniscient who directly knows the entire *loka* and *aloka* with all their attributes and modes of the past, present and future is verily the divinity. He alone comprehends the supersensuous: the knowledge of senses does not grasp even the gross objects with all their modes. The religion preached by him is (1) twelvefold for laymen or householders, and (2) tenfold for monks or houseless (*KA* 302-304).

1. *Darśana-śuddha*: A liberable soul, suitably constituted and qualified, develops *samyaktva* (right faith) which is of three types: *upaśama, kṣāyika* and *kṣayopaśamika.* Even when *samyaktva* is partly attained, there is scope for lapses in it. One endowed with right faith necessarily carries conviction about the many-sided reality stated through sevenfold predication as demanded by the occasion. Through the study of scriptures and by adopting different points of view (*naya*), he recognizes the nine *padārthas.* He is not vain about his family and possessions; but with mental quiet, he feels himself insignificant. Though addicted to pleasures and engrossed in various activities, he knows all that to be worthless, a pursuit in infatuation. He is devoted to the highest virtues, respectful towards the best monks and attached to his co-religionists. The soul, though embodied, is separate from the body, by virtue of its essential attribute of knowledge; the body is just like a garment. He worships God who is free from faults (*doṣa*), reveres religion which enjoins kindness to all beings and respects a teacher who is without any attachment or ties. He regularly reflects that it is his own *karma* — and none else — that brings about his prosperity and adversity, his pleasures and pains and that his death at the due time is a certainty which cannot be averted either by Indra or Jinendra. He understands the various substances with

their modes from a realistic point of view and has no doubts of any kind: in matters beyond his comprehension the words of Jina carry conviction to him. *Samyaktva* or right faith is of the highest value; and it brings respect here and happiness in the next world, even though one does not practise the vows. A man of right faith incurs no more evil *karmas* and whatever he has in stock from earlier birth, he destroys (*KA* 307-327).

2. *Darśana-śrāvaka:* A layman of right faith is firm in his mind and practises his vows without expecting anything in return (*niyana-parihīno*) and is renunciative in his outlook. He does not enjoy abominable items of food and drink, such as flesh, wine, which are full of *trasa* lives (*KA* 328-329).

3. *Vrata-śrāvaka:* A layman with vows practises five *aṇuvratas* and is endowed with *guṇa-vratas* and *śikṣā-vratas:* he is firm, quiet and sensible:

   a. He behaves kindly, treating all others on par with himself; and being introspective and self-critical, he avoids all major sins. He neither commits, nor commissions, nor consents to any injury to *trasa* beings (i.e. beings having more than one sense organ) in thought, word and act.

   b. He does not utter injurious, harsh and rough words, nor does he betray anyone's confidence. His words are beneficial, measured, pleasing to all and glorificatory of religious standards.

   c. He never buys a costly article at a low price, nor does he pick up a forgotten thing; and he is satisfied even with a small gain. He is pure in his intentions and firm in his mind; and he never robs what belongs to others out of treachery, greed, anger or vanity.

   d. Feeling detestation for a woman's body, he looks upon her form and beauty as evil temptations. He observes chastity (broadly) in thoughts, words and acts looking upon other women (than his wedded wife) as mother, sister, daughter, etc.

e. He subjugates greed and is happy with the elixir of contentment. Realizing everything to be transitory, he eradicates all nasty cravings. He puts a limit to his possessions of wealth, corn, gold, fields, etc. taking into account their utility (*KA* 330-340).

1') Like the limit to possessions, putting limits with respect to directions also is an effective curb against one's greed; so one should, knowing the need, limit one's movements in the well-known directions (east, etc.).

2') That concern or activity which achieves no useful purpose but essentially involves sin is something evil which is fivefold with many a variety:

a. Picking up faults of others, yearning for other's wealth, erotic gazing at other women and getting interested in other's quarrels;

b. giving instructions in important matters connected with agriculture, rearing the cattle, business, weddings, etc.;

c. useless activities involving injury to immobile *sthāvara* beings in the form of earth, water, fire and vegetables;

d. maintaining harmful animals, giving weapons, etc. as well as fatal drugs; and

e. attending to works dealing with quarrels, erotics, etc. and finding faults with others.

3') One should put a limit to the enjoyment of food, betel-leaves, clothes, etc. knowing that they are available. A worthy vow is his who relinquishes what he possesses: he who feels himself on his fancies derives no benefit at all (*KA* 341-351).

1") While practising *sāmayika*, the following seven items are to be taken into account: (a) place, (b) time, (c) posture, (d) concentration of mind, (e) purity of mind, (f) purity of speech, and (g) purity of body. These include:

a. The place which is not noisy, nor crowded and not infested with mosquitoes, etc. is suited for *sāmayika*.

b. The *Gaṇadharas* have stated that six *naī(ḍ)ikās* (*nālikā* = about 24 minutes) of the morning, noon and evening are suited for the practice of *sāmayika.*

c. One should sit in the *paryaṅka* posture or stand erect for a fixed period of time, curbing all the activities of sense organs.

d-g. With the mind concentrated on the instructions of Jina, with the body restrained and with the hands folded one should be engrossed in one's Self, reflecting on the significance of the salutation (-formula). One who practises *sāmayika* in this manner, circumscribing the region and avoiding all sinful activities, becomes just like a monk.

2") The man of understanding, who decks himself with (the attitude of) renunciation, relinquishing bath, cosmetics, ornaments, contact with women, scents, incense, etc. and regularly fasts or eats simply or pure food only once on the two *parva* days (of the fortnight, i.e. the eighth and the fourteenth day) has to his credit the *poṣaha* vow.

3") The third *śikṣā-vrata,* which brings happiness, etc. requires a man of understanding, endowed with faith, etc. to give, according to ninefold ways of donating gifts to three kinds of worthy recipients. Gifts can be of four types: food, medicine, scriptures and *abhaya* (security or shelter), the last being unique among the four. By giving food, the remaining three wants also are fulfilled. It is on account of hunger and thirst that there are various diseases; it is the food that sustains a monk in his study of scriptures day and night; and it is by food that all life is nourished. Through detached and devoted gifts one puts the entire *saṅgha* on the path of liberation, consisting of three jewels. Even one worthy gift, given to a single worthy person, brings to one the happiness of Indra.

4") In the fourth *śikṣā-vrata,* the limits put to directions, etc. and pleasures of senses are further circumscribed; greed and erotic temptations are quieted; and sins are reduced.

One who quietly faces the voluntary submission to death (*sallekhanā*), after practising twelve vows, attains heavenly bliss and liberation. Devoted, firm and faultless practice of even a single vow brings immense benefit to one (*KA* 352-370).

4. *Sāmayika* consists in meditating on the consequences of *karmas*, all along fixing one's thoughts on one's own nature, the image of Jina or the sacred syllable, after quietly and courageously giving up attachment for the body and in putting into practice twelve *āvarttas*, two *namanas* and four *praṇāmas* (*KA* 371-372).

5. *Poṣaha* is practised in this way. In the afternoon of the seventh and thirteenth days of the fortnight, one goes to the temple of Jina, offers *kiriyā-kamma* (salutation, etc.) accepts the vow of fourfold fast (from the teacher), abstains from all domestic routine, spends the night in religious thoughts, gets up early in the morning, offers salutations, etc. spends the whole day (eighth and fourteenth) in the study of scriptures concluded with salutation, spends that night in the like manner (as above), offers *vandanā* early morning (of the ninth or fifteenth day), performs *pūjā*, entertains worthy guests of three types and then eats his food. Quietly fasting without any sinful activities easily destroys *karmas*; otherwise fasting is only a physical torture (*KA* 379-383).

6. *Sacitta-virati:* By not eating leaves, fruits, bark, roots, sprouts or seeds which contain life, one becomes *sacitta-virata*. It is all the same whether one eats or makes others eat them. By avoiding such food, one has a full restraint on the tongue, and consequently one is full of compassion to beings and carries out the instruction of Jina (*KA* 379-381).

7. *Rātri-bhojana-virati:* A sensible person neither eats nor serves to others fourfold food at night; by not eating at night one is as good as fasting for six months in a year, and one avoids all sinful activities at night.

8. *Maithuna-tyāga:* He who abstains from women and sex-pleasures in thoughts, words and acts and by committing, commissioning and consenting to, observes the vow of celibacy and is full of kindness to living beings.

9. *Ārambha-tyāga:* He who does not commit, commission and consent to sinful activities and detests harm unto beings avoids all sins.

10. *Saṅga-tyāga:* Ties or possessions are twofold: internal and external. He who gladly relinquishes them both is free from sins. Poor people, naturally, have no external possessions, but it is difficult to relinquish internal ties or distractions.

11. *Anumati-tyāga:* He is an *anumati-virata* who never involves himself even by consent into any household activities causing sin. Being full of attachment and aversion, if one occupies one's thoughts with various useless activities, one commits sins without achieving any purpose.

12. *Uddiṣṭahara-virata:* By going from house to house, one should eat food which is pure in nine ways, which is not specifically solicited, which is proper and which is not specially prepared.

    One who practises the vows of a householder and duly cultivates *ārādhanā* on the eve of his life is reborn as an Indra (*KA* 382-391).

The religious duties prescribed for a monk are tenfold:

1. *Uttama kṣamā:* Forbearance consists in not getting angry even when severe troubles are inflicted.
2. *Uttama mārdava:* Humility or modesty consists in one's being introspective about one's own defects even when one has reached the height of knowledge and austerities.
3. *Uttama ārjava:* Straightforwardness consists in eschewing crookedness in thoughts, words and acts, and in never concealing one's own faults.

4. *Uttama śauca:* Purity means that the dirt of acute greed is washed away by the water of equanimity or peace and contentment, and there is no greed even for food.
5. *Uttama satya:* Truthfulness comprises speaking in conformity with the words of the Jina, even though one is not able to put them into practice and in avoiding lies even in worldly transactions.
6. *Uttama samaya:* Self-restraint consists in not injuring (i.e. giving security to) living beings, even to the extent of cutting grass, in course of one's movements and activities.
7. *Uttama tapas:* Austerity consists of equanimity, being indifferent to the pleasures of this and of the next world and in quietly enduring various physical troubles.
8. *Uttama tyāga:* Renunciation consists in relinquishing dainty food, articles which give rise to attachment and aversion, and home which occasions vanity of possession.
9. *Uttama nirgranthatva:* Non-possession consists in giving up attachment to things, both living and non-living, and in abstaining from all worldly dealings.
10. *Uttama brahmacarya:* Chastity or celibacy, which is ninefold, comprises of having no contact with women, in not observing their form and in not being interested in erotic talks. One who is not distracted by the glances of girls is the greatest hero (*KA* 392-404).

That is the greatest *dharma* in which no harm unto living beings is involved even in the least. Harming living beings in the name of Gods or teachers is sin, and can never be *dharma* which is characterized by kindness to all living beings. The religion preached by the Jina is something unique. By practising this tenfold *dharma* one acquires *puṇya* (merits), but it should not be practised for merits. *Puṇya* involves *saṁsāra;* and only by its destruction, liberation can be attained. If *puṇya* is acquired to gain worldly pleasures, spiritual purity will never be reached. One should aim rather at quieting one's passions than at acquiring *puṇyas* (*KA* 405-413).

One should have faith or conviction, without any doubt, that religion is characterized by:

a. Kindness to living beings and should never involve any injury to them as in a sacrifice.

b. Liberation should be the aim and religion should not be practised through severe penances with the hankering of heavenly pleasures.

c. One should not detest the disgusting physical appearance of those who are endowed with tenfold *dharma.*

d. One who does not consider, out of fear, modesty or gain, harm unto living beings as the religion but is devoted to the words of the Jina, is a man of correct or undeluded perspective.

e. Reflecting on the kārmic consequences, one should never scorn at others' defects and never make public one's own virtues.

f. Those who are shaky in their convictions should confirm on the path of religion by oneself being quite firm.

g. One should talk sweet and show devotion to and follow the religious people.

h. One should preach the tenfold religion to the pious or liberable souls (*bhavya*) and enlighten oneself too.

The greatness of the doctrine preached by Jinas should be established by various arguments and through severe penances. These qualities are cultivated by him who meditates on himself and is averse to pleasures of senses: it is on account of these virtues with reference to *dharma,* as well as to Divinity, teacher and principles that one's right faith gets purified (*KA* 414-425).

Deluded as one is, one understands religion with difficulty and puts the same into practice with greater difficulty. By practising the religion preached by the Jina, one easily gets happiness. Religion is like a seed to give the desired fruit. A religious man is forgiving even to his enemies; he is indifferent to others' wealth; and he looks upon any other woman (other than his wife) as his mother. His mind is pure, he speaks sweetly, he creates confidence all-round and he is reputed everywhere. *Dharma* works out miracles and unexpected results. All efforts fail without the backing of religion: knowing this one should avoid sin and practise religion (*KA* 426-437).

Quietening the senses is, in fine, *upavāsa,* therefore those who have control over their senses are observing *upavāsa* (fast) though eating (some food). The external penances are of six kinds:

a. The *anaśana* austerity consists in easily abstaining from food for a day, etc. only with the object of destroying *karmas*, but if sinful activities are undertaken during a fast, fasting is only a physical torture.

b. The *avamaudārya* austerity consists in eating a little pure and suitable food without any greed and ulterior motives.

c. *Vṛtti-parimāṇa* means eating indifferently tasteless food, anticipated in mind, with the number of houses limited.

d. One who observes *rasa-tyāga* eats tasteless food being oppressed by the misery of *saṁsāra* and constantly thinking that the pleasures of the senses are a poison.

e. One who observes the fifth austerity, stays in a lonely place, such as unhaunted cemetery and forest. He relinquishes positions, etc. which occasion attachment and aversion; and being disgusted with worldly pleasures, he has no craving for houses, etc. He is quiet or peaceful and skilled in the practice of internal penances.

f. One, who is not discouraged by adverse climatic conditions and is triumphant over various troubles, practises the austerity called *kāya-kleśa.*

The internal penances are also of six kinds:

1. *Prāśyascitta:* One is not to commit, commission and consent to a fault in thought, word and deed. If any fault is there through negligence or inadvertence (*pramāda*), it should be confessed, oneself being free from ten defects, before a worthy teacher whose prescriptions one must carry out. Avoiding that fault, one meditates, without any distractions, on the *ātman,* an embodiment of knowledge.

2. *Vinaya:* One should have a pure temperament with reference to *darśana, jñāna, caritra,* twelvefold penance and manifold *upacāra;* and it means devoted attendance on those who are endowed with faith, knowledge and conduct.

3. *Vaiyyāvṛtya:* One should render disinterested service to the aged and suffering monks, and be devoted with the best of intentions to the cultivation of peace and self-restraint, abstaining from worldly activities.

4. *Svādhyāya:* Study of scriptures is indifferent to criticism of others, eliminates wicked thoughts, helps one to ascertain reality and is an aid to meditation or concentration of the mind. Devoted study of Jaina scriptures, without craving for respect and with a view to removing *karmas*, leads to happiness; but if it is attended with vanity, craving and opposition to colleagues, it is harmful. The study of texts dealing with fight and love with a disturbed mind and with a view to dupe other people, bears no benefit. Worthy is that study which enables one to realize one's *ātman,* full of knowledge and quite separated from the body.

5. *Kāyotsarga* means indifference to body, its caressing and needs and being engrossed in self-meditation with perfect detachment with reference to everything outside.

6. *Dhyāna:* Concentration of mind on a certain item for a while is known as *dhyāna* which may be inauspicious or auspicious.

Ārta and *raudra* are inauspicious, while *dharma* and *śukla* are auspicious. Passions are acute in *ārta,* still more acute in *raudra;* but they are temperate in *dharma* and even more temperate in *śukla* which is possessed by one who is free from passions and is possessed of scriptural knowledge and by the omniscient (*KA* 438-472).

Ārta-dhyāna (miserable mood) develops when one wants to escape miserable contacts and when one wants pleasant associations from which one is separated. In *raudra-dhyāna,* one repeatedly revels in injury to living beings and in telling lies; one is not only keen about one's possessions and pleasures but wants to deprive others of them. *Ārta* and *raudra* are a source of sin, and as such they should be studiously avoided.

Dharma means the nature of things, tenfold virtues like *kṣamā*, the three jewels (*ratnatraya*) and protection of living beings. Attachment and aversion, sense-pleasures and extraneous distractions, etc. are avoided and the mind is concentrated on the nature of *ātman;* and one goes on meditating with joy and peace, i.e. *dharma-dhyāna.*

In *śukla-dhyāna*, virtues grow purer, the *karmas* are quieted and eradicated, the *leśyās* are white and one advances in spiritual purification. When all delusion is melted away, when all passions are pacified and when one is engrossed in oneself, there is *śukla-dhyāna* in its four stages (*KA* 473-88).

Chapter 12
Bodhi-durlabha Anuprekṣā (Rarity of Enlightenment or True Insight of the Reality of Things and Right Path of Liberation)

83

उपज्जदि सण्णाणं जेण उवाएण तस्सुवायस्स ।
चिंता हवेइ बोहो अच्चंतं दुल्लहं होदि ॥

upajjadi saṇṇāṇaṁ jeṇa uvāeṇa tassuvāyassa ।
ciṅtā havei boho accaṅtaṁ dullahaṁ hodi ॥

That means an endeavour (*upāya*), which gives rise or generates enlightened or right knowledge (*samyak jñāna*), contemplation of that means (*upayoga*) is true insight or enlightenment (*bodhi*), which is extremely difficult to attain.

In his description of twelve contemplations, Bhudhar Das observes:

> Wealth, grain and gold — all these are easy to get, but acquiring of enlightened or true (*yathārtha*) knowledge is difficult to get in the world.

Human birth is also difficult to get.

Commentary by M.K. Dharma Raja

The focal point of this contemplation is the endeavour through which right knowledge is acquired. Self-realization is attained with the insight that comes from right knowledge. Without the faculty of right knowledge, it is not possible to traverse the path that leads to liberation from the vicious whirlpool of rebirths.

Of all the conditions of mundane existence, it is only human life that it becomes possible to free the Self from sensual desires and to make it shed the shackles of kārmic bondage through ascetic austerities. Only the extremely meritorious souls take birth as humans.

Even in human destiny, it is only rarely that one is able to travel on the path of self-realization. For it is the path of spiritual progress and self-purification that leads to enlightenment of the acquisition of right knowledge. Also there is a chance that makes it possible for one to contemplate on the self-redeeming things.

The extremely fortunate conjunction resulting in a soul taking human birth in which only an infinitesimally few realize true insight providing the threshold to self-realization is the thought emphasized in this verse. That the rarest of rare faculties of true insight ought to be fully harnessed is the quest of eternal bliss is a seminal idea commended by Kundakunda (1990: 87-88).

84

कम्मुदयजपज्जायां हेयं खाओवसमियणाणं तु ।
सगदव्वमुवादेयं णिच्छयत्ति होदि सण्णाणं ॥

kammudayajapajjāyāṁ heyaṁ khāovasamiyaṇāṇaṁ tu ।
sagadavvamuvādeyaṁ ṇicchayatti hodi saṇṇāṇaṁ ॥

Destructive-cum-subsidence (*kṣayopaśamika*) knowledge is the modification (*paryāya*) of knowledge as it has arisen or produced from the coming into operation or rise (*udaya*) of (material) *karmas* [other substance] is worth-abandoning or renouncing (*heya*). Enlightened knowledge is one's own substance (*svaka dravya*), so it is worth-acquiring (*upādeya*).

Commentary

Enlightened knowledge and the true insight of the reality of things as they are worth-acquiring as only through them that it is possible to traverse the path of liberation. Even after one gets human birth, which in itself is difficult, it is even more, i.e. extremely difficult, to get enlightenment (*bodhi*), true insight of the reality of things. Enlightened knowledge is anchored on enlightened worldview, i.e. the true insight of the reality of things as they are.

Commentary by M.K. Dharma Raja

The level of knowledge attained by the Self in its impure state depends on the extent to which it has eliminated and suppressed the *karma*-molecules (*kṣayopaśamika jñāna*). The knowledge possessed at this stage is imperfect knowledge.

It is only the pure soul that is endowed with unbounded infinite knowledge-omniscience. The supreme quality of the pure soul (the pure Self) is thus the only one of the objectives that the aspirant should set for himself. That, indeed, is the work, the destiny of the Self.

Right knowledge is anchored on this firm belief (1990: 88).

85

मूलुत्तरपयडीओ मिच्छत्तादी असंखलोगपरिमाणा ।
परदव्वं सगदव्वं अप्पा इदि णिच्छयणएण ॥

mūluttarapayaḍīo micchattādī asaṅkhalogaparimāṇā ।
paradavvaṁ sagadavvaṁ appā idi ṇicchayaṇaeṇa ॥

Deluded view (*mithyātva*), etc. are the conditions of (knowledge-obscuring, etc.) eight kinds of primary classes or species (*mūla prakr̥tis*) of material *karmas*, which is other substance (*para-dravya*), while the sub-species (*uttara-prakr̥ti*) (of *karmas*) are innumerable on the universe-wide scale. From the internal, self-referential point of view (*niścaya naya*), the Self alone is one's own substance (*svaka dravya*).

Commentary

The spiritual aspirant concentrates on the discriminating insight and knowledge (*bheda-vijñāna*), which emphasizes distinctness between the transcendental pure nature of one's own Self and other substances, including material *karmas*.

In this context, *Samayasāra* 190-192 state:

> It is declared that the psychic states of thought-activity of deluded view (*mithyātva*), perverted knowledge (*ajñāna*), lack of moral self-restraints (*avirati*), and the activities of mind, speech and body (*yoga*) [also anger, etc. passions (*kaṣāyas*)] are the conditions (*hetu*) of knowledge-obscuring, etc. material *karmas*. The absence of these conditions in one having discriminative insight and knowledge (*bheda-vijñāna*) leads to the stoppage (*nirodha*) of the inflow of material *karmas*. When there is stoppage of the inflow of material *karmas*, the inflow of no-*karma* is also stopped. When there is no inflow of no-*karma*, i.e. body-building materials, the process of body-building will completely disappear, which means the cessation of the cycle of births and deaths (*saṁsāra*).

86

एवं जायदि णाणं हेयमुवादेय णिच्छये णत्थि ।
चिंतिज्जइ मुणि बोहिं संसारविरमणट्ठे य ॥

evaṁ jāyadi ṇāṇaṁ heyamuvādeya ṇicchaye ṇatthi ।
ciṁtijjai muṇi bohiṁ saṁsāraviramaṇaṭṭhe ya ॥

Thus arises the perception of knowledge, that is worth abandoning or renouncing (*heya*) and worth acquiring (*upādeya*). But from the internal, self-referential point of view (*niścayena*), there is no thought-construction (*vikalpa*) of that, i.e. of *heya* and *upādeya*. Therefore, the saint (*muni*) should contemplate on *bodhi* (the true insight or the enlightened knowledge of the reality of things as they are) for being non-attached to worldly objects (*saṁsāra-viramāna*).

Commentary by M.K. Dharma Raja

The perception of the precise understanding of the absolute Self (the soul) is summed up in this verse.

An enlightened saint discriminates between what is acceptable as the soul and what are its mere appendages which should be cast away. He knows the difference between the two. To him, therefore, there is no contradiction between them since he sees them as distinct entities. All through its conditions of innumerable transmigrations the pure soul remains distinct from the cloak of impurities cling to it.

The aspiring seeker ought to concentrate all his thoughts on this comprehension (1990: 90).

Kārttikeyānupreksā

Kundakunda describes *bodhi-durlabha anupreksā* in four verses (*BA* 79-82). *Kārttikeyānupreksā* describes it in 78 verses (*KA* 284-361) in these words:

> Dwelling for an infinite period, without beginning in time, in the *nigoda*, the *jīva* somehow comes out, and passing through different grades of beings, such as *sthāvara*, *trasa*, imperfect and perfect *tiryag*, etc. gets human birth, hard to be obtained. Even there, good family, affluence, physical perfection, the body, good character, good company, religious faith, pious life, faith-knowledge-conduct, avoiding mental perversion and passions, godhood, practice of penances: these are rarities among rarities. The human life has a unique signification: it is here that great vows, meditation and attainment of *nirvāṇa* are possible. So one should concentrate respectfully on the cultivation of faith, knowledge and conduct. But to waste human life in the pursuit of pleasures is to burn a precious stone for ashes.

CONCLUDING REMARKS

87

वारस अणुवेक्खाओ पच्चक्खाणं तहेव पडिक्कमणं।
आलोयणं समाहिं तम्हा भावेज्ज अणुवेक्खं॥

vārasa aṇuvekkhāo paccakkhāṇaṁ taheva paḍikkamaṇaṁ ।
āloyaṇaṁ samāhiṁ tamhā bhāvejja aṇuvekkhaṁ ॥

These (the above-mentioned) twelve *anuprekṣās* are of the nature of or themselves constitute a contemplation on one's own true Self (*NS* 83) renunciation or resolve to renounce misdeeds in future (*pratyākhyāna*) and contemplation of one's own true Self (*NS* 95), a repentance (*pratikramaṇa*) of past misdeeds, confession (*ālocanā*), i.e. voluntary acknowledgement of one's own faults existing at present, and contemplation of one's own (*appaṇam*) transcendental, pure nature of the Self, which is distinct from no-*karma* (body) and *karmas* and of attributes (*guṇas*) and modifications (*paryāyas*), which are distortions or defilements of one's own true nature in the sense of being non-relational to or independent of *karmas* (*karma-nirapekṣa*) and contemplates on one's own Self (*NS* 107), and profound meditation, devoid of attachment and equanimity (*samādhi*) (*NS* 122-124) as also contemplation on one's own true Self (*NS* 122).

Commentary by M.K. Dharma Raja

Kundakunda now refers to the virtue and efficacy of the central theme, viz. the twelve contemplations.

All the essential disciplines, which need to be practised in order to direct the mind towards concentration on the Self, are contained in the twelve contemplations. The formulae of these disciplines have been elaborated in the preceding verse.

That the practice of renunciation, expiation for transgression, self-introspection, etc. are exercises for self-realization is prescribed in the canonical texts.

The all-comprehensive scope of the twelve contemplations is elucidated in this verse. The illustrious seer points out that the contemplations, in fact, cover all the self-purificatory disciplines (1990: 91).

88

रत्तिदिवंपडिकमणं पच्चक्खाणं समाहिं सामइयं।
आलोयणं पकुव्वदि जदि विज्जदि अप्पणो सत्ती॥

rattidivaṁpaḍikamaṇaṁ paccakkhāṇaṁ samāhiṁ sāmaiyaṁ ।
āloyaṇaṁ pakuvvadi jadi vijjadi appaṇo sattī ॥

If one has the requisite capacity presently existing, one should contemplate day and night on *pratikramaṇa*, *pratyākhyāna*, *samādhi ālocanā* (see *supra BA* 87) and *sāmayika* meaning steadfast equanimity, which is included in the Samādhi chapter in *Niyamasāra* (125-133), as it is considered the same as *samādhi*.

Commentary by M.K. Dharma Raja

Essential spiritual exercises attune the aspirant to his effort of ridding himself of the kārmic molecules. One should, therefore, endeavour to practise them as best as one can.

The eminent sage here directs the seeker to concentrate intensely on this path of self-discipline (1990: 92).

89

मोक्खगया जे पुरिसा अणाइकालेण वारअणुवेक्खं।
परिभाविऊण सम्मं पणमामि पुणो तेसिं॥

mokkhagayā je purisā aṇāikāleṇa vāra-aṇuvekkhaṁ ।
paribhāviūṇa sammaṁ paṇamāmi puṇo tesiṁ ॥

The souls from beginningless time up to the present had attained liberation (*mokṣa*); they had retained that status through meticulous contemplation on the twelve *anuprekṣās*. Therefore, reverentially bow to them again and again.

Commentary

In this verse, Kundakunda emphasizes the efficacy and significance of the twelve *anuprekṣās* in the path of liberation.

Commentary by M.K. Dharma Raja

Kundakunda emphasizes the sovereign efficacy of the twelve liberating thoughts.

Salvation from the ceaseless travails of the cycle of rebirths is attained through constant meditation on themes contained in these thoughts. They illumine the path of spiritual advance.

Those who achieved emancipation had shown the way to perfection which they traversed by concentrating on the ennobling contemplations. Kundakunda expresses his reference to those Perfected Souls intoning that he paused onto them in repeated salutation (1990: 92).

90

किं पलविएण बहुणा, जे सिद्धा णरवरा गये काले।
सिज्झिहदि जेवि भविया तं जाणह तस्स माहप्पं॥

kiṁ palavieṇa bahuṇā, je siddhā ṇaravarā gaye kāle ।
sijjhihadi jevi bhaviyā taṁ jāṇaha tassa māhappaṁ ॥

Of what use is this lengthy chatter? The excellent souls, who have liberated themselves in the past, thereby attaining the state of *siddhas*, and those who will liberate themselves in future, all that is due to the majesty (*māhātmya*) of *anuprekṣās*.

Commentary by M.K. Dharma Raja

In this penultimate verse, Kundakunda reiterates the redeeming virtues of the twelve supreme contemplations.

Highlighting their sanctifying effect, he draws the attention of the aspirant to the exemplifying footprints of all the Worthy Souls who thus far have ascended the summit of *mokṣa* as well as of those who will follow them in the future. The crowning glory of the purifying contemplations is best illustrated by the sublime example (1990: 93).

91

इदि णिच्छयववहारं जं भणियं कुन्दकुन्दमुणिणाहे।
जो भावइ सुद्धमणो सो पावइ परमणिव्वाणं॥

idi ṇicchayavavahāraṁ jaṁ bhaṇiyaṁ kundakunda-
muṇiṇāhe ।
jo bhāvai suddhamaṇo so pāvai paramaṇivvāṇaṁ ॥

[This verse] is considered an interpolation (*kṣepaka*)]. Lord or master or the doyen of saints Kundakunda has expounded the twelve contemplations from the internal, self-referential (*niścaya*) and external, other-referential (*vyavahāra*) points of view. One, who contemplates on that with the pure mind, is bound to attain supreme liberation.

In addition to the four treatises (viz. *Samayasāra*, *Pravacanasāra*, *Niyamasāra* and *Pañcāstikāyasāra*), mentioned in the Introduction of this treatise (*BA*), the fifth significant work of Kundakunda is *Bārasa Aṇuvekkhā* pertaining to the twelve contemplations (*anuprekṣās*, also called *bhāvanās*).

Even though *Bārasa Aṇuvekkhā* is a short treatise of 91-92 verses, it brings into focus the reality of the changeless permanent (*śāśvata* — *BA* 7 and *NS* 102) "I" beneath the ever-changing, transitory or apparent "I" of the body and the senses (*BA* 6).

Bārasa Aṇuvekkhā emphasizes that the supreme reality of the Self (*āsadā* or *ātmā*), the conscious, sentient in principle, which is distinct or apart from the limitations of the bondage of *karmas* and their fruition, etc. is the only protection, shelter or refuge from birth, old age, death, disease and fear (*BA* 11).

Like *Samayasāra* 38 and 73, *Bārasa Aṇuvekkhā* describes *aham* (I) as *ekko* (*eka*, one alone, solitary, unmixed) (so) of "pure" (*śuddha*) nature, characterized by intuition and knowledge, and that the self-restrained person should contemplate that unity or oneness (*ekatva*) with the Pure Self is worth acquiring (*BA* 20).

Bārasa Aṇuvekkhtar contains reflections on the concept of *ekatva–anyatva*, i.e. unity or oneness and otherness (*BA* 14-23) or *ekatva–vibhakta*, which is the subject matter of *Samayasāra* 5, laying emphasis on the distinctness (*vibhakta*) between one's own substance (*svaka dravya*) and other substances (*para-dravya*) (*BA* 85).

Bārasa Aṇuvekkhā also speaks of the concept of *heya–upādeya* (*BA* 86) (what is worth abandoning or renouncing and what is worth acquiring) by stating that the impure psychic states or modes (*paryāyas*) caused by the coming into operation or rise (*udaya*) of (material) *karmas* are *heya* and that enlightened knowledge (*sat* or *samyak jñāna*), which is one's own (*svaka*) (nature of) Self-substance[1] (*BA* 84). Thus, *Bārasa Aṇuvekkhā* emphasizes the importance and rarity of discriminative insight (*bodhi* or enlightenment) or *bheda-vijñāna*.

At the end, *Bārasa Aṇuvekkhā* declares that all the living beings, who have attained liberation since beginningless

[1] This verse is similar to *Niyamasāra* 38.

time, have attained that status due to the efficacy of twelve contemplations alone (*BA* 89).

Commentary by M.K. Dharma Raja

Reconciliation of the apparently contradictory, the real and the conventional, standpoints and alienating the strands of the twelve contemplations is an outstanding excellence of Kundakunda's treatise. He emphasizes in this concluding verse that it is this integrated and holistic approach that leads to a correct appraisal of the problems of mundane existence. It is also the synoptic view which guides the aspirant on the path of self-purification.

To those who seek to follow the path to perfection, the supreme code of contemplations is commanded by Acharya Kundakunda, the enlightened examplar of the order of ascetics (1990: 94).

Kārttikeyānuprekṣā

Kundakunda has described his concluding remarks in four verses (*BA* 87-90) (*BA* 91 being interpolation is excluded). *Kārttikeyānuprekṣā* describes the concluding remarks in three verses as follows:

Svami Kumar has expounded with great devotion these *anuprekṣās* with a view to comprehend the words of the Jina and to restrain the fickle mind. A study of these *anuprekṣās*, which are explained according to Jināgama (Jaina scriptures), leads to eternal bliss (*KA* 489-490).

(In the last verse (*KA* 491)), Svami Kumar, the author of *Kārttikeyānuprekṣā*, offers prayers to Vasupūjya, Malli, Nemi, Pārśva and Mahāvīra who are the prominent Lords to the three worlds and who practised penance as Kumāras, i.e. before coronation.

Note: In Devendra Kumar Shastri's *Bārasa Aṇuvekkhā*, verse 19 (shown on p. 189 of this book) is given as the last verse (verse 92) as interpolation. This verse is originally of *Darśana Pāhuḍa* (verse 3) and is coming in *Bhagavatī Ārādhanā* as verse 738.

Select Bibliography

Akalaṅka, 1993, *Tattvārtha-Vārttika* (*Rāja-Vārttika)* (also called *Tattvārtha Rāja-Vārttika* commentary on *Tattvārthasūtra*), vol. 2, New Delhi: Bharatiya Jnanapeetha.

Amitgati, 1975 (1918). *Dvatrimsatika*, in *Tattvanusasanadi samgraha*, Manikchandra Digambara Jaina Granthmala, no. 13, Bombay: Bombay Vaibhav Press.

——, 1968, *Śrāvakācāra*, tr. into English by Dayanand Bhargava, *Jaina Ethics*, Delhi: Motilal Banarsidass.

——, 2004, *Maraṇakaṇḍikā*, commentary by Vishuddhmati Mataji, ed. Chetan Prakash Patni, Dhariavada, Udaipur: Shrutodaya Trust.

Amrtachandra, 1964, *Samayasāra Kalaśa*, tr. into Hindi by Phulchandra Siddhantashastri, Songarh: Shri Digambar Jain Svadhyaya Mandir Trust.

Antaraatma Swamiji, 2005 (January), *Vicharsetu: The Path of Introspection* (monthly), Thrissur, Kerala: Narayanashrama Tapovanam.

Asadhara, 2018, *Dharmāmṛta Anāgāra*, tr. Kailash Chandra Shastri, New Delhi: Bharatiya Jnanapeetha.

——, 1967, *Sāgāradharmāmṛta* (*SDHA*), as translated in Kamal Chand Sogani, 1967, *Ethical Doctrines in Jainism*, Sholapur: jaina Sanskrit Saiharakshaka Sangha.

Atmaram, 1936, *Tattvārthasūtra Jaināgama Samanvaya*, Rohtak.

Begley, S., 2007, *Train Your Mind and Change Your Brain*, New York: Ballantine Books.

Bhargava, Dayanand, 1968, *Jaina Ethics*, Delhi: Motilal Banarsidass.

Chakravarti, A., 1971, *Samayasāra*, Varanasi: Bharatiya Jnanapeetha.

Chakravartinayanar, A., 1975, *Pañcāstikāyasāra: The Building of the Cosmos,* New Delhi: Bhartiya Jnanapeetha.

Chaudhury, Ishan, 2015, "Dormant Is not Inactive", *Economic Times*, 1 May.

Chitrabhanu, G.S. 1980, *Twelve Facets of Reality: The Jaina Path to Freedom*, ed. Clare Rosenfield, New York: Jain Meditation International Center.

Deresiewicz, William, 2009, "The End of Solitude: Selected Essays on Culture and Society", *Chronicle of Higher Education*, 55(21).

Dharma Raja, M.K. (ed. & tr.), 1990, *Bārasa Aṇuvekkhā* (*Twelve Contemplations*) *of Kundakunda*, New Delhi: Kund Kund Bharati.

Drukpa, Gyalwang, 2016, "Be Totally Free, Drop all Attachments", *The Times of India: The Speaking Tree*, 25 December.

Gazzaniga, M.S., 1998, *The Mind's Past*, Berkeley, CA: University of California Press.

Goldstein, Joseph, 2002, *One Dharma: The Emerging Western Buddhism*, San Francisco: Harper Collins.

Handiqui, Krishna Kanta, 1949, *Yaśastilaka and Indian Culture*, Sholapur: Jaina Sanskriti Samrakshaka Sangha (reprinted in 2011 under the title *Somadeva's Yaśastilaka: Aspects of Jainism, Indian Thought and Culture*, New Delhi: Rashtriya Sanskrit Sansthan and D.K. Printworld).

Hemachandra, 2002, *The Yoga Shastra of Hemachandra*, tr. Olle Quarnström, Cambridge, MA: Harvard University, Department of Sanskrit and Indian Studies.

Jaffe, Dennis T. and C.D. Scott, 1984, *From Burnout to Balance: A Workbook for Peak Performance and Self-Renewal*, New York: McGraw-Hill.

Jain, Champat Rai, 1929, *Jaina Psychology*, Allahabad: The Indian Press.

Jain, Duli Chand, 1993, *Jinavāṇī ke Motī*, Madras: Jain Vidya Anushthan Pratishthan.

Jain, Jagdish Prasad (ed.), 2001, *Jain Agama*, vol. 2, New Delhi: Jain Mission, nos 2 and 3, July-December.

——, 2001, "Bhavana: Affirmative Messages", *Jain Agam* (2-3, July-December): 16-17.

—— (ed.), 2005, *Fundamentals of Jainism*, New Delhi: Radiant Publishers.

——, 2007, *The Art and Science of Self-Realization: Puruṣārtha Siddhyupāya of Amrtachandra*, New Delhi: Radiant Publishers.

——(ed.), 2014, *The Essence of Jaina Scriptures: Pravacanasāra of Kundakunda*, with *Tattva-dīpikā* commentary by Amrtachandra Suri, English tr. Barend Faddegon, New Delhi: Kaveri Books.

—— (ed.), 2022, *Ratnakaraṇḍa Śrāvakācāra of Samantabhadra: The Spiritual Life of the Householder*, New Delhi: Kaveri Books.

——(ed.), 2024, *Advaita Vedānta and Jaina Advaita*, New Delhi: Kaveri Books.

Jain, Kamla, 1998, *Aparigraha: The Humane Solution*, Varanasi: Parshwanath Vidyapeeth.

Jain, Mahendra Kumar (ed.), 1949, *Bārasa Aṇuvekkhā*, Murtidevi Jaina Granthmala, No. 4, Benares: Bharatiya Jnanapeetha.

—— (ed.), 2009, *Tattvārthavārttika (Rāja-Vārttika)* of Śrī Akalaṅkadeva, part 2, Commentary on Tattvārthasūtra, New Delhi: Bharatiya Jnanapeetha.

Jain, Suresh Chand, 1990, "From the Publishers", in *Bāras Aṇuvekkhā (Twelve Contemplations) of Kundakunda*, ed. M.K. Darma Raja, New Delhi: Kundkunda Bharati.

Jaini, J.L. (ed.), 1956, *Tattvārthasūtra* by Umāsvāmi, Delhi: Barrister Champat Rai Jain Trust.

——(ed.), 1990, *The Sacred Books of the Jainas*, vol. 5: *Gommaṭsāra Jīva-Kāṇḍa (The Soul)* by Nemichandra Siddhanta Chakravarti, Lucknow: The Central Jaina Publishing House.

Kahneman, Daniel, 2011, *Thinking Fast and Slow*, cited in *The Economist* (London), 29 October-4 November.

Kaundeya, Manikchand, 1969, *Tattvārtha-Śloka-Vārttika*, Commentary on *Tattvārthasūtra*, ed. Pandit Vardhaman Parshvanath Shastri, vol. 7, Sholapur: Pandit Vardhaman Parshvanath Shastri.

"Knowledge@Wharton", University of Pennsylvania, reproduced in *Economic Times*, 11 August 2006.

Kosambi, D.D. (ed.), 1940, *Viśuddhimaggo of Buddhaghoṣacarīya*, Bombay: Bharatiya Vidya Bhavan.

Kundakunda, n.d. *Aṣṭa-Pāhuḍa*, Sonegar: Shri Digambar Jain Swadhyaya Mandir Trust.

Libet, Benjamin, 2003, "Can Conscious Experience Affect Brain Activity", *Journal of Consciousness Studies*, 10: 24-25.

Mahaprajna, Acharya, 1995, *Aabha Mandal*, Churu, Rajasthan: Aadarsha Sahitya Sangha.

———, 2010, *Abstract Thinking*, tr. R.K. Seth, Ladnun: Jain Vishva Bharati.

Malhotra, Rajiv, 2006, "What Is Dharma", *The Times of India, Speaking Tree*, 9 October.

Manikchandra (ed.), 1923, *Mūlācāra* of Vaṭṭakera, Digambar Jain Granthmala, No. 23, Bombay.

Maraṇa-Samādhi (*Prakīṇaka-daśakam*), 1927, Bombay: Agamodaya Samiti.

Mardia, K.V., 1990, *The Scientific Foundations of Jainism*, Delhi: Motilal Banarsidass.

Mehta, Mohan Lal, 1957, *Jaina Psychology: A Psychological Analysis of the Jaina Doctrine of Karma*, Amritsar: Sohanlal Jaindharma Pracharak Samiti.

Mehta, Mona, 2017, "Meet Bapu's Mentor", *The Times of India, Speaking Tree*, 4, November.

Muni Kishanlal, 1994, *Sādhanā: Prayoga and Pariṇāma*, Ladnun: Jain Vishva Bharati.

Nadkarni, Vithal C., 2011, "Angels vs. Devils", *The Economic Times*, 17 November.

"New 3-Point Planto Chase Away the Blues!", *Weekly World News* (Lantana, FL), 18 June 1996, p. 16.

Nyayavijaya, Muni, 1935, *Jain Darshan*, Pune: Jaina Sahitya Mandir.

——, 2000, *Jain Darshan*, tr. Nagin J. Shah under the title *Jaina Philosophy and Religion*, Delhi: Motilal Banarsidass.

Pūjyapāda, 1944, *Sarvārthasiddhi* commentary *on Tattvārthasūtra* of Pūjyapāda, tr. Phoolchand Shastri, New Delhi: Bharatiya Jnanapeetha.

——, 1960, *Sarvārthasiddhi*, tr. S.A. Jain, Calcutta: Vira Sasana Sangha.

——, 1992, *Sarvārthasiddhi* commentary on the *Tattvārthasūtra*, English tr. S.A. Jain, Madras: Jwalamalini Trust.

Rajchandra, Shrimad, 1988, *Bhāvanā Bodha*, tr. into English by Dinubhai Muljibhai Patel, Agas, Gujarat: Shrimad Rajchandra Ashram.

Rajjan Kumar, 2001, *Samādhi-Maran*, Varanasi: Parshvanath Vidyapeetha.

Sadasukhadas, Pandit, 1863, *Ratnakaraṇḍa Śrāvakācāra*, Ajmer: Pandit Sadasukha Granthmala.

Samantabhadra, 1917, *Ratnakaraṇḍa Śrāvakācāra*, 1917, tr. Champat Rai Jain, Arrah, Bihar: Central Jaina Publishing House.

Sangave, Vilas, 1990, "Foreword", in *Bārasa Aṅuvekkhā (Twelve Contemplations)* of Kundkunda, ed. and tr. M.K. Dharma Raja, New Delhi: Kundakunda Bharati.

Santideva, 1901, Prajñāpāramitā's commentary to the *Bodhicaryāvatāra*, ed. Louis de La Vallee Poussin, Calcutta: Asiatic Society.

Schubring, Walter, 1935, *Die Lehre der Jainas*, Berlin and Leipzig: De Gruyter.

Sharma, Pulkit, 2017, "To Feel Happy, Just Rewire Yourself", *Times of India*, 11 January.

Shastri, Devendra Kumar (tr.), 1991, *Bārasa Aṇuvekkhā* (in Hindi), Jaipur: Pandit Todarmal Smarak Trust.

Shital Prasad, Brahmachari, 1931, *Twelve Meditations* (English tr. with text and Sanskrit rendering) by Sri Kundakunda Acharya, Madras.

Shiv Kumar, Muni, 2000, *The Doctrine of Liberation in Indian Religion with Special Reference to Jainism*, New Delhi: Munishiram Manoharlal.

Shubhachandra, 1927, *Jñānārṇava*, Rayachandra Jaina Shastramala, Bombay: Revashankar Jagjivan Zaveri.

———, 1975, *Jñānārṇava*, tr. into Hindi by Pannalal Bakliwal, Agas, Gujarat: Paramshruta Prabhavak Mandal.

Siddhasena, 1930, *Bhāṣya-ṭīkā*, Part II, Bombay.

Singh, Naranjan, 2016, "Oneness to Humanness as a Favoured Value", *The Times of India*, 19 November.

Sivarya, 1990, *Bhagavatī Ārādhāna* in Prākr̥t language with *Vijayodaya* commentary and introduction by Acharya Aparajit Suri, ed. and tr. into Hindi by Kailash Chandra Siddhantshastri, Phaltan, Maharashtra: Shri Hiralal Khushal Chand Joshi.

———, 2004, *Bhagavatī Ārādhanā*, commentary by Aparajita Suri, Jivaraj Jain Granthmala — Hindi Vibhaga No. 36, Sholapur, Maharashtra.

Sogani, Kamal Chand, 1967, *Ethical Doctrines in Jainism*, Sholapur, Maharashtra: Jaina Sanskrti Sangharakshaka Sangha.

Suru, N.G. (ed.), 1931, *Ovavaiya Suttam*, Pune: N.G. Suru.

Svami Kumar, 1945, *Kārttikeyānuprekṣā,* tr. Kailash Chandra Shastri, Agra: Shrimad Rajchandra Ashram.

Taneja, Anup, 2015, "Remember, It Can Always Be Done", *Times of India*, 3 June.

Tatia, Nathmal, 1998, *That Which Is*, tr. of *Tattvārthasūtra*, San Francisco: Harper Collins.

Tattvārthasūtra, 1930, Commentary by Siddhasena Ganin, Bombay.

Upadhye, A.N., 1935, *Pravacanasāra*, Bombay: Shetha Manilal Revashankar Jhaveri.

———, 1983, *Upadhye Papers* Mysore: University of Mysore.

Vattakera, 1923, *Mulachara*, part 2, Manikchand Digambar Series, Bombay.

Vishuddhmati Mataji, 2004, *Maraṇakaṇḍikā,* ed. Chetan Prakash Patni, Dhariavada, Udaipur: Shrutodaya Trust.

Vivekananda (Swami), 1902, *Lectures on Jaina Yoga*, New York: The Vedanta Society.

Vidyanandi (Swami), 1918, *Tattvārtha-Śloka-Vārttika*, vol. 7, Bombay: Nirnaya Sagar Press.

——, 1969, *Tattvārtha-Śloka-Vārttika*, Commentator Manikchand Kaundeya, ed. Pandit Vardhaman Parshvanath Shastri, Sholapur: Pandit Vardhaman Parshvanath Shastri.

Yugantar, Jugal Kishore Mukhtar, 1956, *Jain Sāhitya or Itihāsa para Viśada Prakāśa,* Calcutta: Veer Shasan Sangh.

Williams, Robert, 1991, *Jaina Yoga: A Survey of Mediaeval Sravakacharas,* Delhi: Motilal Banarsidass.

Name Index

Title Index

Word Index

Subject Index